DESCARTES' SYSTEM OF NATURAL PHILOSOPHY

Towards the end of his life, Descartes published the first four parts of a projected six-part work, *The Principles of Philosophy*. This was intended to be the definitive statement of his complete system of philosophy, dealing with everything from cosmology to the nature of human happiness. Stephen Gaukroger examines the whole system, and reconstructs the last two parts, 'On Living Things' and 'On Man', from Descartes' other writings. He relates the work to the tradition of late Scholastic textbooks which it follows, and also to Descartes' other philosophical writings, and he examines the ways in which Descartes transformed not only the practice of natural philosophy, but also our understanding of what it is to be a philosopher. His book is the first comprehensive examination of Descartes' complete philosophical system.

Stephen Gaukroger is Professor of History of Philosophy and History of Science at the University of Sydney. His books include *Explanatory Structures* (1978), *Cartesian Logic* (1989), *Descartes, An Intellectual Biography* (1995), and *Francis Bacon and the Transformation of Early Modern Philosophy* (2001).

D1614329

DESCARTES' SYSTEM
OF NATURAL PHILOSOPHY

STEPHEN GAUKROGER

CAMBRIDGE
UNIVERSITY PRESS

PUBLISHED BY THE PRESS SYNDICATE OF THE UNIVERSITY OF CAMBRIDGE
The Pitt Building, Trumpington Street, Cambridge, United Kingdom

CAMBRIDGE UNIVERSITY PRESS
The Edinburgh Building, Cambridge CB2 2RU, UK
40 West 20th Street, New York, NY 10011-4211, USA
477 Williamstown Road, Port Melbourne, VIC 3207, Australia
Ruiz de Alarcón 13, 28014 Madrid, Spain
Dock House, The Waterfront, Cape Town 8001, South Africa

http://www.cambridge.org

© Stephen Gaukroger 2002

This book is in copyright. Subject to statutory exception
and to the provisions of relevant collective licensing agreements,
no reproduction of any part may take place without
the written permission of Cambridge University Press.

First published 2002

Printed in the United Kingdom at the University Press, Cambridge

Typeface Baskerville Monotype 11/12.5 pt.   *System* LATEX 2ε   [TB]

A catalogue record for this book is available from the British Library

Library of Congress Cataloguing in Publication data

Gaukroger, Stephen.
Descartes' system of natural philosophy / Stephen Gaukroger.
p.   cm.
Includes bibliographical references and index.
ISBN 0 521 80897 9 (hardback) – ISBN 0 521 00525 6 (paperback)
1. Descartes, René, 1596–1650.   I. Title.
B1873 .G38   2002
194 – dc21   2001043655

ISBN 0 521 80897 9 hardback
ISBN 0 521 00525 6 paperback

Contents

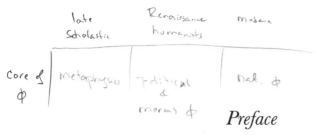

Preface

This book is part of an ongoing project in which my aim is to understand how the process of shaping cognitive values around scientific ones began in the early modern era, and it is in many ways a companion to my *Francis Bacon and the Transformation of Early Modern Philosophy* (Cambridge, 2001). Descartes and Bacon are two of the founders of early modern thought, in many respects *the* founders of early modern thought. Both of them see natural philosophy as the core of the philosophical enterprise, by contrast, on the one hand, with Renaissance humanist philosophers, who saw moral and political philosophy in this role, and, on the other, with late Scholastic philosophers, who saw metaphysics as the core enterprise. They approach their task from different traditions – Bacon from the humanist tradition, and Descartes, at least in the *Principia*, from that of late Scholasticism – but both end up transforming not only natural–philosophical practice but the understanding of what it is to be a philosopher.

Earlier versions of material for the book have been presented at seminars and conferences at the Australian National University, the University of British Columbia, Eötvös University Budapest, the Universities of Chicago, Harvard, Helsinki, Hong Kong, Melbourne, and Ottawa, All Souls College Oxford, the State and Federal Universities of Rio de Janeiro, the Sorbonne, and the Universities of Sydney and Toronto. I am grateful to audiences at these events for some probing questions and fruitful discussion. I have particularly benefited from discussions with Peter Anstey, Roger Ariew, Colin Fowler, Dan Garber, Ettore Lojacono, John Schuster, John Sutton, and Margaret Wilson. The research for the book has been funded by an Australian Research Council Large Grant, which has been invaluable in allowing me significant relief from teaching and enabling travel for research.

References to Descartes' works

Descartes' works are referred to by their original titles, in the original language, with original orthography. References to these works are to the standard edition: Charles Adam and Paul Tannery (eds.), *Oeuvres de Descartes*, 2nd edn (11 vols., Paris, 1974–86). The edition is abbreviated to AT throughout, and reference is made to volume number and page number by roman and arabic numerals respectively: for example, AT IV. 123. In the case of the *Principia* and *Les Passions*, however, references are to Part and Article number, since this is a more convenient way of locating the relevant passage. In chapters 3 to 6, which cover Parts I to IV of the *Principia* respectively, where the reference is to an article in the respective Part, I have ommitted the Part number in the reference, so that in chapter 3, for example, a reference to art. 20 refers to Part I art. 20 unless otherwise indicated.

As regards reproductions of Descartes' figures, those that accompanied the 1647 French translation of the *Principia*, which Descartes supervised, have finer detail than those of the original 1644 Latin edition, and for this reason I have reproduced the former. In some cases these figures are mirror images of those in the 1644 edition, but this is irrelevant for the understanding and interpretation of the figures.

The only complete annotated English translation of the *Principia* is V. R. and R. P. Miller, *René Descartes: Principles of Philosophy* (Dordrecht, 1991). Stephen Gaukroger, *Descartes, The World and Other Writings* (Cambridge, 1998) contains full annotated translations of *Le Monde*, *L'Homme*, and a full translation of *La Description du corps humain*. There is a full annotated translation of *Les Passions* in Stephen H. Voss, *René Descartes: The Passions of the Soul* (Indianapolis, 1989). I have often followed these translations, as well as those in John Cottingham et al., *The Philosophical Writings of Descartes* (3 vols., Cambridge, 1984–91).

Introduction

Natural philosophy lay at the core of Descartes' philosophical enterprise, and he instituted the most comprehensive reform of philosophy that has ever been attempted. His achievement was wide-ranging: he completely reformulated metaphysics by exploring its epistemological credentials in a wholly novel and indeed unprecedented fashion; he led the way in seventeenth-century cosmology up until Newton; he was one of the founders of modern geometrical optics; his contribution to mathematics was second to none in the seventeenth century; and he not only discovered reflex action, but developed a mechanistic approach to physiology which set the parameters for much thinking about physiology in the eighteenth and nineteenth centuries. The variety of Descartes' interests is not always immediately evident, however. This is partly because – unlike philosophers of similar standing such as Plato, Aristotle, and Kant – Descartes is usually approached through a single concern, namely the foundationalist metaphysics that is set out in similar ways in *La Discours de la Méthode*, the *Meditationes*, and the *Principia Philosophiæ*. It is also partly because we can discern a plausible systematic connection between many of the parts of the Platonic or Aristotelian or Kantian corpus, which we cannot do in the case of Descartes. These two points are connected: Descartes' foundationalist metaphysics is so notoriously problematic that it is difficult to get beyond it to what it is supposed to provide the foundation for, and, in any case, if the foundations are not viable, there would seem to be little to be gained in asking what plausible systematic connection there could be between them and what is built upon them. The problem here derives in large part from a widespread but manifestly mistaken conception of the relation between the foundations and the rest of the system in Descartes. Descartes' system of natural philosophy is not generated by inference from first principles, but has been established quite independently of these first principles. In structuring his system around first principles, what Descartes hopes to achieve is a particular

NB

kind of legitimation of the whole project.)Why he seeks to legitimate his philosophy in the first place, and why he goes about legitimating it in this way, are matters that will concern us in what follows, where we shall be reconstructing Descartes' mature system of natural philosophy, and investigating the systematic connections between its various parts.

At the beginning of 1641, Descartes began work on what was initially envisaged as a six-part treatise. The first four parts were published as *Principia Philosophiæ* in 1644. These dealt with the 'principles of human knowledge', the 'principles of material objects', the 'visible universe', and 'the Earth'. In article 188 of Part IV of the *Principia*, Descartes tells us that he had intended to write 'two other parts: a fifth, concerning living things, or animals and plants, and a sixth, concerning man', but that he had not had the leisure to finalise these parts. He proceeds to describe what he had intended to cover, however, and it quickly becomes clear that the material for the last two parts is available, in one form or another, elsewhere in his writings. We shall be concerned not just with the work that was published under the title of *Principia Philosophiæ*, but also with the two projected final parts of the *Principia*, which I shall be reconstructing from these other materials.

Drawing on related material to reconstruct Descartes' project is not as problematic as it might first seem.⟨The content of the *Principia* is not *sui generis*, nor even a novel departure from his earlier writings. Descartes reworked earlier material, including earlier published material as well as material intended for publication, throughout his writings. The published parts of the *Principia* are an exemplary instance of this. Part I reworks material already presented in the *Meditationes*, which itself revises material already presented in *La Discours*. Parts II and III rework material from *Le Monde*, and Part IV reworks material published in *Les Meteores*, which itself relies upon parts of *Le Monde*.⟩

The content of the projected Part V is not difficult to reconstruct. *Le Monde* had covered the same material as Parts II to IV of the *Principia*, and had been succeeded by *L'Homme*, which dealt with animal physiology. It is true that Descartes mentions 'animals and plants' as being the subject of Part V, and *L'Homme* does not deal with plants, but we shall see that he holds there to be a continuity between plant and animal physiology, something entirely in keeping with his unified mechanistic reduction of organic processes. *L'Homme* was put to one side in 1633, but Descartes kept up work in anatomy and physiology through the 1630s and early 1640s, and he in part rewrote and updated *L'Homme* in the 1640s in *La Description du Corps Humain*, which remained unfinished. This material is summarised very briefly at the beginning of *Les Passions de l'Ame*, published in 1649. *Les Passions* takes us from the physiology and psycho-physiology of the projected Part V into the intricacies of the mind/body as they relate to affective states. It is a treatise on human psychology, and, in the last instance, on the nature of morality. It is, in short, the basis for Part VI of the *Principia*.

As regards the sources of the *Principia*, as well as Descartes' earlier projects, there was a late Scholastic textbook tradition which offered a comprehensive treatment of philosophy, and the *Principia* was modelled on these textbooks. Descartes' first proposal had in fact been to write a double textbook, his own followed by a reprinting of the *Summa philosophiæ* (1609) of Eustachius a Sancto Paulo, with his annotations to this. He subsequently abandoned this project, but stuck with the idea of presenting his work in the form of a textbook. The textbook tradition provided a format for a comprehensive account of natural philosophy, identifying the topics to be included and their ordering, and, although Descartes reshapes this arrangement to his own purposes, his account is in many respects in line with the textbook tradition and is couched in the language of late Scholastic philosophy. However, late Scholastic metaphysics, and the natural philosophy it grounds, is theologically driven, whereas Descartes' foundationalist metaphysics is driven by epistemology. This is particularly important because there is no evidence of any interest in a foundationalist metaphysics before the abandonment of *Le Monde*, and its introduction, as we shall see, was a legitimatory device that was directly provoked by the view of the Inquisition that condemned Galileo in 1633 that claims for the physical reality of a cosmology could not be settled on purely natural–philosophical grounds. Descartes' project was to show that his natural philosophy was not just one amongst many, but the only one that could be reconciled with a particular set of metaphysical considerations whose distinguishing feature was that they could not be faulted or even doubted.

In other words, there was nothing internal to Descartes' project in natural philosophy that required metaphysical foundations, and there was nothing crucial to his natural philosophy that could only be generated from such metaphysical foundations. This does not mean, however, that the foundationalist metaphysics he provides is simply an added extra that can be stripped from the natural philosophy he sets out. On the contrary, Descartes makes it clear that it is in virtue of such a metaphysics that his natural philosophy is not simply one amongst many, but the one uniquely suited to revealing the ultimate constituents and structure of the cosmos. That his natural philosophy is a metaphysically grounded one is a key part of Descartes' project, and this is something important not only in the physical theory of Parts II, III, and IV, but also in the physiology and psycho-physiology of Parts V and VI. The constraints on this metaphysics are provided by a number of sources, not least the Scholastic vocabulary he takes up, but above all by the dictates of his natural philosophy. Indeed, the fact that natural philosophy ultimately provides the tasks for his metaphysics, rather than these tasks being generated directly by a definition of the subject matter of natural philosophy provided by metaphysics, is one of the features of Descartes' project that marks it out from the late Scholastic approaches against which he is pitting his own system.

The reconstructed *Principia* provides us with a comprehensive account of Descartes' mature philosophy, beginning with metaphysical foundations of natural philosophy, and ending with the implications of his natural philosophy for morality. In the course of this, Descartes completely reshapes the relations between metaphysics and natural philosophy, and develops the first mechanist physical cosmology, the first non-mythological theory of the formation of the Earth, the first mechanist physiology and embryology, the first mechanist account of animal sentience, an account of the nature of mental functioning that goes beyond anything devised to that time and which has largely shaped discussions of the mind since, and an account of human passions that demonstrates the need for a unified conception of the person. This is the 'system of natural philosophy' that we shall be exploring in what follows.

CHAPTER I

Before the Principia

In each of the decades of his maturity, Descartes embarked upon an unfinished project: the *Regulae* in the 1620s, *Le Monde/L'Homme* in the 1630s, and the *Principia* in the 1640s. The first two of these projects inaugurate major changes of direction in Descartes' thinking, while the third attempts to consolidate a major development begun in *La Discours de la Méthode* and the *Meditationes*. There are some themes that persist, however, and this is particularly true of *Le Monde/L'Homme*, which provides much of the material for the final project. Indeed, in thinking through this final project, Descartes talks of teaching *Le Monde* 'to speak Latin' before bringing it into the world, and 'naming it *Summa Philosophiæ* to make it more welcome to the Scholastics, who are now persecuting it and trying to smother it before its birth'.[1]

Between the abandonment of *Le Monde* and the publication of the *Principia*, Descartes formulated some of his results in method, optics, meteorology, and geometry in the form of four essays, published in 1637, and then he turned away from explicit natural philosophy for a while. Developing a theme that had already been evident in the first of these essays, *La Discours*, he set out a sceptically driven epistemology as a way of indicating the tasks of a foundational metaphysics in the *Meditationes*. Then, 'when I thought that these earlier works had sufficiently prepared the minds of my readers to accept the *Principia Philosophiæ*, I published these too'.[2] The *Principia* is the work in which the foundational tasks are carried out, and it begins its account with a number of fundamental claims about the nature of knowledge, claims that had been worked out in detail in *La Discours* and in the *Meditationes*. In these texts, Descartes had provided a metaphysical foundation for knowledge, something wholly absent from *Le Monde*, and indeed from anything he wrote before the mid 1630s. The remaining three books, then, present a revised version of

---

[1] Descartes to Huygens, 31 January 1642; AT III. 523.   [2] AT IXB. 16.

Le Monde, with some important additions (such as the rules of collision and the account of the formation of planets) and some important revisions (such as the doctrine of the reciprocity of motion). The *Principia* appears, in sum, as a revised version of the project of *Le Monde / L'Homme*, prefaced by a foundationalist metaphysics which reshapes some of the natural–philosophical doctrines of the earlier writings, and – taking *Les Passions de l'Ame* as providing a version of the final part of the exercise – culminating in an account of human psychology and the attainment of a moral life.

The *Principia*, in its projected complete form, offers us the mature Cartesian system, and, in order to come to terms with it, it is important that we understand what this system developed from, why it developed in the way it did, and just why Descartes chose to set out his system in the form of the *Principia*. To this end, my aim in this chapter is to explore the first and second of these questions by looking at Descartes' own earlier projects, particularly as they bear upon the *Principia* and its projected two final parts, and then, in the next chapter, to explore the third question by looking at possible models for the *Principia*.

'PHYSICO-MATHEMATICS'

'Physico-mathematicians are very rare', wrote Isaac Beeckman in a diary entry for December 1618, shortly after meeting Descartes for the first time, and he notes that Descartes 'says he has never met anyone other than me who pursues his studies in the way I do, combining physics and mathematics in an exact way. And for my part, I have never spoken with anyone apart from him who studies in this way.'[3] It was Beeckman who introduced Descartes to a quantitative micro-corpuscularian natural philosophy, one that he was to reshape and make into his own very distinctive system of natural philosophy.[4]

Descartes' earliest writings, which derive from late 1618/early 1619, deal with questions in practical mathematical disciplines. He composed a short treatise on the mathematical basis of consonance in music, exchanged letters with Beeckman on the problem of free fall, and worked

---

[3] *Journal tenu par Isaac Beeckman de 1604 à 1634*, ed. Cornelius de Waard, 4 vols. (The Hague, 1939–53), I. 244.

[4] On the details of Descartes' relationship with Beeckman, see Klaas van Berkel, 'Descartes' Debt to Beeckman: Inspiration, Cooperation, Conflict', in Stephen Gaukroger, John Schuster, and John Sutton, eds., *Descartes' Natural Philosophy* (London, 2000), 46–59. On how Descartes reshaped his early work with Beeckman see Stephen Gaukroger and John Schuster, 'The Hydrostatic Paradox and the Origins of Cartesian Dynamics', *Studies in History and Philosophy of Science*, forthcoming.

with him on a number of problems in hydrostatics.[5] The second, and particularly the third, of these exercises are of interest. In the correspondence on free fall,[6] Beeckman poses Descartes a mathematical question about the relation between spaces traversed and times elapsed in free fall, but Descartes seems keen to steer the question in the direction of dynamics, seeking the nature of the force responsible for the continued increase in motion. The move is not successful, and in fact it leads Descartes to misconstrue the original problem, but it is indicative of what will be an important and productive feature of his thinking about mechanical problems, and later about physical problems more generally.

The hydrostatics manuscripts[7] are of even greater interest in this respect. Here Descartes turns his attention to a paradoxical result that Simon Stevin had proved in hydrostatics, namely that the pressure exerted by a fluid on the base of its container is independent of the weight of the fluid and, depending on the shape of the vessel, can be many times greater than its weight. Here, Descartes takes a question which has been solved in rigorous mathematical terms and looks for the underlying physical causes of the phenomenon. He construes fluids as being made up from microscopic corpuscles whose physical behaviour causes the phenomenon in question, and he asks what kinds of behaviour in these corpuscles could produce the requisite effect. This is, in effect, an attempt to translate what Stevin had treated as a macroscopic geometrical question into a dynamically formulated micro-corpuscularian account of the behaviour of fluids. In the course of this, Descartes develops a number of rudimentary dynamical concepts, particularly his notion of *actio*, which he will use to think through questions in physical optics in the mid 1620s, and then questions in cosmology in 1629. This is of particular importance because his whole approach to cosmological problems, for example, is in terms of how fluids behave, and, as we shall see, it is fluids that carry celestial bodies around in their orbits.

THE *REGULAE*

Later in 1619, Descartes began work on the *Regulae*. His principal interest had shifted to mathematics by this time, and this interest was stimulated by reflection upon an instrument called a proportional compass, which had limbs that were attached by sliding braces so that, when the compass was opened up, the distances between the limbs were always in the same

5 On these see my *Descartes, An Intellectual Biography* (Oxford, 1995), ch. 3.
6 AT x. 58–61, 75–8, 219–22.   7 AT x. 67–74, 228.

a dist. in
posterior analytics

proportion.[8] The proportional compass enabled one to perform geometrical operations, such as trisection of angles, and arithmetical ones, such as calculation of compound interest, and Descartes asked how it was possible for the same instrument to generate results in two such different disciplines as arithmetic, which dealt with discontinuous quantities (numbers), and geometry, which deals with continuous quantities (lines). Since the principle behind the proportional compass was continued proportions, he realised that there was a more fundamental discipline, which he initially identified with a theory of proportions, later with algebra. This more fundamental discipline had two features. First, it underlay arithmetic and geometry, in the sense that, along with various branches of practical mathematics such as astronomy and the theory of harmony, these were simply particular species of it, and for this reason he termed it *mathesis universalis*, 'universal mathematics'. Its second feature was that this universal mathematics was a problem-solving discipline: indeed, an exceptionally powerful problem-solving discipline whose resources went far beyond those of traditional geometry and arithmetic. Descartes was able to show this in a spectacular way in geometry, taking on problems, such as the Pappus *locus*-problem, which had baffled geometers since late antiquity, and he was able to show how his new problem-solving algebraic techniques could cut through these effortlessly. In investigating the problem-solving capacity of his universal mathematics, however, Descartes suspected that there might be an even more fundamental discipline of which universal mathematics itself was simply a species, a master problem-solving discipline which underlay every area of inquiry, physical and mathematical. This most fundamental discipline Descartes termed 'universal method', and it is such a method that the *Regulae* sought to set out and explore.

When Descartes began work on the *Regulae*, it was intended to be in three parts, each part to contain twelve 'Rules'. What was offered was a general treatise on method, covering the nature of simple propositions and how they can be known (first twelve Rules), how to deal with 'perfectly understood problems' (second set of Rules), and 'imperfectly understood problems' (projected third set). The composition proceeded in two stages, however, and the nature of the work shifted somewhat between stages.[9] In 1619–20, Descartes completed the first eleven Rules, and then apparently

thinking about the proportional compass led D to realise that there is a more fundamental mathematical discipline

mathesis universalis [the theory of proportion: later: algebra]

pursuing questions re mathesis universalis led him to believe that there was an even more fundamental discipline at the basis of every field of inquiry - universal method

---

[8] See my *Descartes, An Intellectual Biography*, ch. 4 for details.

[9] On dating see Jean-Paul Weber, *La Consitution du texte des Regulae* (Paris, 1964) and John Schuster, 'Descartes' Mathesis Universalis, 1619–28', in Stephen Gaukroger, ed., *Descartes, Philosophy, Mathematics and Physics* (New York, 1980), 41–96.

abandoned them. When he took up the *Regulae* again in 1626–8, he revised two of these (Rules 4 and 8) and added Rules 12 to 18, with titles
only for Rules 19–21. The thrust of the work remains methodological,
and mathematics is still taken very much as model – which is what we
would expect, since the fact that the move to universal method comes
through universal mathematics is what provides the former with its plausibility. But the complete Rules of the second Part, particularly Rules 12
to 14, focus on the question of how a mathematical understanding of
the world is possible by investigating just what happens in quantitative
perceptual cognition, that is, just what happens when we grasp the world
in geometrical terms. The change in focus is interesting, but it is not thoroughgoing, and severe problems arise in reconciling universal method
with universal mathematics, which has now become algebra.

Specifically, the problem that Descartes faced was that universal
method was supposed to provide a general form of legitimation of knowledge, including mathematical knowledge, but algebra also provided its
own specific kind of legitimation of mathematical knowledge, and the
point at which the *Regulae* break off and are abandoned is exactly that
at which it becomes clear that these two forms of legitimation come into
conflict. The general form of legitimation provided by universal method
is one in which problems are represented in the form of clear and distinct ideas, and Rule 14 spells out just what this means in the case of
mathematics: it means representing the pure abstract entities that algebra deals with in terms of operations on line lengths, and in this way the
truth or falsity of the proposition so represented is evident. To take a simple example, the truth of the proposition $2 + 3 = 5$ is not immediately
evident in this form of representation, but it is evident if we represent the
operation of addition as the joining together of two lines, as in Figure 1.1.

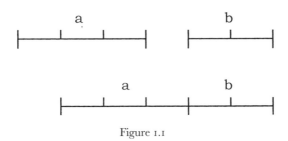

Figure 1.1

In this case we can see how the quantities combine to form their sum (and
this is just as evident in the case of very large numbers the numerical value

of whose sum we cannot immediately compute). This is a very insightful and profound move on Descartes' part. The problem he is concerned with is that of identifying those forms of mathematical demonstration not merely in which we can grasp that the solution or conclusion follows from the premises, but in which we can track how the solution or conclusion is generated. The difficulty that arose was that the range of operations for which this kind of basic legitimatory procedure held did not extend to the more sophisticated kinds of operation with which Descartes' algebra was able to work. And it is just such operations that begin to be envisaged in Rules 19–21, namely the extraction of higher-order roots, where no manipulation of line lengths is going to generate the result.

It is at this point that the *Regulae* are abandoned, and this also marks the end of the attempt to model knowledge on mathematics, at least in anything other than a merely rhetorical sense. When mathematics is invoked from now on, it will be invoked as a paradigm of certainty, but, in contrast to the work of the 1620s, it will cease to be accompanied by an attempt to capture at any level of mathematical detail just what this certainty derives from or consists in. Indeed, Descartes' interest in methodological questions in his later writings comes to be overdetermined by metaphysical, epistemological, and natural–philosophical issues.

LE MONDE AND L'HOMME

At the end of 1629, Descartes began work on a new project, which he later described to Mersenne in these terms:

Since I tried to explain the principles in a Treatise which certain considerations prevented me from publishing, I know of no better way of making them known than to set out here briefly what it contained. I had as my aim to include in it everything that I thought I knew before I wrote it about the nature of material things. But just as painters, not being able to represent all the different sides of a body equally well on a flat canvas, choose one of the main ones and set it facing the light, and shade the others so as to make them stand out only when viewed from the perspective of the chosen side; so too, fearing that I could not put everything I had in mind in my discourse, I undertook to expound fully only what I knew about light. Then, as the opportunity arose, I added something about the Sun and the fixed stars, because almost all of it comes from them; the heavens, because they transmit it; the planets, comets, and the Earth, because they reflect light; and especially bodies on the Earth, because they are coloured, or transparent, or luminous; and finally about man, because he observes these bodies.[10]

The work described here was again intended to be in three parts. The first part (*Le Monde*), which covers inanimate nature, and the second, which covers animal and human non-conscious functions (*L'Homme*), were to have been complemented by a third part, on the 'rational soul', but, just as with the *Regulae*, this third part never appeared. And, again as with the *Regulae*, the project was abandoned, but, whereas the *Regulae* was abandoned because problems internal to the project became evident, in the case of this second project the problems were wholly external: *Le Monde* had set out to derive the truth of a heliocentric system from first principles, and the 1633 condemnation of Galileo's defence of Copernicanism by the Roman Inquisition stopped Descartes in his tracks.

Le Monde sets out a theory of the physical world as something consisting exclusively of homogeneous matter, which can be considered as comprising three types of corpuscle, distinguished solely by size. On the basis of laws describing the motion of these corpuscles, a mechanistic cosmology is set out which includes both a celestial physics and an account of the nature and properties of light. Descartes begins with an argument to the effect that the world may be different from our perceptual image of it, and indeed that our perceptual image may not even be a reliable guide to how the world is. This is in no sense a sceptical argument, and, once Descartes has established the nature of the world, it is clear that it is in fact very different from our perceptual image of it. He begins with the nature of fire, partly because fire is the only terrestrial form of production of light and one of his main tasks is to offer a theory of light, and partly because it showcases his very economical theory of matter. The aim is to show how a macroscopic phenomenon can be accounted for plausibly in micro-corpuscularian terms, and fire is a good example for Descartes' purposes: all we need to postulate in order to account for the burning process, he argues, is the motion of parts of the wood resulting in the separation of the subtle parts (flame and smoke) from the gross parts (which remain as ashes).

Matter theory is developed in a more systematic way from the beginning of chapter 3, Descartes drawing attention to the prevalence of change in nature by arguing that the total amount of motion in the

[10] AT VI. 41–2.

universe is conserved, although this motion may be redistributed among bodies. The general principle from which he works is that, given that all bodies can be divided into very small parts, a force is required to separate these parts if they are stationary with respect to one another, for they will not move apart of their own accord. If the very small parts of which the body is constituted are all at rest with respect to one another, then it will require significant force to separate them, but, if they are moving with respect to one another, then they will separate from one another, at a rate which may even be greater than that which one could achieve by applying a force oneself. The former bodies are what we call solids, the latter what we call fluids, and in the extreme cases they form the ends of a spectrum on which all bodies can be ranked, with rigid solids at one terminus and extremely fluid bodies at the other. This ranking on a spectrum of fluidity provides the basis for Descartes' theory of matter, for it enables him to reduce the properties of matter to the rate at which its parts move with respect to one another. At the extreme fluid end of the spectrum comes, not air as one might expect, but fire, whose parts are the most obviously agitated, and whose degree of corpuscular agitation is such that it renders other bodies fluid.

On Descartes' account, all bodies, whether fluid or solid, are made from the one kind of matter. He argues that the degree of fluidity of a body cannot be proportional to the amount of vacuum that exists between its constituent parts, trying to establish that, if voids did exist, there must be more space between the parts of a solid than between those of a liquid, because the moving parts of a liquid 'can much more easily press and arrange themselves against one another' than can the parts of a solid. His main conclusion is that if there is a vacuum anywhere it cannot be in fluids but must be in solid bodies, and he is more concerned to make sure that we accept that there are no interstitial vacua in fluids than to show the absence of such vacua in solids. This is because his account of the basic structure of the universe effectively subsumes it under fluid mechanics, and hence his interest is really in fluids. This begins to become evident in the subsequent discussion of how motion is possible, and in his interconnected accounts of the nature of light and the differentiation of matter into 'elements'. In the former case, the question arises of how bodies can move at all if there are no empty spaces for them to occupy, and the answer Descartes gives is that 'all the motions that occur in the world are in some way circular'. Among the images Descartes uses to fill out this idea is that of a fish swimming through a relatively dense medium by making the water circulate around it. On the second question, Descartes' model of light is one drawn from fluid mechanics: it is something that acts by means of mechanical pressure, and what needs to be explained is how this mechanical pressure is generated in the first place, how it is propagated, and why light so construed behaves in particular geometrically defined ways when it encounters opaque and transparent bodies. Light is generated by fiery bodies, transmitted through the air, and is refracted and reflected by terrestrious bodies. The traditional elements of fire, air, and earth have, then, a cosmological analogue. These three elements are, for Descartes, simply three different sizes of corpuscle: very fine, fine, and gross respectively.

Chapter 6 of *Le Monde* begins with Descartes' construction of a hypothetical world on the basis of the theory of matter set out in the first five chapters. The ultimate aim is to show that a world constructed in this manner, one without forms or qualities, is indistinguishable from the actual world. The traditional Aristotelian forms and qualities are excluded because they could not form part of a properly mechanist explanation. Indeed, if we strip the world of the traditional forms and qualities, what we would be left with would, in Descartes' view, be its genuine properties. His new world is to be conceived as 'a real, perfectly solid body which uniformly fills the entire length, breadth, and depth of the great space at the centre of which we have halted our thought'. This perfectly solid body is 'solid' in the sense of being full and voidless, and it is divided into parts distinguished simply by their different motions. At the first instant of creation, God provides the parts with different motions, and after that He does not intervene supernaturally to regulate their motions. Rather, these motions are regulated by laws of nature which Descartes now sets out.

The three laws of nature that Descartes provides are designed to describe the behaviour of bodies in collision. They deal quite separately with the power of moving and the determination of a body. The first law tells us that a body conserves its motion except in collision, when, the second law tells us, the total motion of the colliding bodies is conserved but may be redistributed amongst them. It is left to the third law to tell us about direction, and according to this law, because a body's tendency to move is instantaneous, this tendency to move can only be rectilinear, because only rectilinear motion can be determined in an instant: 'only motion in a straight line is entirely simple and has a nature which may be grasped wholly in an instant'. Motion in a circle or some other path would require us to consider 'at least two of its instants, or rather two of its parts, and the relation between them'. What path the body will

[margin notes, handwritten:]
3 traditional elements have cosmological analogues in D's system, but are understood merely in terms of corpuscle size

• first element (fire): very fine corpuscles comprise light producing bodies & fill the space btwn 2nd & 3rd elements

• second element (air): fine corpuscles comprise the celestial fluid, the medium through which light is transmitted

• third element (earth): gross corpuscles, comprise bodies that reflect & refract light

actually take, however, will be a function of the collisions to which it is subject.

The first law states that certain states of bodies are conserved: they will remain unchanged unless something acts to change them. Among these are a body's size, shape, its position if it is at rest, and also its motion, for once a body has begun to move, 'it will always continue in its motion with an equal force until others stop or retard it'. This rule of conservation of state has always been considered to hold for the first three items, and many others, Descartes tells us, but not for the last, 'which is, however, the thing I most expressly wish to include in it'. In defence of the first law, Descartes spells out the conception of motion that it employs and contrasts this with the Aristotelian conception. His suggestion is that motion is simply to be equated with change of place or translation. The second law of motion is a law of the conservation of motion (or perhaps a law of conservation of the total 'force of motion') in collisions. In its defence, Descartes points to its advantages over the traditional accounts of continued projectile motion. Aristotelians were in disagreement amongst themselves about how to account for the continued motion of projectiles, and their accounts were premised upon a distinction between terrestrial and celestial motions. Descartes changes the question, so that it now becomes that of explaining why the motion of the projectile decays rather than why it continues to move, and the answer he provides is the air's 'resistance'.

Whereas the first two laws deal with the power of motion, the third deals with what Descartes regards as a separate issue: the direction of motion. It asserts that, whatever the path of a moving body, its tendency to motion, or *action*, is always rectilinear. The evidence presented for this is, first, that a stone released from a sling will not continue to move in a circle but will fly off along the tangent to the circle, and, second, while in the sling the stone will exert a force away from the centre causing the string to stretch, showing 'that it goes around only under constraint'. But there is a notorious discrepancy in Descartes' account here. The trouble is that, while the third law as stated in chapter 7 would seem to establish the uniqueness of rectilinear motion as an inertial motion, when he elaborates further on the law in chapter 13, he apparently counts a circular component in the motion of the stone as inertial as well. Why, after giving a clear statement of rectilinear inertia and providing an explanation of why rectilinear motion is the only inertial motion in terms of its 'simplicity', does he appear to blatantly contradict this? There are two complementary answers to this question, I believe, and both derive from Descartes' attempt to use hydrostatic model in his physical theory. The first is that a statement of a principle of inertia does not seem to be the point of the exercise. In one sense Descartes was not, and could not have been, concerned with inertia. He is not concerned to specify how a body behaves in the absence of forces, for example, because the bodies he deals with always move within a system of constraints, just as in statics: the aim is to understand the instantaneous collisions of inelastic bodies. One does not ask what would happen if the forces were removed, because the understanding of the action of these forces is the point of the exercise. The second is that what Descartes is concerned with in chapter 13 is not so much circular inertia as circular equilibrium, namely, the idea that a body moves in a continuous circular orbit because the forces acting upon it are exactly balanced, so that the net force is zero. The confusion arises because Descartes slides between this static notion of equilibrium (which involves the extremely problematic assumption that some motions are dynamically unbalanced) and the dynamic notion of inertia.

Chapters 8 to 12, using the theory of matter and laws of nature which have now been elaborated, set out the details of a heliocentric cosmology in the form of an account of a hypothetical 'new world', from the formation of the Sun and the stars (ch. 8), the planets and comets (ch. 9), the Earth and the Moon (ch. 10), and, finally, weight or gravity (ch. 11) and the tides (ch. 12). The key to this whole cosmology is Descartes' account of vortices. Because the universe is a plenum, for any part of it to move it is necessary that other parts of it move, and the simplest form of motion which takes the form of displacement is going to be a closed curve, although we have no reason to think that the universe turns around a single centre: rather, we may imagine different centres of motion. The matter revolving furthest away will be the largest or most agitated because it will describe the greatest circles, owing to its greater capacity to realise its inclination to continue motion in a straight line. Whatever differences in size and agitation we may imagine there to have been in the early stages of the universe, however, except for the large clumps of third element we can imagine that the constant motion and collision caused the difference in sizes of matter to be reduced as 'the larger pieces had to break and divide in order to pass through the same places as those that preceded them'. Similarly, differences in shape gradually disappear as repeated collisions smooth off the edges and all matter (of the second element) becomes rounded. Some pieces of matter are sufficiently large to avoid being broken down and rounded off in this way: these are what

Descartes refers to as the third element, and such pieces of matter form the planets and the comets. Finally, the collisions yield very small parts of matter, which accommodate themselves to the space available so that a void is not formed but this first element is formed in a greater quantity than is needed simply to fill in the spaces between pieces of second and third element, and the excess naturally moves towards the centre because the second element has a greater centrifugal tendency to move to the periphery, leaving the centre the only place for the first element to settle. There it forms perfectly fluid bodies which rotate at a greater rate than surrounding bodies and exude fine matter from their surfaces. These concentrations of first element in the form of fluid, round bodies at the centre of each system are suns, and the pushing action at their surfaces is 'what we shall take to be light'.

The universe, as Descartes represents it (Fig. 1.2), consists of an in-definite number of contiguous vortices, each with a sun or star at the centre, and planets revolving around this centre carried along by the sec-ond element. Occasionally, however, planets may be moving so quickly as to be carried outside the solar system altogether: then they become comets. Descartes describes the difference between the paths of planets and comets in terms of an analogy with bodies being carried along by rivers, the latter being like bodies that will have enough mass and speed to be carried from one river to another when rivers meet, whereas the former will just be carried along by the flow of their own river. Planets eventually enter into stable orbits, the less massive they are the closer to the centre, and once in this orbit they are simply carried along by the celestial fluid in which they are embedded. The stability of their orbits arises because, once a planet has attained a stable orbit, if it were to move inward it would immediately meet smaller and faster corpuscles of second element which would push it outward, and if it were to move outward, it would immediately meet larger corpuscles which would slow it down and make it move inward again.

This accounts for the motions of comets, and the motion of planets proper around the Sun, and Descartes now moves on to explain the motions of planetary satellites and the diurnal rotation of a planet like the Earth. The celestial matter in which the Earth is embedded moves faster at one side of the planet than at the other, and this gives the Earth a 'spin' or rotation, which in turn sets up a centrifugal effect, creating a small vortex around itself, in which the Moon is carried. Turning next to consider what the weight (*pesanteur*) of the Earth consists in, Descartes rejects the idea of weight as an intrinsic property. In earlier writings he

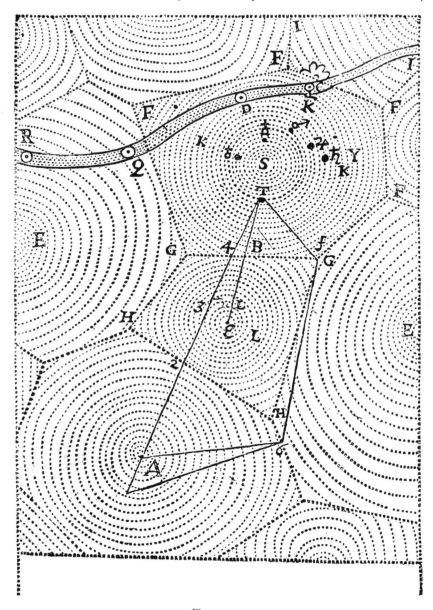

Figure 1.2

had defined weight in functional terms as 'the force of motion by which a body is impelled in the first instant of its motion'.[11] In a homogeneous plenum, where there is not only one kind of matter but one density of matter, this functional approach to weight is clearly crucial and he continues to think in functional terms in *Le Monde*.

Finally, the phenomenon of the tides is explained using the same materials. Direct evidence for the orbital and rotational motion of the Earth was not available in the seventeenth century, but the tides, which are difficult to explain on the assumption of a non-rotating Earth, do offer indirect evidence. Tides are a very complicated phenomenon, however, involving daily, half-monthly, monthly, and half-yearly cycles. Descartes was especially pleased with his account and wrote to Mersenne at the time that accounting for the tides had given him a great deal of trouble, and that, while he was not happy with all the details, he did not doubt the success of his account.[12] Although he will revise it over the next ten years, he will not alter its fundamentals. Indeed, the theory of the tides is really the first genuinely quantitative ingredient in *Le Monde*, but the fact that the earlier material is not quantitative should not blind us to the significance of Descartes' success in presenting a thoroughly mechanist cosmology which takes as its foundations a strictly mechanist conception of matter and the three laws of motion. *Le Monde* presents a fully mechanist alternative to Aristotelian systems, one which effectively derives heliocentrism from first principles, which offers a novel and apparently viable conception of matter, and which formulates fundamental laws of motion – laws that are clearly open to quantitative elaboration. But the jewel in the crown of *Le Monde* is the theory of light set out in the last three chapters, for, especially if we read these together with Descartes' other work in optics at this time, later set out in *La Dioptrique* and *Les Meteores*, we have an empirical, quantitative account of a physical question whose explanation derives directly from his mechanist cosmology.

Descartes' purpose in the last three chapters is to show how the behaviour of light rays can ultimately be explained in terms of his theory of the nature of matter and the three laws of motion. Indeed, the theory of matter turns out to be motivated directly by the requirements of Descartes' physical optics, for the first element makes up those bodies that produce light, namely suns and stars; the second element makes up the medium in which light is propagated, namely the celestial fluid; and those bodies that refract and reflect light, such as the planets, are

---

[11] AT x. 68.   [12] AT i. 261.

made up from the third element. Moreover, it is the laws of motion that underpin and explain the laws of refraction and reflection of light, and the accounts of phenomena such as the rainbow and parhelia that are based on these.

The laws of motion show us that, given the rotation of the Sun and the matter around it, there is a radial pressure which spreads outwards from the Sun along straight lines from its centre. This pressure is manifested as 'a trembling movement', a property which is 'very suitable for light'. Indeed, the inhabitants of Descartes' proposed new world 'have a nature such that, when their eyes are pushed in this way, they will have a sensation which is just like the one we have of light'. The question that Descartes now poses is whether this model accounts for the known properties of light. Setting out twelve 'principal' properties of light which a theory of light must account for, he proceeds to show that his account is not only compatible with all of these, but can actually explain them.

Descartes' achievement in *Le Monde* is twofold. In the first place, his vortex theory explains the stability of planetary orbits in a way that presents an intuitively plausible picture of orbital motion which requires no mysterious forces acting at a distance: the rapid rotation of the Sun at the centre of our solar system, through its resultant centrifugal force, causes the 'pool' of second matter to swirl around it, holding planets in orbits as a whirlpool holds bodies in a circular motion around it. Moreover, it explains this motion in terms of fundamental quantifiable physical notions, namely centrifugal force and the rectilinear tendencies of moving matter. In other words, the heliocentric theory is derived from a very simple theory of matter, three laws of motion, and the notion of a centrifugal force. Secondly, this account also enables Descartes to account for all the known principal properties of light, thereby providing a physical basis for the geometrical optics that he had pursued so fruitfully in the 1620s.

Le Monde was not to appear in Descartes' lifetime, however. At the end of November 1633, he wrote to Mersenne:

I had intended to send you my *Le Monde* as a New Year gift ... but in the meantime I tried to find out in Leiden and Amsterdam whether Galileo's *Sisteme du Monde* was available, as I thought I had heard that it was published in Italy last year. I was told that it had indeed been published, but that all copies had been burned at Rome, and that Galileo had been convicted and fined. I was so surprised by this that I nearly decided to burn all my papers, or at least let no one see them. For I couldn't imagine that he – an Italian and, I believe, in favour with the Pope – could have been made a criminal, just because he tried, as he certainly did, to establish that the Earth moves. . . . I must admit that if this view is false, then so too are the entire foundations of my philosophy, for it can be demonstrated from them quite clearly. And it is such an integral part of my treatise that I couldn't remove it without making the whole work defective. But for all that, I wouldn't want to publish a discourse which had a single word that the Church disapproved of; so I prefer to suppress it rather than publish it in a mutilated form.[13]

Galileo's *Dialogo . . . sopra i due Massimi Sistemi del Mondo* had in fact been withdrawn shortly after its publication in Florence in March 1632, and it was condemned by the Roman Inquisition on 23 July 1633. The condemnation had clear implications for *Le Monde*. Galileo's *Dialogo* provided physical evidence both for the Earth's diurnal rotation, in the tides, and for its annual orbital motion, in cyclical change in sunspot paths. It also provided a detailed and ingenious account of why our perceptual experience apparently does not accord with the Earth's motion, in the principle of the relativity of motion (albeit a very different principle from the one that Descartes will propose in *Principia*). The Inquisition's condemnation focused on the question of the physical reality of the Copernican hypothesis. A core issue in dispute in both the 1616 and 1633 condemnations of Copernicanism was whether the heliocentric theory was 'a matter of faith and morals' which the second decree of the Council of Trent had given the Church the sole power to decide.[14] Galileo and his defenders denied that it was, maintaining that the motion of the Earth and the stability of the Sun were covered by the first criterion in Melchior Cano's handbook of post-Tridentine orthodoxy, *Locorum Theologicorum Libri Duodecim*, namely that when the authority of the Church Fathers 'pertains to the faculties contained within the natural light of reason, it does not provide certain arguments but only arguments as strong as reason itself when in agreement with nature'. Opponents of Galileo treated Scripture as a source of scientific knowledge, and argued that the case was covered by different criteria, such as the sixth, which states that the Church Fathers, if they agree on something, 'cannot err on dogmas of the faith'. In the 1633 condemnation, the latter interpretation was effectively established, and this meant that the physical motion of the Earth could not be established by natural–philosophical means. In other words, the kind of arguments that Galileo offered in the *Dialogo* had no power to decide the issue, and this in effect meant that the kind of arguments that Descartes had offered in *Le Monde* had no power to decide the issue either.

[13] AT I. 270–1.
[14] For details see Richard J. Blackwell, *Galileo, Bellarmine, and the Bible* (Notre Dame, 1991).

Descartes was clearly devastated by the condemnation of Galileo, and he abandoned any attempt to publish *Le Monde* as a result.[15] Because *L'Homme* is a continuation of *Le Monde* – it is part of the same project in natural philosophy, extending the mechanist programme into physiology, and relying on the matter theory and mechanics established in *Le Monde* – it, too, had to be abandoned. In some ways, *L'Homme* was even more radical than *Le Monde*. The idea that mechanism might allow one to account for everything from physical processes to the behaviour of celestial bodies was certainly contentious, not least in the Copernican consequences that Descartes draws from this. But the project was common ground among quite a few natural philosophers in the 1630s: Beeckman, Mersenne, and Gassendi for example. A mechanistic physiology was a different matter: this was both far more ambitious and far more threatening. In *Le Monde*, Descartes postulated a single kind of matter in the universe and this matter is inert, homogeneous, and qualitatively undifferentiated. The boundaries of bodies are determined by motion relative to surrounding matter, and any variation in properties is a function of the size, speed, and direction of the matter. It is with this notion of matter that Descartes attempts to account for all functions and behaviour of animals.

L'Homme follows much the same course as *Le Monde*. It does not purport to describe the physiology of real human beings, but of 'a statue or machine made of earth' that God could have created,[16] just as *Le Monde* purports to describe an imaginary world and not the real one. At the end of each work the aim is to establish that, if we compare the imaginary constructs with the real thing, we will find in both cases that they are indistinguishable; and, although the text breaks off before this point in *L'Homme*, Descartes writes to Mersenne that he has discovered nothing in his extensive dissections that he cannot explain, that is, that he cannot explain in micro-mechanical terms.[17] The only difference is that a full account of human beings would also include their souls, whereas Descartes is concerned here only with their bodies.

Animal physiology is introduced right from the beginning of *L'Homme* as the workings of a machine.[18] The digestion of food is described in a mixture of mechanical and chemical terms. The food is first broken

---

[15] That it was indeed the condemnation of Galileo that prevented publication is clear not just from the letter to Mersenne just quoted, but also from his request to Mersenne to tell Naudé that the only thing stopping him publishing his physics was the prohibition on advocating the physical reality of the Earth's motion: Descartes to Mersenne, December 1649; AT III. 258.

[16] AT XI. 120. [17] Descartes to Mersenne 20 February 1639; AT II. 525. [18] AT XI. 120.

down into small parts and then, through the action of heat from the blood and that of various humours which squeeze between the particles of blood, the food is gradually divided into excrementary and nutritive parts. The heat generated by the heart and carried in the blood is the key ingredient here, and Descartes devotes much more attention to the heart and the circulation of the blood than to functions such as digestion and respiration. He accepts that blood circulates throughout the body, but, like most of his contemporaries, rejects Harvey's explanation of circulation in terms of the heart being a pump, preferring to construe the motion as being due to the production of heat in the heart. The heart is like a furnace, or rather like the sun, for it contains in its pores 'one of those fires without light',[19] which are comprised of the first element that also makes up the sun. In fact, Descartes really had little option but to reject Harvey's account. To accept that the motion of the blood was due to the contractive and expansive action of the heart would have required providing some source of power for its pumping action, and it was hard to conceive how he could do this without recourse to non-mechanical powers, whereas at least he can point to phenomena such as natural fermentation in defending his own account of thermogenetic processes creating pressure in the arteries. The most important feature of the circulation of the blood from the point of view of Cartesian psycho-physiology is the fact that it carries the 'animal spirits', which it bears up through the carotid arteries into the brain. These are separated out from the blood and enter the brain through the pineal gland, at the centre of the cerebral cavities. This is a mechanical procedure in that the animal spirits are the subtlest parts of the blood and hence can be filtered into the pineal gland through pores too fine to admit anything larger.[20]

Having dealt with the heart – the heat of which is the 'principle of life' – and the circulation of the blood, Descartes turns to the nervous system. The nervous system works by means of the animal spirits, which enter the nerves and change the shape of the muscles, which in turn results in the movement of the limbs, an analogy being drawn with the force of water in fountains. He sets out his programme as follows:

I wish to speak to you first of the fabric of the nerves and the muscles, and to show you how – from the sole fact that the spirits in the brain are ready to enter into certain of the nerves – they have the ability to move certain members at that instant. Then, having touched briefly on respiration and other such simple and ordinary movements, I shall say how external objects act upon the sense

---

[19] AT XI. 123.   [20] AT XI. 128.

organs. After that I shall explain in detail all that happens in the cavities and pores of the brain, what route the animal spirits follow there, and which of our functions this machine can imitate by means of them. For, were I to begin with the brain and merely follow in order the course of the spirits, as I did for the blood, I believe what I have to say would be much less clear.[21]

The pineal gland is also responsible for the discharge of the animal spirits to the muscles via the nerves, which are hollow tubes with a double membrane continuous with the brain's pia mater and dura mater.[22] In general terms, what happens is that external stimuli displace the peripheral ends of the nerve fibres, and a structural isomorph of the impression made on the sense organ is transmitted to the brain. This results in changes in the patterns formed by the animal spirits in the brain, which can produce changes in the outflow of spirits to the nerves. At the muscle, a small influx of spirit from the nerve causes the spirits already there to open a valve into its antagonist. Spirits then flow from the antagonist which causes it to relax, as well as causing the first muscle to contract.

Descartes deals in turn briefly with the control of breathing, swallowing, sneezing, yawning, coughing, and excretion, before turning to 'automatic motions', which we shall be looking at in chapter 7. He then deals with the external senses, concentrating on vision, before turning to an account of the internal senses, where he not only attempts to explain traditional areas such as imagination and memory in corporeal terms, but also provides a sketch of various temperaments in terms of animal spirits. The treatment of the latter simply translates various temperaments and humours into their supposed microscopic correlates in an intuitive but simplistic way. Generosity, liberality, and love, for example, are attributed to abundance of animal spirits; confidence and courage are attributed to strong or coarse animal spirits; promptness, diligence, and desire are attributed to unusually agitated animal spirits; tranquillity is attributed to the exceptionally uniform action of animal spirits; on the other hand, malice is attributed to lack of animal spirits, timidity to weak animal spirits, tardiness to lax spirits, and so on.[23] Various conditions such as sneezing and vertigo are explained in a similarly primitive way, as is the difference between the sleeping and the waking state: the brain in a waking state is characterised as having all its fibres tense and

---

[21] AT xi. 132.

[22] AT xi. 133. In reflex action, as we shall see, the pineal gland is bypassed, so that the discharge of animal spirits will be independent of the action of the pineal, and it will be the cerebral ventricles that direct the animal spirits.

[23] AT xi. 166–7.

its animal spirits strong, whereas the sleeping brain is characterised as having lax fibres.[24]

Some parts of Descartes' account do go beyond this simplistic picturing of micro-corpuscularian mechanisms, however, and memory and perceptual cognition, for example, are given particularly sophisticated treatment. We shall be looking at these in chapter 7.

LA DISCOURS AND *LES ESSAIS*

As we have seen, Descartes abandoned *Le Monde*, and with it *L'Homme*, in 1633. As far as *L'Homme* is concerned, it is evident that Descartes continued his research in this area, as there are manuscript notes on anatomy, physiology, and embryology dating from the 1630s and early 1640s.[25] This work culminates in the incomplete *La Description du Corps Humain*, dating from the winter of 1647/8. In his published writings, however, the only mentions of his work in physiology are in Part V of *La Discours*, which summarises *L'Homme*, focusing on the circulation of the blood, and in the opening sections of *Les Passions de l'Ame*.

The situation with regard to *Le Monde* is different. In 1637, in his first published work, Descartes offered a 'discourse on method' and three 'essays', on geometrical optics, meteorology, and analytic geometry respectively. The first two of these essays bear on the project of *Le Monde*. As regards the first, optics had been a key concern of *Le Monde*, but within the context of cosmology, where it had been tightly tied in with his heliocentrism. So, for example, the fact that the sun was the source of light had been premised on its being composed of the finest type of matter – that responsible for heat and light on Descartes' scheme – which was pushed into the centre as larger bodies exercised their inertial and centrifugal tendencies more freely, revolving closer to the periphery, where their orbits approximated more closely to a straight line. And the uniform radiation of light from the sun had been explained in terms of its rotation around the centre of the system, the centrifugal tendencies at its surface causing light matter to be projected radially outwards. ⟨The cosmological setting for Descartes' theory of light is ignored in *La Dioptrique*, where the concern is with geometrical optics, rather than physical optics, and the contentious cosmological consequences of his physical optics are avoided⟩

[24] AT XI. 174–5, 197–9.   [25] See the collections of texts in AT XI. 505–638.

Most of the material in the essay on meteorology is very traditional (we shall look at the *Principia* version of this material, which includes Descartes' contentious theory of the formation of the Earth, in chapter 6), but one section, that on the rainbow, is novel, and indeed Descartes identifies it as the example of his 'method'. It is of interest in countering those views of Descartes that construe him as deducing his results in natural philosophy from first principles. In *La Discours*, he describes the procedure by which he has proceeded in *La Dioptrique* and *Les Meteores* in the following terms:

The order which I have followed in this regard is as follows. First, I have attempted generally to discover the principles or first causes of everything which is or could be in the world, without in this connection considering anything but God alone, who has created the world, and without drawing them from any source except certain seeds of truth which are naturally in our minds. Next I considered what were the first and most common effects that could be deduced from these causes, and it seems to me that in this way I found the heavens, the stars, an Earth, and even on the Earth, water, air, fire, the minerals and a few other such things which are the most common and simple of all that exist, and consequently the easiest to understand. Then, when I wished to descend to those that were more particular, there were so many objects of various kinds that I did not believe it possible for the human mind to distinguish the forms or species of body which are on the earth from the infinity of others which might have been, had it been God's will to put them there, or consequently to make them of use to us, if it were not that one arrives at the causes through the effects and avails oneself of many specific experiments. In subsequently passing over in my mind all the objects which have been presented to my senses, I dare to say that I have not noticed anything that I could not easily explain in terms of the principles that I have discovered. But I must also admit that the power of nature is so great and so extensive, and these principles so simple and general, that I hardly observed any effect that I did not immediately realise could be deduced from the principles in many different ways. The greatest difficulty is usually to discover in which of these ways the effect depends on them. In this situation, so far as I know the only thing that can be done is to try and find experiments which are such that their result varies depending upon which of them provides the correct explanation.[26]

In a letter to Antoine Vatier of 22 February 1638, Descartes elaborates:

I must say first that my purpose was not to teach the whole of my method in *La Discours*, where I set it out, but only to say enough to show that the new views in *La Dioptrique* and *Les Meteores* were not random notions, and were perhaps worth the trouble of examining. I could not demonstrate the use of this method

[26] AT VI. 63–5.

in the three treatises which I gave, because it prescribes an order of research which is quite different from the one I thought proper for exposition. I have however given a brief sample of it in my account of the rainbow, and if you take the trouble to re-read it, I hope it will satisfy you more than it did the first time; the matter is, after all, quite difficult in itself. I attached these three treatises to *La Discours* which precedes them because I am convinced that if people examine them carefully and compare them with what has previously been written on the same topics, they will have grounds for judging that the method I adopt is no ordinary one and is perhaps better than some others.[27]

The point is reiterated in *Les Meteores* itself, where Descartes tells us that his account of the rainbow is the most appropriate example 'to show how, by means of the method which I use, one can attain knowledge which was not available to those whose writings we possess'.[28]

One of the central problems in *Les Meteores*, to which Book 8 is devoted, is that of explaining the angle at which the bows of the rainbow appear in the sky. He begins by noting that rainbows are not only formed in the sky, but also in fountains and showers in the presence of sunlight. This leads him to formulate the hypothesis that the phenomenon is caused by light reacting on drops of water. To test this hypothesis, he constructs a glass model of the raindrop, comprising a large glass sphere filled with water, and, standing with his back to the sun, he holds up the sphere in the sun's light, moving it up and down so that colours are produced (Fig. 1.3). Then, if we let the light from the sun come

from the part of the sky marked AFZ, and my eye be at point E, then when I put this globe at the place BCD, the part of it at D seems to me wholly red and incomparably more brilliant than the rest. And whether I move towards it or step back from it, or move it to the right or to the left, or even turn it in a circle around my head, then provided the line DE always marks an angle of around 42° with the line EM, which one must imagine to extend from the centre of the eye to the centre of the sun, D always appears equally red. But as soon as I made this angle DEM the slightest bit smaller it did not disappear completely in the one stroke but first divided as into two less brilliant parts in which could be seen yellow, blue, and other colours. Then, looking towards the place marked K on the globe, I perceived that, making the angle KEM around 52°, K also seemed to be coloured red, but not so brilliant.[29]

Descartes then describes how he covered the globe at all points except B and D. The ray still emerged, showing that the primary and secondary bows are caused by two refractions and one or two internal reflections of the incident ray. He next describes how the same effect can be produced

[27] AT I. 559–60.   [28] AT VI. 325.   [29] AT VI. 326–7.

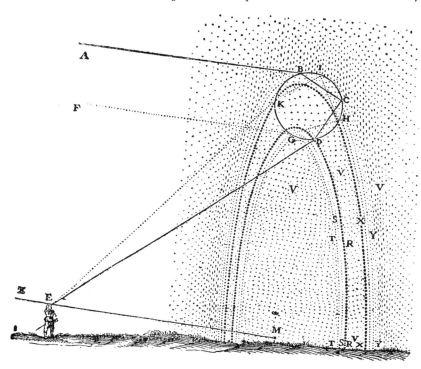

Figure 1.3

with a prism, and this indicates that neither a curved surface nor reflection are necessary for colour dispersion. Moreover, the prism experiment shows that the effect does not depend on the angle of incidence and that one refraction is sufficient for its production. Finally, Descartes calculates from the refractive index of rainwater what an observer would see when light strikes a drop of water at varying angles of incidence, and finds that the optimum difference for visibility between incident and refracted rays is for the former to be viewed at an angle of 41° to 42° and the latter at an angle of 51° to 52°,[30] which is exactly what the hypothesis predicts.

In so far as there is a method of discovery in Descartes, this is it. But the later writings, most notably the *Meditationes* and the *Principia*, are even less concerned with discovery than *La Discours*: their concern is with the legitimation of Descartes' natural philosophy.

[30] AT VI. 336.

[handwritten margin note: articulating 'method of discovery' is (much) less important, esp. in later works, than the project of legitimating Descartes' natural phil.]

METAPHYSICS AND THE LEGITIMATION
OF NATURAL PHILOSOPHY

The outcome of the crisis provoked by the condemnation of Galileo's heliocentrism was a new direction in Descartes' work. He does not abandon interest in natural philosophy, and to the end of his life continues to think it has been his most important contribution. In a letter to Elizabeth of 28 June 1643, he tells her that the principles of metaphysics must be understood, but once understood one need spend no more time upon them: rather one should then proceed to devoting one's time 'to thoughts in which the intellect co-operates with the imagination and the senses',[31] that is, natural philosophy. The same point is made to Burman in 1649, ⟨Descartes insisting that one should not waste too much time on metaphysical questions, especially his *Meditationes*, as these are just preparation for the main questions, which 'concern physical and observable things'.[32]⟩

Descartes' post-1633 preoccupation is to legitimate mechanistic natural phil. by articulating a metaphysics & epistemology that grounds such a natural philosophy

But Descartes' interest in natural–philosophical areas such as optics, mechanics, and cosmology after 1633 is confined largely, if not exclusively, to polemics and systematisation, and above all to the legitimation of a mechanist natural philosophy by metaphysical and epistemological means, a completely different enterprise from that pursued in the pre-1633 works, of which *Le Monde* and *L'Homme* are the culmination. Setting out the kind of metaphysics that gives just the right fit with his natural philosophy, indeed grounds the kind of natural philosophy he wants, is the preoccupation of the *Meditationes* and the first Part of the *Principia*, which reworks the *Meditationes*.

The *Meditationes* uses a sceptically driven epistemology to systematically strip down the world – the world of common sense and the world of Aristotelian natural philosophy – so that the assumptions that lie behind this picture are laid bare, and found wanting. Descartes then proceeds to build up the world metaphysically from first principles, using a notion of clear and distinct ideas, backed up by a divine guarantee. What this yields is a sharp distinction between the mind and the corporeal realm, and an account of the corporeal realm radically different from that with which the *Meditationes* began. Because our new starting point is clear and distinct ideas (the paradigm for which is the *cogito*), we cannot ask about the existence of the corporeal world without having a clear and distinct idea of what it is that we are asking for the existence of. The question of existence only becomes determinate, and thereby answerable on Descartes' account, when we ask whether something with

---

[31] AT III. 695.   [32] AT v. 165.

particular characteristics exists, where the characteristics in question are not only fully specified, but also securely grasped. Unless we start from things which we clearly and distinctly grasp, we can never be sure we are actually getting anywhere⟩ The question is whether there are any conceptions of the corporeal world available to us which offer a grasp of this kind. Descartes' answer is that he knows of only one, namely a mathematical grasp of the world. Corporeal things, he tells us at the end of the *Meditationes*,

> may not all exist in a way that exactly corresponds with my sensory grasp of them, since sensory understanding is often very obscure and confused. But at least they possess all things that I perceive in them clearly and distinctly, that is to say, all those things which, generally speaking, come under the purview of pure mathematics.[33]

If the arguments of the *Meditationes* go through, what Descartes has established is that our starting point in natural philosophy must be a world stripped of all Aristotelian forms and qualities, and consisting in nothing but geometrically quantifiable extension. The only natural philosophy compatible with such a picture is mechanism, in particular, mechanism of the kind set out by Descartes in the matter theory and mechanics of *Le Monde*. If we grant him his matter theory, and the two basic principles of his mechanics, the principle of rectilinear inertia and that of centrifugal force, then, if the argument of *Le Monde* is correct, we have heliocentrism, for this is all he needs. In this way, the *Meditationes* connect up directly with *Le Monde*, providing a metaphysical route to the natural philosophy of the latter and providing a legitimation of the whole enterprise.

[margin note: link btwn D's metaphysics & his natural philosophy]

But the *Principia*, which begins with what is, despite a reordering of some arguments, in effect a summary of the *Meditationes*, does not simply lead into *Le Monde*. Much the same ground is covered, but the material is reworked in terms of a metaphysical vocabulary wholly absent from *Le Monde*, not required for the natural–philosophical (as opposed to the legitimatory) thrust of the *Principia*, and it is occasionally unhelpful in illuminating the natural–philosophical questions it raises.[34]

---

[33] AT vii. 80.

[34] This is particularly so on the vexed question of force. As Alan Gabbey points out, Descartes clearly has a realist view of forces (something determined by natural–philosophical considerations), but his metaphysics of substance and modes seems to leave no place for it, so its ontological status is very unclear: 'New Doctrines of Motion', in Daniel Garber and Michael Ayers, eds., *The Cambridge History of Seventeenth-Century Philosophy* (Cambridge, 1998), 649–79: 656.

Descartes did not decide immediately on the textbook format for the development of his ideas in natural philosophy after the *Meditationes*, and there exists what is probably a first experiment in setting out his post-*Meditationes* natural philosophy, *La Recherche de la vérité*. Interestingly, this unfinished dialogo pulls us in a very different direction from that evident in the *Principia*.

La Recherche de la vérité par la lumiere naturelle – 'the search for truth through the natural light [of reason]' – begins by telling us that 'this light alone, without any help from philosophy or religion, determines what opinion *un honnête homme* [literally, a good or honest man] should hold on any matter that may occupy his thought, and penetrates into the secrets of the most difficult sciences'.[35] The dialogue contrasts the fitness for natural philosophy of three characters: Epistemon, someone well versed in Scholasticism; Eudoxe, a man of moderate intelligence who has not been corrupted by false beliefs; and Poliandre, who has never studied but is a man of action, a courtier, and a soldier (as Descartes himself had been). Epistemon and Poliandre are taken over the territory of sceptical doubt and foundational questions by Eudoxe, but in a way that shows Poliandre's preparedness for, or capacity for, natural philosophy, and Epistemon's lack of preparedness. Preparedness here is in effect preparedness for receiving instruction in Cartesian natural philosophy. The *honnête homme*, Descartes tells us,

came ignorant into the world, and since the knowledge of his early years rested solely on the weak foundation of the senses and the authority of his teachers, it was close to inevitable that his imagination should have been filled with innumerable false thoughts before his reason could guide his conduct. So later on, he needs to have either very great natural talent or the instruction of a very wise teacher, to lay the foundations for a solid science.[36]

The thrust of Descartes' discussion is that Poliandre has not had his mind corrupted, because, in his role as an *honnête homme*, he has not spent too much time on book-learning, which 'would be a kind of defect in his education'.[37] The implication is that Epistemon has been corrupted in this way, and so is not trainable as the kind of natural philosopher Descartes seeks. It is only the *honnête homme* who can be trained, and it is Poliandre whom Eudoxe sets out to coax into the fold of Cartesian natural philosophy, not Epistemon.

[35] AT x. 495.   [36] AT x. 496.   [37] AT x. 495.

This is in stark contrast with the *Principia*, where the aim is to engage Scholastic philosophy, to some extent on its own terms, and in effect to reform and transform Scholasticism into Cartesian natural philosophy. Descartes sets out to convince his readers (the text is primarily aimed at students who would otherwise be reading the late Scholastic textbooks that Descartes himself was raised on) that they too should be Cartesians in natural philosophy. It is true that we might think of the procedure of radical doubt, and the purging that results, as a way of transforming everyone into an *honnête homme*, and to some extent it is, although, as we shall see, in his account of the passions Descartes makes it clear that, once we leave the programmatic level, ridding ourselves of prejudices and preconceived ideas is not so simple, and it requires the cultivation of a particular mentality, which is really what we witness in *La Recherche*. *La Recherche* does not so much contradict the trajectory of the *Principia* – as we shall see, the questions it raises are appropriate to the projected Part VI of the *Principia* – as provide a radically different route to thinking about how one achieves the ends of establishing a Cartesian natural philosophy. *La Recherche* raises such questions right at the beginning of the exercise, whereas the *Principia* (on my reconstruction) defers them until the end.

Descartes decided in favour of the *Principia*, abandoning *La Recherche* unfinished. To understand this choice, and to grasp what is going on in the *Principia*, we need to understand the Scholastic textbook tradition that it engages.

CHAPTER 2

The Principia *and the Scholastic textbook tradition*

On 30 September 1640, Descartes wrote to Mersenne:

I should like to reread some of the philosophy [of the Jesuits], which I have not done for twenty years, to see if it looks any better now than it did previously. In this respect, I ask that you send me the names of authors who have written textbooks [*cours*] of philosophy, and to tell me which are the most commonly used, and whether there have been any new ones in the last twenty years. I remember only some of the Conimbricenses, Toletus, and Rubius. I would also like to know whether anyone has made an abridgement of the whole of Scholastic philosophy, as this would save the time it would take to read their huge volumes. I think there was a Carthusian or a Feuillant who made an abridgement of this kind, but I don't remember his name.[1]

Mersenne presumably informed Descartes that the abridgement or abstract he was seeking was the *Summa Philosophiæ* of Eustachius a Sancto Paulo (first published 1629), for six weeks later he tells Mersenne that it seems to him 'the best book of this kind ever written'.[2] Nevertheless, his general opinion of the material it abstracts is low, and he tells Mersenne that he does not believe 'the diversity of views among the Scholastics makes their philosophy difficult to refute, for it is easy to overturn the foundations, on which they all agree, and, this being done, all their disagreements will seem beside the point [*inepti*]'.[3]

Descartes then spells out his plan to write 'a complete textbook of philosophy' in which he will: 'simply put down my true conclusions, with all the true premises from which I derive them, which I think I could do without too many words'. In the same volume, he adds, he will also include a traditional textbook with notes at the end of each proposition,

---

[1] Descartes to Mersenne, 30 September 1640; AT III. 185.
[2] Eustachius' textbook was one of the most widely used, in both Catholic and Protestant countries: see Charles Lohr, 'Renaissance Latin Aristotle Commentaries: Authors D–F', *Renaissance Quarterly*, 30 (1976), 714–45: 725–6.
[3] Descartes to Mersenne, 11 November 1640; AT III. 232.

in which his own views and those of others are compared.[4] He seems to have decided on Eustachius' *Summa* as the textbook, but he also mentions the textbook of Abra de Raconis, *Summa totius Philosophiae* (1629) which he intends to look at in the hope that it is shorter than Eustachius' (which is 800 pages), in which case he would use that instead,[5] but on examining it he concludes that: 'it is less suited to my plan than that of Eustachius'.[6] However, by 21 January 1641, on learning of the recent death of Eustachius, he has changed his mind about the idea of printing a textbook along with his own work.[7]

This does not mean that the plan of pitting his project against the Scholastic one has been abandoned, and in 1642 he wrote to Constantijn Huygens that he was thinking of calling the work *Summa Philosophiæ*, the same title as Eustachius' textbook, 'to make it more welcome to the Scholastics, who are now persecuting it and trying to smother it before its birth'.[8] The point is made at greater length in the long self-justificatory letter, appended to the seventh set of replies to objections to the *Meditationes*, to Dinet, a Jesuit who had taught at La Flèche. Dinet was a man of influence in his order and someone whom Descartes hoped to win over. His enemies, Descartes tells Dinet,

grow in number every day, and as often happens the enthusiasm with which they seek every chance to disparage me has not been matched by my supporters in my defence. So I began to fear that their clandestine attempts to discredit me may meet with some success, and that they will cause me greater trouble if I were to stick to my plan of publishing nothing than if I were to openly confront them; for by setting before them in its entirety the work of which they are so afraid, I can at least make sure that they will have nothing further to be afraid of. I have therefore decided to submit to the public the whole of my few reflections on philosophy, and to fight for the widest possible acceptance of my views, if they are true. Because of this I shall not present them in the same order and style as I adopted when I wrote about many of these matters previously, namely in the treatise [*Le Monde/L'Homme*] which I outlined in *La Discours de la Méthode*, but instead I shall try to use a style more suited to the current practice in the Schools. That is, I shall deal with each topic in turn, in short articles, and

---

[4] AT III. 233. Cf. Descartes to [Charlet], [December 1640]; AT III. 270, where he talks of 'a full comparison between the philosophy of the Schools and my own'. This letter, addressed to a Jesuit assumed to be Charlet, is interesting because of its rather threatening tone. Descartes does not speak of himself publishing the book, but rather of 'a friend' publishing the book, comparing Descartes' philosophy favourably with that of the Jesuits, because the latter have spoken disparagingly of his philosophy.

[5] AT III. 234.   [6] Descartes to Mersenne, 3 December 1640: AT III. 251.

[7] Descartes to Mersenne, 21 January 1641; AT III. 286.

[8] Descartes to Huygens, 31 January 1642; AT III. 523.

present the topics in such an order that the proof of what comes later depends solely on what has come earlier, so that everything is connected together into a single structure. In this way I hope to be able to provide such a clear account of the truth of all the issues normally discussed in philosophy, that anyone who is seeking the truth may be able to find it in my book without difficulty.⁹

There can, in short, be no doubt that Descartes sees his project as being in direct competition with the Scholastic textbook, and he contrasts his project, which is inspired by the desire for truth, with the Scholastic one, motivated by the desire for controversy and contradiction.[10]

What he does in the *Principia* is to rewrite his philosophy in Scholastic terms, and to present it as a total system in the way in which the Scholastic textbooks presented their system. The plan for an explicit comparison is abandoned, but there can be no doubt that there is an implicit one. The question is why, when he clearly has such a low view of at least the content of the Scholastic textbook tradition, having rejected the idea that this is a productive way of pursuing natural philosophy twenty years earlier – and, given his evident lack of familiarity with anything at all in the area written since then, he had clearly not returned to it – he now finds it necessary to engage this tradition in such a large-scale way. For, in engaging it, he not only has to recast the presentation of his own philosophy into a traditional format, he has also to rewrite this philosophy in Scholastic terms so that comparison is possible, and in doing this he has to engage doctrines the motivation for which lies outside his own project in natural philosophy. Each of these carries an element of risk: Descartes is fighting the enemy on their own terrain, so to speak, and under their rules of engagement. He can do this only because he is so sure of his own position: after all, as we have just seen, his view is that Scholastic philosophy can be refuted easily because it rests on untenable assumptions. Still, he could presumably demonstrate the untenability of these assumptions, and then proceed to set out his own programme on his own terms. Why, having refuted the assumptions underlying Scholastic philosophy, does he then follow the Scholastic route of encyclopedic presentation? The answer can only be that he did not simply want to destroy Scholastic philosophy, he wanted to replace it with his own, so his aim is, at least in part, to show that his own philosophy meets the needs of Scholastic philosophy, that is, meets the kinds of requirements that Christianised Aristotelianism set for itself and failed to realise.[11] Descartes was not the only one of

⁹ AT VII. 577.   ¹⁰ Descartes to Mersenne, 22 December 1641; AT III. 465.
¹¹ While there can be no doubt that he failed to convince his Scholastic contemporaries of his account, by the beginning of the eighteenth century we do begin to find some accommodation

his contemporaries to see the question in these terms: Gassendi also believed that Aristotelianism had failed in its attempt to secure a viable and orthodox natural philosophy, and he tried to replace it with a revived version of Epicureanism.[12] As well as producing a viable metaphysics and natural philosophy, adopting the textbook genre means that a number of considerations about orthodoxy – that is, compatibility with Christian teaching – that did not necessarily correspond to anything in the internal trajectory of Descartes' work needed to be accommodated in one way or another.

To understand what lies behind Descartes' adoption of the textbook format, we need first to understand what the rationale behind the textbook tradition was, what topics were included and why, and why they were ordered in the way they were. The late Scholastic textbook was not merely the most convenient way of presenting a comprehensive body of information, it was also a way of keeping control over the topics it had selected as being constitutive of the philosophical enterprise, marking out this enterprise as distinctively its own, and keeping competitors at bay. Above all, by the late sixteenth century it was as much as anything else a holding operation, a way of consolidating a philosophical system that had begun to come apart at the seams.

THE PROBLEM OF NATURAL PHILOSOPHY

The key problem that underlies the textbook tradition is the relation between metaphysics and natural philosophy, and the depth and complexity of this problem, as well as its importance for Descartes' project, are such that some detail is needed if we are to appreciate just what was at stake.[13]

Aristotle had divided knowledge or science into the theoretical, the practical, and the productive sciences. There were three theoretical sciences: mathematics (which deals with those things that do not change and have no independent existence), physics or natural philosophy (which

with Cartesianism in Jesuit textbooks of Buffier, Rapin, and Regnault: see Desmond M. Clarke, *Occult Powers and Hypotheses: Cartesian Natural Philosophy under Louis XIV* (Oxford, 1989), 241–4.

[12] See, for example, the Introduction to the *Syntagma*, where he points out that just as the medieval Christian philosophers were able to expunge his serious errors, his task is to expunge the errors of Epicurus so as to make Epicureanism the philosophy of Christianity: *Opera Omnia*, 6 vols. (Lyons, 1658), I. 5 cols. 1–2. On this project, see Barry Brundell, *Pierre Gassendi* (Dordrecht, 1987), ch. 3.

[13] The material in this section is drawn from work in progress, in which my aim is to understand the origins of modernity. Part of the argument of this project is that the failure to reconcile Aristotelian natural philosophy and a theologically driven metaphysics plays a key role in the early development of modernity.

deals with those things that do change and have an independent existence), and metaphysics or first philosophy (which deals with those things that do not change and have an independent existence). Natural philosophy was the pivot on which everything else turned here: both the relation between natural philosophy and metaphysics, and that between natural philosophy and mathematics, were problematic.

The latter became a problem of general significance only in the wake of the 1616 Condemnation of Copernicanism, however, and, while there were occasionally questions raised about the standing of mathematics within the Aristotelian tradition, when it did become a problem this was due to a conflict between Aristotelianism's qualitative approach to natural–philosophical explanation and competing conceptions of natural philosophy in which the quantitative understanding of natural processes was the chief aim. The relation between metaphysics and natural philosophy, on the other hand, had a much longer history. It is the single most problematic and important theme of the textbook tradition, and indeed it had been the major source of philosophical concern since the revival of interest in Aristotle in the Christian West.

From the middle of the twelfth century, almost as quickly as the texts of Aristotle were being translated into Latin for the first time, a series of commentaries began to be produced at the University of Salerno,[14] and these and other sources made Aristotle's work available to theologians and philosophers at centres such as Paris for the first time in the Christian West around the beginning of the thirteenth century.[15] The introduction of Aristotle's works was accompanied by a series of condemnations, beginning in 1210, when the University of Paris banned all public and private teaching of Aristotle's natural philosophy in the Arts Faculty, under penalty of excommunication. The ban was renewed on several occasions, until 1255, when Aristotle's works were finally allowed to be taught; but, in 1270, the Bishop of Paris, Étienne Tempier, issued a condemnation of Aristotelian philosophy, and in 1277 the condemnation, with the encouragement and support of Pope John XXI, was extended to 40 theological and 179 philosophical propositions. The 1277 Condemnation drew into the open a number of fundamental ambiguities about just what the relative standing of theology, metaphysics, and natural philosophy was, and it was instrumental in establishing or

---

[14] See Danielle Jacquart, 'Aristotelian Thought in Salerno', in Peter Dronke, ed., *A History of Twelfth-Century Western Philosophy* (Cambridge, 1988).
[15] On the history of Latin translation of Aristotle see Bernard Dod, 'Aristoteles Latinus', in N. Kretzman et al., eds., *The Cambridge History of Later Medieval Philosophy* (Cambridge, 1982).

reinforcing a set of constraints on how questions were decided as being metaphysical or natural–philosophical. These constraints would be widely contested in the course of the next three and a half centuries, but, at least until the early decades of the sixteenth century, were contested within a framework that was established in the thirteenth century.

The introduction of Aristotelian philosophy undermined a traditional, secure understanding of the relation between theology, natural philosophy, and metaphysics, which Augustine did more than anyone else to establish. In the Patristic period, we witness the gradual 'Christianisation' of philosophy (metaphysics, natural philosophy, ethics etc.), begun by the early Church Fathers and brought to completion by Augustine. In its early stages, the project is that of nurturing what is worthwhile in pagan thought in the nourishing atmosphere of Christian teaching with Clement of Alexandria, for example, presenting himself as Christ's gardener, cutting twigs from the rank, dried-back and brittle bushes of pagan literature, and grafting them onto the stock of Christ's truth.[16] In its later development, especially in the writings of Augustine, the project amounts to nothing short of a total translation of all philosophy into Christian terms. Christianity is conceived of as the final form of philosophy. Using the language of the classical philosophers to formulate his theology, Augustine attempts to show that Christianity is able to answer all the questions of classical metaphysics. In general terms, not only does Christianity supplement classical philosophy here, it appropriates the teachings of this philosophy, denying that they were ever the property of the ancients in the first place, and it construes every philosophical question in terms of Christian teaching.

This appropriation of earlier thought by Christianity made it possible for it to present itself as the final answer to what earlier philosophers were striving for, and it meant four things. First, it effectively meant that it had no external competition. No system of thought was alien to it, not even paganism, because it had effectively appropriated all other intellectual systems and made them its own, and in the strongest possible way: by providing what (it considered) they all lacked in its Christianisation of earlier philosophies. Second, it had assimilated a relatively sophisticated body of philosophical doctrine, derived above all from Stoicism and Neoplatonism, which, with the decline of speculative philosophical schools at the end of the Hellenistic era, meant that it assumed an intellectual leadership. Third, it meant that philosophy – in which one

---

[16] Peter Brown, *The Body and Society* (London, 1989), 124.

should primarily include moral philosophy, metaphysics, and natural philosophy – could not threaten theology because philosophy was evaluated with respect to the contribution it made to the whole, a whole that was ultimately governed by revealed religion. This did not mean that the reconciliation of various philosophical systems – or more usually selected ingredients from various philosophical systems – with revelation and Christian dogma was not contested during the Patristic era,[17] but Christian natural theology was shaped within what was very much a shared framework. Finally, it meant there were no irreconcilable truths: there was one truth, one reality, that of Christianity.

In sum, the situation holding before the thirteenth-century disputes over Aristotelianism is that, from the Patristic era – and above all from Augustine – onwards, there is a conception of the unity of philosophy and theology in which Christian theology is conceived as an indispensable ingredient in any viable metaphysics, and it is this that marks out Christian metaphysics from the metaphysical systems of pagan philosophers, systems which are unwittingly engaged in the same project, while lacking the key to the problem that Christianity provides. This somewhat ecumenical view of the continuity of ancient philosophy and Christian natural theology is reflected in the later responses to non-Christian systems, for example in the work of Anselm and, later, Lull, where the problem is identified as being resolved by a kind of philosophical reflection on the nature of God which must lead anyone, whether Christian, Muslim, or Jew, to the orthodox Christian conception. Although the classical and Hellenistic sources of Christian philosophy – whether that of Plato (the only work of Plato's that had been transmitted through the Middle Ages was the *Timaeus*, which is his one contribution to natural philosophy) or Aristotle, or that of Neoplatonists or Stoics or Epicureans – had always been concerned with the structure of the world, natural philosophy figures in this conception only in a rather marginal way, and is effectively subsumed under metaphysics. However, the Neoplatonic metaphysics that Augustine took over, which is single-mindedly devoted to providing a foundation for theology, is quite impoverished by the standards of antiquity and the revival of classical thought in Arab commentators, and (with one late exception[18]) lacks any engagement with

---

[17] See Jaroslav Pelikan, *Christianity and Classical Culture* (New Haven, 1993).
[18] Some aspects of the metaphysical problem of universals had been discussed in the twelfth century by Roscelin and Abelard, just before the revival of Aristotle's works. Martin Tweedale, 'Logic (i): From the Late Eleventh Century to the Time of Abelard', in Peter Dronke, ed., *A History of Twelfth-Century Philosophy* (Cambridge, 1988), 196–226.

core classical metaphysical questions such as particulars and universals, the nature of substance, and the one and the many.

All of this changes radically with the introduction of Aristotelianism in the thirteenth century. The basic problem identified in the various condemnations of Aristotelianism that came to a head in 1277 was that Aristotelian natural philosophy had embraced doctrines in clear and indisputable conflict with Christian teaching, doctrines such as the eternity of the world, and the denial of the possibility of creation *ex nihilo*. Yet thinkers such as Aquinas were concerned both with the formulation of a natural theology based on a viable metaphysics and with developing a natural philosophy: and both of these relied heavily on Aristotle. If Aristotelian metaphysics was somehow to keep its intimate connection with theology, Aristotle's natural philosophy had to be separated from his metaphysics. Aristotelianism had (as a first approximation) to be split into two: Aristotelian metaphysics as a science of the nature of being, and Aristotelian natural philosophy as the study of natural phenomena. In Neoplatonic thought, these had been part of the same enterprise, much to the cost of natural philosophy,[19] but it seemed that they could have a life of their own, under the umbrella of a very broadly conceived form of Christianised Aristotelianism. The details of just what their connection was, however, was not at all straightforward.

We can think of natural philosophy in two ways, as a sub-species of metaphysics, and as something that, although still part of a general conception which was guided by Aristotelian metaphysics, was concerned with a set of problems that were sufficiently distinctive to allow them to be pursued largely independently of metaphysics. Which way we choose to think of the matter makes a significant difference. Just what this difference amounts to became evident as the centre of gravity of philosophy began to shift after the Condemnation of 1277: treatments of metaphysics in the fourteenth century moved from the exploration of the relation between theology and metaphysics, which had been the staple of Christian philosophy up to this point, to that between metaphysics and natural philosophy.[20] The key problem is now the reconciliation of metaphysics and natural philosophy.

The background to Tempier's Condemnation can be set out schematically in terms of four different approaches. The first is that pursued by

---

[19] The only significant exception is Philoponus: see Richard Sorabji, ed., *Philoponus and the Rejection of Aristotelian Science* (London, 1987).

[20] Charles Lohr, 'Metaphysics', in Charles B. Schmitt, Quentin Skinner, and Eckhard Kessler, eds., *The Cambridge History of Renaissance Philosophy* (Cambridge, 1988), 591.

Augustine, Anselm, and Bonaventure in the West and Avicenna in the East, whereby philosophy is a dependent and subordinate part of theology. Peter of Spain, who, as Pope John XXI, gave his authority to the 1277 Condemnation, was probably the closest to this tradition in the thirteenth century. The trouble is that the pieces no longer fit together as they did in Augustine's synthesis, for elements of genuinely different traditions are being juxtaposed. Augustine's relatively narrow range of philosophical interests and sources helps hold together his account under philosophically artificial conditions. With the reintroduction of Aristotle's texts, these artificial conditions are exposed for what they are, and the old Augustinian unity of doctrine is no longer attainable. Peter of Spain's own response falls apart: as Gilson puts it, 'one has the uncomfortable impression of meeting already-known formulas, which have come from elsewhere and have lost their meaning during the journey'.[21] And this is no less true of the thought of the greatest representative of this tradition in the thirteenth century, Bonaventure, whose philosophy is in many respects an unreconciled mixture of elements taken from Augustine, Neoplatonists, and Aristotle, as well as Arab Aristotle commentators.[22] Despite revivals in the fifteenth century among Neoplatonists, in the sixteenth among Protestants,[23] and in the seventeenth century among some French Catholics,[24] Augustinianism, although it has some bearing upon how early Protestant thinkers like Melanchthon conceived of the standing of natural philosophy,[25] could offer no distinctive understanding of natural philosophy and was not a serious participant in the debates over natural philosophy in the early modern period.

A second approach, which we can refer to as transcendentalism, characterises the non-Thomist form of Aristotelianism in the late thirteenth and fourteenth centuries, and in many ways continues a direction already evident in the move from Anselm to Aquinas. Anselm had seen theological and philosophical truths as being so intimately connected that the one could be demonstrated from the other. Aquinas rejects this, and limits the number of theological truths that can be established on a philosophical basis. Duns Scotus, writing at the end of the thirteenth century – and, Gilson believes, writing in a way that reflects the new

---

[21] Etienne Gilson, *History of Christian Philosophy in the Middle Ages* (London, 1955), 321.
[22] See Etienne Gilson, *La Philosophie de St. Bonaventure* (Paris, 1945).
[23] See D. C. Steinmetz, *Luther and Staupitz* (Durham NC, 1980).
[24] See Henri Gouhier, *Cartésianisme et Augustinisme au XVIIᵉ Siècle* (Paris, 1978).
[25] See Sachiko Kusukawa, *The Transformation of Natural Philosophy: The Case of Philip Melanchthon* (Cambridge, 1995).

balance forced by the 1277 Condemnation[26] – takes this further, and, opening up a gulf between God and his creation, makes a sharp separation between supernatural theology and natural philosophy. Ockham cements this distancing of the supernatural and the natural, denying the possibility of any rational knowledge of God. From the late thirteenth to the fifteenth centuries, the main areas of contention, as they bear upon natural philosophy,[27] are effectively shaped by disputes between Thomism and transcendentalism. These had in common a conception of the nature of metaphysics which marked them out from the Augustinian idea of metaphysics – ultimately indebted to Neoplatonism – as the science of God. Aquinas, Scotus, and Ockham all treated metaphysics primarily as the science of being. The transcendentalist programme was a source of concern, however, and by the fifteenth century theologians such as Gerson were becoming worried by the way in which natural philosophy was being pursued, where reconciliation with theology was no longer paramount.[28]

The third approach is the Thomist one. Aquinas' mentor, Albertus Magnus, is in some respects, like Peter of Spain, within the Augustine/ Avicenna mould, but he offers a conception of philosophy as a discipline which achieves something different from theology, since philosophy is concerned with natural truths, and he defends the idea of philosophy as something which, within theologically determined limits, can be pursued for its own sake. This forms the basis for Aquinas' attempt to keep separate foundations and sources for Aristotelian philosophy and Christian theology, but, given this, to attempt then to reconcile them in the form of an Aristotelian/Christian amalgam. Finally, the fourth approach, associated with Averroes, envisages a separation of philosophy and theology whereby the two become different and perhaps irreconcilable sources of truth.

Thomism and Averroism are the key to the fortunes of natural philosophy in the sixteenth century. Aquinas attempts to formulate theology within the framework of Aristotle's classification of the sciences. He used revelation as the basis for theology, and Aristotelian metaphysics as the foundation of philosophical doctrine. However, whereas for Averroes the

[26] Gilson, *History of Christian Philosophy*, 465.
[27] Other questions are determined differently: the question of free will, for example, was shaped by disputes between defenders of Augustine, such as Gregory of Rimini, and defenders of Ockham, such as Gabriel Biel. It must also be remembered that political questions were high on the agenda in the fourteenth century, with the 'Babylonian captivity' of the pope at Avignon (1309–77), and the Great Schism (1378–1417).
[28] See Lohr, 'Metaphysics', 597.

two may not be able to be reconciled, for Aquinas they must be consonant with each other, but there is no synthesis of an Augustinian kind:
nor in a sense could there be, because Augustinian theology was formulated within Neoplatonic terms, taking a Neoplatonic conception of
the divinity and 'Christianising' it,[29] whereas Christianised Aristotelian
metaphysics has to start with a Neoplatonically formulated Christianity
and reshape it as best it can. It is a mixture, or at best an amalgam, with
an internal balance that is much more delicate than anything needed in
the Augustinian synthesis, and which is pursued via the doctrine of analogy. But it also has a flexibility which the Augustinian synthesis lacked.
And, indeed, it is this flexibility that makes sure that Christian philosophy can adapt, and indeed remake itself, at least in the short to middle
term, when natural–philosophical questions come to the centre of the
philosophical enterprise.

   The attempt to solve the problems of transcendentalism and Averroism took the form of a revival of Thomism. With the failure of the
Council of Basle (1431–49) and the restoration of the supremacy of the
papacy, there was a renewed interest in the Thomist programme, with
its distinction between truths of reason and truths of revelation, and
its attempted balance between the claims of theology, metaphysics, and
natural philosophy. The institutional attractiveness of Thomism, particularly at the all-important University of Paris, cannot be underesti-
mated. As far as the Theology Faculty was concerned, Aquinas' epistemology, with its Aristotelian stress on sense perception as the basis
for knowledge, left open a space for revelation, because God necessarily transcends human faculties. In particular, Aquinas' denial of some
higher intellectual knowledge which allows one to penetrate revealed
religion (a doctrine dear to Neoplatonists) retained a unique role for
the clergy in interpreting revelation. And there were advantages for
the secular Arts programme as well. As Lohr has pointed out, 'the
idea of a philosophy autonomous in its own realm, but guided both
positively and negatively by revelation, represented a kind of prag-
matic sanction, defining the powers of the clergy in its relation to
science . . . Just as the papacy had to recognise the authority of secular rulers in the temporal sphere, so also the clergy – whose function had

---

[29] The authority of such a reading derived not just from Augustine but also from the Neoplatonically
      formulated mystical theology of the sixth-century Neoplatonic writer, Pseudo-Dionysius the
      Aeropagite, who was wrongly identified (by some right up to the nineteenth century) with the
      first-century Dionysius whom Paul converted. His writings had an immense authority because
      of his assumed closeness to the origins of Christianity, and to its de facto founder, Paul.

traditionally been that of teaching – had to admit the self-sufficiency of the secular sciences and to concede the limitation of its role to that of surveillance.'[30]

THEOLOGY, METAPHYSICS, AND NATURAL PHILOSOPHY

Threats to the Thomist balance between a Christianised metaphysics and natural philosophy did not come from outside the Aristotelian model – the strengths of Neoplatonism were always in theology (if only because Neoplatonism had provided the conceptual apparatus of, and the language for, Christian theology), not in any other area of philosophy[31] – but from within. That is to say, within Aristotelian terms, the balance simply did not work. This is reflected in that bastion of orthodoxy, the late Scholastic textbook tradition. The 'first wave' of this textbook tradition, beginning in the work of Toletus in the 1560s and culminating in the Coimbra commentaries later in the century, was by and large Thomist, at least on the issues that bore crucially on the relation between theology, metaphysics, and natural philosophy. The 'second wave' of textbooks – such as those of Eustachius, Abra de Raconis, and Dupleix – while following the Coimbra commentaries, often to the point of verbatim repetition, nevertheless differ from them in a number of crucial respects, and by 1630 had largely displaced them.[32] They are no longer commentaries on Aristotle but condensations of this thought,

---

[30] Lohr, 'Metaphysics', 600.

[31] The Italian Neoplatonic revival, begun in earnest in Ficino's *Theologia Platonica*, which appeared between 1469 and 1474, culminated (as far as natural philosophy is concerned) in a distinctively Platonic natural philosophy in Patrizi's *Nova de universis philosophia* of 1591. This turned out to be of some importance in the development of early modern philosophy, but its distinctive natural–philosophical claims became caught up in a general Italian 'naturalist' movement which also included revivers of Stoicism and pre-Socratic thought – notably Telesio – as well as Averroist Aristotelians such as Pomponazzi. Even Kepler's early Neoplatonically inspired cosmology is formulated within the terms of Aristotelìan natural philosophy.

[32] I say 'largely' because there was also a 'third wave' of textbooks, which took the form of a conservative reaction to the Jesuit textbooks. This 'third wave' comprises the ultra-Thomist commentaries of the Complutenses, based at the Philosophical College of the Discalced Carmelites at Alcalá (Lat. *complutum*), and Salmanticenses, based at the Theological College at Salamanca. The Complutenses commentaries began with the logic commentary of Diego de Jesus, which was first published in 1608, and they appeared in a definitive five-volume version in 1670. Although they dealt with natural–philosophical questions, they seem to have had no influence on natural–philosophical disputes outside Catholic clerical circles, and none at all on Descartes. The Salamancan commentaries began to appear in 1630 with the theological works of Antonio de la Madre de Dios, and the last volume of the definitive collection of these commentaries appeared in 1704. These commentaries were primarily concerned with theology rather than natural philosophy, and were treated as the embodiment of Thomist orthodoxy in the Roman Catholic Church from the eighteenth century onwards.

which is quite a radical shift of genre.[33] Moreover, they are less orthodox, and on the crucial question of our knowledge of God follow the
transcendentalist doctrine of Scotus.[34]

The root of the problem is that Christianised Aristotelian metaphysics
straddles theology on the one side and natural philosophy on the other.
On the one hand, since metaphysics deals with whatever is unchanging
and independent, and natural philosophy with whatever is changing and
independent, we seem to have straightforwardly distinct domains. But
Aristotelian metaphysics in its Christianised version included under its
rubric both uncreated or infinite being, and created or finite being, so
that topics such as the nature of the soul, which could be seen as straightforwardly natural–philosophical issues, could also be seen to fall under
metaphysics, and not just under metaphysics, but under a metaphysics
which graded reality in degrees from inert matter to God, so that the
apparently sharp distinction between truths of reason and truths of revelation became even more blurred.[35] This is true of Aquinas, writing in
the thirteenth century, but it is also true of the writers following in the
wake of the fifteenth-century Thomist revival. Suárez, for example, in the
most influential Scholastic treatise on metaphysics of the early modern
era, tells us that we must provide firm foundations in metaphysics before
proceeding to theology, but that we must not forget that philosophy 'is
the servant of divine theology'.[36]

So, while there can be no doubt that, during the fourteenth century,
natural philosophy – thought of in distinction to the transcendentalist
construal of theology – begins to take on a degree of autonomy, as it
is conceived less as a species of the general science of being and more
as a distinct discipline with less direct implications for metaphysics, and

---

[33] See Laurence W. B. Brockliss, 'Rapports de structure et de contenu entre les *Principia* et les cours de
philosophie des collèges', in Jean-Robert Armogathe and Giulia Belgioioso, eds., *Descartes: Principia
Philosophiæ, 1644–1994* (Naples, 1996), 491–516. Brockliss makes the intriguing suggestion (494–5)
that Descartes may not have been aware of these condensations until 1640, but that when he
was introduced to them he realised their potential as a means of popularising his own mechanist
natural philosophy. It is worth noting in this respect that the new condensations laid a far greater
emphasis on natural philosophy than the older commentaries had done: see Charles B. Schmitt,
'The Rise of the Philosophical Textbook', in Charles B. Schmitt et al. eds., *The Cambridge History
of Renaissance Philosophy* (Cambridge, 1988), 792–804: 803.

[34] See Roger Ariew, *Descartes and the Last Scholastics* (Ithaca, 1999), ch. 2.

[35] This had always been the case in the Platonist tradition, where the distinction between natural
theology and revelation was always grey, and Renaissance Platonists devoted much time to
uncovering the divine revelation they considered to lie beneath Plato's doctrines, which many of
them believed he may have learned from Moses. But, clearly, the causes of, or motivation behind,
the blurring in the Platonist and Aristotelian cases are very different.

[36] Francisco Suárez, *Disputationes Metaphysicae* (1st pub. 1597, repr. Hildesheim, 1965), Preface, unpag.

hence for theology, there can also be no doubt about the grounds on which theology and natural philosophy could be pulled back together again in the fifteenth-century Thomist revival. Metaphysics bridges the two, so that, while natural philosophy can be pursued independently to some degree, ultimately it must be subordinated to theology via this metaphysical bridge. In other words, metaphysics begins to act as a way of connecting theology and natural philosophy, and the skill comes in trying to develop these two in their own directions while keeping them consonant with one another.

The beginning of the end of this project comes in the early decades of the sixteenth century. If the 1277 Condemnation marks the failure of an Augustinian synthesis of Christian revelation and a Neoplatonic philosophy and theology, and the beginning of a reconciliation between a (Neoplatonically formulated) Christian theology and an Aristotelian metaphysics and natural philosophy, then the fifth Lateran Council (1512–17) marks the beginning of the end of this reconciliation, as a wedge was driven between theology and natural philosophy. This is not to say that the exact nature of the wedge is always clear, however. There is some case to be made that it divides natural philosophy and metaphysics from theology, so that metaphysics becomes constitutive of philosophy in the sixteenth century, with theology left to float off on its own,[37] but the full situation must be more complex than this because metaphysical discussion in the seventeenth century can still engage core theological questions about the nature of God, as in Descartes' account of the nature of eternal truths, or in Leibniz's theodicy.

What is clear is that what drives the wedge is not the kind of thing that might have driven it in the fourteenth and fifteenth centuries, namely a transcendentalist conception of God, but rather a revival of the heresy that stood at the centre of the 1277 Condemnation: Averroism. More specifically, it was the doctrine of 'double truth', namely, the idea that natural philosophy and theology might, each in their own way, generate independently legitimate but apparently contradictory truths: that there is no metaphysics that can reconcile them. Matters came to a head on the issue of 'mortalism', associated above all in the sixteenth century with the Paduan philosopher, Pietro Pomponazzi, and condemned by the Lateran Council in 1513. Pomponazzi accepted on faith the Church teaching of the personal immortality of the soul, and he argues that Aquinas decisively refuted Averroes' view that there cannot be individual

---

[37] See Lohr, 'Metaphysics', 605ff.

souls. But he also argues that Aquinas' own proposal makes no sense in terms of Aristotelian metaphysics/natural philosophy. Philosophically speaking, the soul was the form of the body, and there was no such thing as an uninstantiated form, so that the death and corruption of the body resulted in the disappearance of the soul.[38]

Pomponazzi's dilemma is that two completely different lines of thought, each of which he has every reason to believe to be completely compelling and neither of which he was prepared to renounce, lead to incompatible conclusions. Somehow one must embrace both.[39] The one question can be contextualised and pursued in two completely different ways, with every expectation that they will lead to the same solution, but what in fact happens is that we end up with two contradictory solutions, each achieved by perfectly legitimate means. Note also that the Lateran Council's solution to this dilemma is not simply to condemn Aristotelian natural philosophy, but to instruct theologians and philosophers to reconcile philosophy with theology on this issue.[40]

The problems here turned out to be insuperable. As I have indicated, the Augustinian synthesis had been viable only because it worked with philosophical resources which, by the standards of the revival of Aristotle, were impoverished. Once this had become clear to philosophers and theologians, as it had to many by the end of the thirteenth century, Aristotelianism took command of the philosophical resources deployed, and the task became that of reconciling a Christian theology which had been developed from, and thought through in terms of, a Neoplatonic metaphysics and natural philosophy, with Aristotelian metaphysics and natural philosophy. But the metaphysics of Neoplatonism and Aristotelianism were wholly antithetical, as were their natural philosophies. Moreover, the relative priorities of metaphysics differed; in Neoplatonism natural philosophy was, generally speaking, wholly subordinate to metaphysics, whereas there were two possible views of the priority in Aristotelianism, metaphysical priority and independence. But even Aristotelian metaphysical priority was profoundly different from that of

[38] Pietro Pomponazzi, *De immortalitate animae* (Padua, 1516).
[39] See the discussion in Paul Oskar Kristeller, *Renaissance Thought and its Sources* (New York, 1979), ch. 11. On the details of the Pomponazzi case see Etienne Gilson, 'Autour de Pomponazzi: problématique de l'immortalité de l'âme en Italie au début du XVIe siècle', *Archives d'histoire doctrinale et littéraire du moyen âge* 18 (1961), 163–279.
[40] This is something that Descartes will famously try to do in his doctrine of the soul or mind as a separate substance in the *Meditationes*. See AT VII. 3: 'The Lateran Council ... condemned those who take [the Averroist] position, and expressly enjoined Christian philosophers to refute their arguments and use all their powers to establish the truth; so I have not hesitated to attempt this task as well.'

Neoplatonism. Neoplatonic metaphysics *generated* its natural philosophy, whereas Aristotelian metaphysics offered a general account of the nature of being, defining the province of natural philosophy and, for those who considered metaphysics prior to natural philosophy, providing constraints of compatibility and consistency dictated by the metaphysics.

It is possible that, to a large extent, the attempt to subordinate natural philosophy to metaphysics derives from the attempt to replace Neoplatonism with Aristotelianism without sacrificing the structural features of a Christian Neoplatonic theology/metaphysics. That is to say, the construal of Aristotelian metaphysics as constraining natural philosophy in anything more than the provision of a definition of the subject area might be an artificiality placed upon Aristotelianism. Of course, one could always go back to the texts of Aristotle and attempt to vindicate the substantive subordination in textual terms, but that is not the issue. The point is that the directions originally open to Aristotelianism on this question were closed off with its construal as the philosophy of Christianity, and it was pushed in a direction that was more natural for (that is, less liable to generate anomalies for) Neoplatonism than for Aristotelianism. That Aristotelianism was not up to the task of realising an agenda that had been framed within the context of a Neoplatonic philosophy seemed clear not only to the sixteenth-century Neoplatonist critics of Aristotelianism, such as Patrizi, who tried to revive a Christian/metaphysical synthesis, but also to those like Telesio, who advocated a return to pre-Socratic and Stoic conceptions of the universe. The failure was equally apparent to non-Scholastic Aristotelians such as Pomponazzi, who saw the solution in the separation of metaphysics and natural philosophy, and in the seventeenth century to Gassendi, who believed that atomism would serve the purposes of Christian philosophy better than those of Aristotelianism, as well as to early advocates of mechanism, such as Descartes and Hobbes.

The sixteenth-century crisis of natural philosophy turns on the failure to reconcile Aristotelian natural philosophy and a Christian theology which had been reformulated in terms of Aristotelian metaphysics. This failure throws open the questions of the standing of Aristotelian natural philosophy, the standing of a Christian theology formulated in terms of Aristotelian metaphysics, the relation between natural philosophy and metaphysics, the relation between natural philosophy and theology, and the relation between metaphysics and theology. In some ways, the questions raised by the Pomponazzi affair were questions that had been at issue in the 1277 Condemnation. What is significantly different is that Aristotelianism is now calling the shots, and it is armed with a metaphysics and natural philosophy far more penetrating, detailed, and complex than anything the Augustinian synthesis had to offer in the thirteenth century. It was able to provide a level of metaphysical engagement that was far more profound, and it was much better able to prise open the philosophical issues than any of the various Neoplatonic, Epicurean, Stoic, or other systems that sought to usurp it. The greatest damage to Aristotelianism was done from inside, from the discrepancy between naturalistic and Scholastic readings of Aristotle.

If we ask how, within Aristotelianism, one would decide on the degree of independence of natural philosophy and a theologically driven metaphysics, we can begin to appreciate the nature of the constraints. Subordinating natural philosophy to metaphysics leads one to intractable problems about such questions as the nature of soul/mind, where we seem to get conflicting doctrines, sometimes even in the same text – for example the naturalistic treatment of the mind/soul in the first two books of the *De Anima* by contrast with the treatment of the soul in the third book,[41] which is more reminiscent of that of the *Metaphysics*. But, on the other hand, the fragmentation of the Aristotelian system is a high price to pay for the autonomy of natural philosophy. It must be remembered that competing philosophies – Neoplatonism, Stoicism, Epicureanism – each constituted a total world-view, however impoverished these world-views might have been by the standards of Aristotelianism. In the case where world-views were at stake, a clear internal consistency, constrained by a clear internal hierarchy, was of very great significance.

THE UNITY OF ARISTOTELIAN PHILOSOPHY: THE TEXTBOOK TRADITION

The response to this need took the form of the late Scholastic textbook tradition. In the letter to Mersenne quoted at the beginning of this chapter, Descartes writes that he remembers 'only some of the Conimbricenses, Toletus, and Rubius'. The Jesuit commentators based at Coimbra, the Jesuit commentators based at the Collegio Romano, of whom Toletus is the most distinguished representative, and Rubius, who

---

[41] In chapter 5 of Book 3 of *De Anima* (430a10–25), Aristotle talks of active and passive intellects, and this seemed to imply to Muslim and Christian commentators the existence of two different intellects, one of which was not bound to the body and was not perishable. On early interpretations of this passage, see Ross' discussion in his introduction to his edition of *De Anima* (Oxford, 1961), 41–8.

compiled textbooks both during his twenty-five years in Mexico and then at the Jesuit College at Alcalá, were the three main sources of Jesuit textbooks in the late sixteenth and early seventeenth centuries. These 'first-wave' textbooks were the origin of Descartes' knowledge of Scholastic philosophy in his schooldays at La Flèche. Their explicit aim was the systematic reconstruction of Aristotle's metaphysics and natural philosophy from first principles, rearranging material in Aristotle as necessary.[42] It should be noted that, despite their general advocacy of Thomism, not only did these commentaries set out to supplant Aquinas – whom Descartes did not read at La Flèche, and whom he does not seem to have read until 1628 – but in many ways they were meant to supplant Aristotle as well.[43] They recast the whole Aristotelian tradition with two main aims: to show how the truths of a Christianised Aristotelianism could be derived from first principles, and to show how this was a single, coherent, comprehensive system.

The project traded on a traditional feature of Aristotelianism, whereby understanding ultimately took the form of *scientia* ('science'). Research or discovery was not part of *scientia* as such, but rather a prerequisite for *scientia*, which was constituted by the derivation of true and certain conclusions from first principles that were both evident and indemonstrable: that is, neither in need of, nor capable of, further demonstration. *Scientia* is built up and consolidated as more and more conclusions are drawn from the basic principles, and the ultimate aim is a wholly exhaustive and encyclopedic account of theoretical knowledge, that is, knowledge concerned with understanding how things are and why they are as they are.[44]

The three theoretical *scientiae* are metaphysics, mathematics, and natural philosophy, and the ultimate aim was to build these up

[42] See the discussion in Charles H. Lohr, 'The Sixteenth-Century Transformation of the Aristotelian Division of the Speculative Sciences' in D. R. Kelley and R. H. Popkin, eds., *The Shapes of Knowledge from the Renaissance to the Enlightenment* (Dordrecht, 1991); and Lohr, 'Metaphysics'.

[43] See Joaquim F. Gomez, 'Pedro da Fonseca: Sixteenth Century Portuguese Philosopher', *International Philosophical Quarterly* 6 (1966), 632–44: 633–4. The later Carmelite Complutenses commentaries set out to reverse this trend.

[44] There is a good account of these questions in Charles H. Lohr, 'Metaphysics and Natural Philosophy as Sciences: the Catholic and Protestant Views in the Sixteenth and Seventeenth Centuries', in Constance Blackwell and Sachiko Kusukawa, eds., *Philosophy in the Sixteenth and Seventeenth Centuries* (Aldershot, 1999). Alan Gabbey has pointed out that 'the scholastics believed their explanatory schemes and ontological categories coped adequately with the universal range of natural phenomena, and one gets the impression in reading their treatises that no empirical discovery or philosophical upheaval, present or future (or indeed from their recent past) could lead to a revision or displacement of that scheme', 'The *Principia Philosophiae* as a Treatise in Natural Philosophy', in Jean-Robert Armogathe and Giulia Belgioioso, eds., *Descartes: Principia Philosophiae, 1644–1994* (Naples, 1996), 517–29: 524–5.

demonstratively from first principles, where 'demonstratively' ideally meant syllogistically. The case of mathematics was exceptional in that there was already a formal deductive exposition of geometry based on first principles, in the *Elements* of Euclid. There were attempts to rewrite this deductive exposition in syllogistic terms, the most concerted attempt being that of Conrad Dasypodius and Christian Herlinus, *Analyseis geometricae sex librorum Euclidis* (1566).[45] The Jesuit mathematician Christopher Clavius, who also thought geometry should be reworked into syllogistic terms, tried to defend the standing of mathematics by arguing it was intermediate between metaphysics and physics, because metaphysics 'is separated from all matter in reality and in theory', physics 'is connected to matter in reality and in theory', and mathematics 'treats things which are considered without sensible matter, even though they are in reality impressed in matter'.[46] But, generally speaking, in the textbook tradition mathematics is of very marginal interest. Instead, attention centres around metaphysics and natural philosophy. These are the basic *scientiae*.

Eustachius, in his *Summa*, points out that some philosophers consider the subject of metaphysics to be God, whereas others say it is being taken in its broadest sense, i.e. in the sense that includes both the being of real things and the being of things that are merely of reason (the objects of mathematics). He rejects the former as being too narrow and the latter as being too broad, but he comes down on the side of metaphysics as a science of being, and he proceeds to explain that the principal function of metaphysics is to determine the subject matters of the other sciences, and to provide them with their basic principles. In this sense, metaphysics is a kind of master-science, and this is a view shared by the other textbooks.

As for natural philosophy, this deals with those things that change and exist independently of us, and the scope of natural philosophy considered in this way needs some clarification. There are three fundamental differences between Aristotelian and most early modern conceptions of natural philosophy that are particularly worth drawing attention to. First, we are inclined to see the most fundamental division in natural phenomena in terms of the living and the non-living. The theoretical division between the physical sciences and the life sciences is a nineteenth-century phenomenon, which comes about with the establishment of biology as a discipline: eighteenth-century natural history, by contrast, had included both living things and minerals under its purview. But there is in the

[45] See Neal W. Gilbert, *Renaissance Concepts of Method* (New York, 1960), 89–90.
[46] Christoph Clavius, *Opera mathematica*, vol. 1 (Mainz, 1611), 5.

early modern period a shifting recognition of the fundamental character of the distinction between the living and the non-living, manifest for
example in the hostility to attempts, such as those of Descartes, to construe organic processes, such as foetal development, as something purely
mechanical. What lies at the basis of Aristotle's classification of natural
phenomena is completely different: not a distinction between the living
and the non-living, but a distinction between those things that have an
intrinsic principle of change, and those things that have an extrinsic principle of change. Acorns, and stones raised above the ground, both come
in the first category; the former has within itself the power to change its
state, into an oak tree, the latter has within itself the power to change
its position, to move to the ground. In neither case is anything external
required. Aristotle thinks that we explain and understand things by understanding their natures. To give the nature of something is to give the
ultimate characterisation of it. If we ask why a stone falls, the answer is
simply that it falls because it is a heavy object – that is how heavy things
behave – just as, if we are asked why a particular tree puts out broad
flat leaves in spring and keeps them through the summer, we may reply
that it does that because it is a beech. In other words, it is not necessary
to look outside the thing to account for its behaviour. And wherever we
can explain a thing's behaviour without looking outside the thing, then
that behaviour, and the feature that it acquires or retains, is natural. It
is natural for stones to fall, it is the nature of beeches to have broad flat
leaves. The fundamental distinction is between natural objects and processes, and artefacts and constrained processes (making furniture out of
trees, raising bodies above the ground).[47]

Second, there has been an increasing tendency from at least the nineteenth century to explain biological phenomena in physical (e.g. bio-
chemical) terms, but never physical process in biological terms. Aristotle,
by contrast, uses a biological model to enable him to think through all
natural processes. Natural objects have within themselves the source of
their own making, artefacts do not: the paradigm case that is invoked
to understand this is the process of organic growth, and the crucial distinction he wants to capture is that between growth and manufacture.
The category of natural things and processes, as opposed to artefacts and
artificial or externally induced processes, is what 'physics' or natural philosophy is concerned with. Not only does this category of things include
living things, but the general model that Aristotle uses is biological in its

47 There is a good account of these issues in William Charlton, *Aristotle's Physics I, II* (Oxford, 1970).

orientation. That is to say, what we would regard as physical processes proper – the movement of inanimate objects, for example – is ultimately conceived on a biological model. The placing of considerations of motion firmly within the central metaphysical doctrines of form and substance makes the account that Aristotle gives quite different from that which we find in the work of natural philosophers from the seventeenth century onwards. His account of substance is dominated by biological examples and metaphors. The substantial form of a thing is supposed to provide it with an identity for example, and Aristotle's examples are always of animals. Even though the doctrine is supposed to apply to all physical things, he never gives us examples of inanimate things, and it is hard to see how it is to be extended to these. Biological models and examples saturate his account. The inorganic tends to be modelled on the organic.[48]

Third, Aristotle defines metaphysics, physics, and mathematics in terms of their subject matters: metaphysics is concerned with whatever does not change and has an independent existence, physics is concerned with those things that change and have an independent existence, mathematics with those things that do not change and do not have an independent existence. The aim of scientific inquiry on his account is to determine what kind of thing the subject matter is by establishing its essential properties. The kinds of principles one employs to achieve this are determined by the subject matter of the science. To establish the essential properties of a natural object, one needs to use principles consonant with that subject matter, i.e. principles that are designed to capture the essence of something which is independent and changing. This has a very significant bearing upon the connections between the theoretical sciences, and it is particularly marked in the complex question of the relation between physics and mathematics, for it leads to the idea that

---

[48] This is *not* to say that he conceives of inorganic things as being organic. The Stoics held something like this, but Aristotle did not. He has a biological model: he does not advocate a biological reduction. The division of the subject matter of natural philosophy into natural processes and artificial or constrained processes, and the use of a biological model to think through natural processes generally, are separate questions. What marks out natural processes is the fact that they occur as a result of something internal to the body, something that follows from the nature of the body, as opposed to something imposed from outside. It has nothing to do with biological versus non-biological processes: there are artificial biological processes – grafting, for example – just as there are artificial non-biological ones, and there are natural non-biological processes – bodies falling to the earth – just as there are natural biological ones. The fact that biology helps Aristotle model natural processes does not mean that he treats these processes as biological: in contrast to the Stoics, who were inclined to do so, for example in their occasionally animistic construal of the cosmos.

physical principles must be used in physical inquiry, and mathematical principles in the very different kind of subject matter that constitutes mathematics. The two cannot be mixed, for physical and mathematical principles are essentially concerned with different kinds of subject matter. Although there are many qualifications we need to make to this in exploring the Aristotelian account in detail, the general thrust of the Aristotelian position is that physical inquiry or demonstration cannot be pursued mathematically, any more than mathematical inquiry can be pursued physically. The point can be made in a different way by asking what one does in a physical explanation, and in particular by asking what it is that makes a physical explanation informative. Aristotle, and the whole ancient and medieval tradition after him, thought that one has explained a physical phenomenon when one has given an account of why that event occurred in the way it did, and that this ultimately comes down to providing an account of why bodies behave as they do. In accounting for this behaviour, one needs to distinguish between accidental features of a body and its essential properties, and any behaviour which can be said to be due to the body itself is due to the essential properties it has. These essential properties explain its behaviour. Such properties are physical, and Aristotle argued that they have cannot be captured by employing mathematical or quantitative concepts.

The comprehensive, encyclopedic, late Scholastic textbooks, while they centre on metaphysics and natural philosophy, also include two other areas, logic and ethics, neither of which is a theoretical science. Logic or dialectic is included above all because it is the method by which the basic principles of the various *scientiae* are discovered, and by which one then demonstrates conclusions from these basic principles. The principal rationale for the inclusion of ethics in the textbook tradition is, as Eustachius points out at the beginning of his treatment of ethics, that the aim of philosophy is human happiness, and

> this happiness has been taken to consist partly in the contemplation of truth, and partly in action in accordance with virtue. Hence as well as the contemplative *scientiae* there must be some *scientia* that provides an account of what is right and honourable, and instructs us in virtue and moral probity. This *scientia* is called ethics, that is, moral learning, or the science of morals, and is traditionally taken to be one of the chief parts of philosophy.[49]

But what is particularly interesting about the inclusion of logic and ethics is the way in which, as often as not, they seem to go together, as if they

---

49 Eustachius, *Summa*, Part II, Præfatio.

precede metaphysical and natural–philosophical inquiry, and this is the case not just in the textbook authors but also in Descartes. It is therefore important that we ask just what insights the ordering of the material provides us with.

CONTENT AND ORDERING

The question of what topics would be included in a comprehensive ordering of knowledge, and the order in which these topics should be presented, is an instructive one.[50] Restricting our attention to three well-known textbooks, namely the two that Descartes mentions, those of Eustachius and d'Abra de Raconis, and that of Scipion Dupleix, we find that logic, physics, metaphysics, and ethics each have a book devoted to them. These are also just the topics that Descartes takes us through in the *Discours*. The two textbook alternatives to the Scholastic textbook tradition, both deriving from the 1640s, Descartes' *Principia* and Gassendi's *Syntagma*, each exclude a section. Gassendi excludes metaphysics, and Descartes' *Principia*, in the projected full version, excludes logic. More schematically, we have:

Eustachius *Summa* (1610)	Dupleix *Corps de Philosophie* (1603–10)	Abra de Raconis *Summa* (1629)	Descartes *Discours* (1637)	Descartes *Principia* (1640s)	Gassendi *Syntagma* (1640s)
1 Logic	1 Logic	1 Logic	1 Logic	1 Metaphysics	1 Logic
2 Ethics	2 Ethics	2 Ethics	2 Ethics	2 Physics	2 Physics
3 Physics	3 Physics	3 Physics	3 Metaphysics	3 Ethics	3 Ethics
4 Metaphysics	4 Metaphysics	4 Metaphysics	4 Physics		

The ordering of material in the Scholastic textbook – logic, ethics, physics, metaphysics – is significant.[51] That logic should be put first is

[50] Roger Ariew looks at the question of ordering, but focuses on the analysis/synthesis question. See Roger Ariew, 'Les *Principia* et la *Summa Philosophica Quadripartita*', in Jean-Robert Armogathe and Giulia Belgioioso, eds., *Descartes: Principia Philosophiae, 1644–1994* (Naples, 1996), 473–89. See also Brockliss, 'Rapports de structure et de contenu entre les *Principia* et les cours de philosophie des collèges'. Brockliss ignores the two last projected books of the *Principia*, however, and treats the project as comprising solely metaphysics and physics (496–7), which distorts what is at stake.

[51] Note that the ordering of the material in the textbook does not reflect the order of appearance of the parts. Dupleix's work, for example, appeared in the following order: logic (1603), physics (1603), metaphysics (1610), ethics (1610). Once the material was arranged into textbook form, however, it assumed the standard order, with ethics interposed between logic and physics.

not surprising since, amongst other things, this provides the language for building one's system, and it provides the basic categories and techniques by which we must proceed if we are to progress scientifically. But what lies behind the ordering of the other topics? The placing of metaphysics after natural philosophy follows a traditional hierarchical ordering of subject matters, working from the most concrete to the most abstract forms of knowledge: knowledge is a pyramid, as it were, with metaphysics, as the highest science, at its apex. In his *Syntagma*, Gassendi puts a very radical gloss on this, collapsing metaphysics into natural philosophy.[52] He rejects the idea of metaphysics (which he calls theology) as a discipline separate from natural philosophy, a separation he traces back to Plato, and follows the Hellenistic division of philosophy into logic, natural philosophy, and ethics:

The Stoics, Epicureans, and others combined theology with physics. Since the task of theology is to contemplate the natures of things, these philosophers considered that the contemplation of the divine nature and of the other immortal beings was included, especially since the divine nature reveals itself in the creation and government of the universe.[53]

Gassendi's idea was that, in pursuing natural philosophy, one automatically pursues questions about the nature of God because one finds abundant evidence of divine purpose, and hence of the nature of divine causation. He criticises Descartes for failing, in Meditation III, to follow the 'Royal Way' of philosophising, namely the discovery of design and purpose in nature.[54] This conception reverses the traditional theology/natural philosophy priority, so that now natural philosophy, rather than being guided or constrained by a theologically driven metaphysics, is taken as a starting point, with a natural theology being derived from natural philosophy. Indeed, this approach was to be fostered in a striking way in the seventeeth century, particularly in England, and natural philosophy began to produce its own version of God, as deism was born.

Descartes' approach is different again. The order in which he goes through the topics in the *Discours* deviates from that of the textbooks. Having started with logic (i.e. 'method') and ethics, we might have expected him to go from concrete to abstract and proceed from physics to

---

[52] On this aspect of Gassendi's approach see Olivier Bloch, *La philosophie de Gassendi* (The Hague, 1971), and Brundell, *Pierre Gassendi*.
[53] Petrus Gassendi, *Opera Omnia*, I. 27 col. I.
[54] See the discussion in Brundell, *Pierre Gassendi*, 72–3.

metaphysics. However, he puts metaphysics before physics, because, by the mid-1630s, as we saw in the previous chapter, his approach to physics or natural philosophy, to the extent to which it is driven by questions of legitimation, is via metaphysics. What is of interest for present purposes is that he explicitly sees the division of philosophy into the traditional four areas as being constitutive of the philosophical enterprise. Stripped of logic, for reasons we shall come to shortly, the remaining three areas are seen as constitutive of the philosophical enterprise in the prefatory letter to the French translation of the *Principia*:

> The first part of true philosophy is metaphysics, which contains the principles of knowledge; among which is the explanation of the principal attributes of God, of the immateriality of our souls, and of all the clear and simple notions which are in us. The second is physics, in which, once we have discovered the true principles of material things, we examine, in general, the composition of the universe as a whole, and then, in particular, the nature of this Earth and of all the bodies most commonly found in it, such as air, water, fire, the lodestone, and the other minerals. Having done this, we must then examine the nature of plants, animals and, above all, man, so that we might subsequently be able to discover all the other useful branches of knowledge. Thus philosophy as a whole is like a tree, of which the roots are metaphysics, the trunk physics, and the branches emerging from this trunk all the other branches of knowledge. These branches can be reduced to three principal ones, namely medicine, mechanics, and ethics: by which I mean the highest and most perfect ethics, which presupposes a complete knowledge of the other branches of knowledge and is the final stage of wisdom.[55]

Bearing this in mind, let us now turn to the question of where ethics fits into the scheme. All the Scholastic textbook authors place ethics second, after logic. Gassendi by contrast places ethics last, explicitly following the Hellenistic classification in which ethics is the culmination of the exercise. Moreover, Hellenistic ethics is profoundly naturalistic, and considerations of nature and our place in it precede and shape, and in the case of Epicureanism largely dictate, our moral theory.

In the *Principia*, Descartes also places ethics last: his model of roots, trunk, and branches puts ethics at the end of the project, as, arguably, does his view of ethics as the final stage of wisdom. But this should not be taken to put him on the side of Gassendi rather than of the Scholastic textbooks. Note, first, that in the *Discours* Descartes places ethics between logic and metaphysics. Second, although ethics is designed to occupy the

---

[55] AT IXB. 14. This ordering, with logic restored, in the form of Cartesian method, is followed in Cartesian textbooks such as Pierre-Sylvain Régis, *Système de philosophie, contenant la logique, la métaphysique, la physique et la morale*, 3 vols. (Paris, 1690).

sixth and final Part of the *Principia*, in the prefatory letter to *Les Principes* – the French translation of the *Principia* – Descartes warns that the very first thing one must do if we aim to instruct ourselves, is 'to devise for oneself a code of morals sufficient to regulate the actions of one's life'.[56] In other words, ethics has a place both at the beginning of the *Principia* and at the end of it. One thing this might mean is that ethics is too important to be put to one side while one embarks on a systematic programme of instruction about the world. Unlike knowledge of terrestrial and cosmological questions, where, in the *Principia* version of things, we must start with something approaching a *tabula rasa* as we follow Descartes' arguments through to their conclusions, we cannot suspend our morality until we reach Cartesian enlightenment. But if this is all there were to the question, we should ask why single out morality here: surely the same considerations would have held in the case of basic Christian theology. After all, just as one cannot begin from a position of amorality, so one cannot begin from atheism. It is true that the existence and nature of God are established right at the beginning of the *Principia*, whereas the ethics is missing from the work, but would this really explain why ethics is picked out? After all, it is surely odd to remark that we must operate with a *provisional* ethics unless we are to be presented with a definitive one, and the *Principia* as published – and the Preface is, of course, a preface to the published version – does not offer an ethics at all. Most puzzling of all, however, is why we need an ethics, provisional or otherwise, in order to pursue natural philosophy.

This is really the key to Descartes' project: he seems to be insisting that we do indeed need an ethics of some kind, just as we need a logic of some kind, if we are to proceed in metaphysics and natural philosophy in the first place. As I have indicated, metaphysics and natural philosophy were deeply contested in the history of philosophy from the thirteenth century onwards, and the situation became even more heated at the beginning of the sixteenth century. At La Flèche, where Descartes studied, metaphysics, natural philosophy, and ethics were reserved for élite senior students, and masters were required to have attended advanced courses in theology and show evidence of orthodoxy to be qualified to teach such courses, and even then contentious parts of Aristotle's *Metaphysics* were avoided altogether.[57] We are dealing here with questions of orthodoxy and obedience to Church teaching, and therefore with moral questions. One must come to the study of contentious and potentially dangerous

[56] AT IXB. 13.   [57] See my *Descartes, An Intellectual Biography*, 52.

areas such as metaphysics and natural philosophy in the right frame of mind, and this right frame of mind is to be secured through both what might be termed good will and a capacity to reason properly. This is made very clear in the 'Preface to the Reader' with which Eustachius' *Summa* opens. Following Aristotle in dividing philosophy into two parts, theoretical and practical, he divides the latter into ethics and logic. He begins with the practical because,

since man must first be purged, illuminated, or perfected, we will begin this work of ours with those parts of philosophy which have been set out for the purging of the two chief parts of the soul, the understanding and the affections; whether in the rational by logic or in the moral by ethics.[58]

What is advocated here is very close to what is offered in *La Recherche de la verité*. The combination of 'method' (the analogue of logic in Descartes' system) and ethics as a prerequisite for the life of natural philosophy – as part of the required endowment or education of the natural philosopher – is part of the project of *La Recherche*, and we shall return to this question in chapter 8. The prefatory letter to *Les Principes* seems to suggest that they should be part of the project of the *Principia* as well, but, if they are, it is only implicitly. The reason for this, as I hope will become apparent in the chapters that follow, is that, whereas the route to natural philosophy offered in the *La Recherche* is dictated by considerations of what is needed to train someone to become a (Cartesian) natural philosopher, the route offered in the *Principia* serves a different function, that of establishing the credentials of Cartesian natural philosophy, and this requires a very different kind of preparation, where a quite different means of purging, namely hyperbolic doubt, is called upon.

THE STRUCTURE OF THE *PRINCIPIA*

In the context of the textbook tradition, Descartes' *Principia* has two distinctive features: it excludes something, namely logic, that we might well have expected to be present, and it includes something, namely metaphysics, the necessity for which is not obvious, at least if we compare the *Principia* with its predecessor, *Le Monde*.

In the prefatory letter to *Les Principes*, he writes that, once one has availed oneself of the standard sources of information about the world – grasp of clear notions, sense perception, conversation with others, and

---

[58] Eustachius, *Summa*, Part II, Præfatio in universum hoc opus philosophicum: Ad lectorum.

knowledge gleaned from books[59] – and has formulated a moral code by which to regulate one's life, one must study logic, 'but not that of the Schools, for that is properly speaking only a dialectic that teaches the means of making others understand what one knows, or even the means of speaking without judgement and at length about things which one does not know'.[60] In other words, Scholastic logic does not provide a method of discovery, only a method of presentation, and the problem with a method of presentation is that the skills it teaches are independent of whether one actually knows the material one is presenting. What we need to study is, rather, 'that logic that teaches one how to use one's reason correctly in order to discover the truths of which one is ignorant; and because this depends greatly upon practice, one should drill oneself at length, using the rules of logic on simple and easy questions, like those of mathematics'.[61] Underlying this approach is a firmly held view that we cannot be taught to reason, that reasoning is a natural faculty we all have which is corrupted by the artificial logical rules of Aristotelian syllogistic, but which can be made explicit and sharpened through practice in problem-solving, mathematics being a particularly fertile area in this respect.

The solution is, of course, not as simple as replacing logic with mathematics. Mathematical problem-solving techniques cannot simply be applied to everything; rather, the point is to capture just what it is that makes these problem-solving techniques so successful, to isolate and analyse this, and ask whether and how it can be manifested in areas other than mathematics.[62] This is exactly what Descartes tried to do in the 1620s. Rejecting syllogistic as a method of discovery, he believed that he could generalise his newly discovered 'universal mathematics', which he treated – with some justification – as a method of mathematical discovery, into a general method of discovery, a 'universal method.' However, in the late 1620s he realised that he was unable to reconcile the precepts of his generalised method, which required analysis of numbers and shapes into line lengths and operations on these, with the kinds of algebraic operations he was now able to carry out. What resulted from this was a rather complex situation. On the one hand, he believed he had hit upon a genuine method of discovery in the case of mathematics, and he believed that the driving force behind this, which he termed 'analysis', should be at least a reflection of some more general underlying

[59] AT IXB. 5.   [60] AT IXB. 13–14.   [61] AT IXB. 14.
[62] The contrast here is with writers such as Clavius, who, as we have seen, tried to bring out what they believed was the syllogistic structure lying behind mathematics.

principles. But when he uses the notions of analysis and synthesis in the context of non-mathematical arguments, in the Replies to Meditation II, they are contrasted not so much as methods of discovery and presentation respectively, but as different methods of presentation, one reflecting how the proposition in question was discovered but not carrying the same degree of conviction that the synthetic means of presentation does.[63] The relation between analysis and synthesis as employed in a mathematical context, on the one hand, and this usage, on the other, is at best a very loose analogy, and is of little help in explicating the latter; nor, indeed, is the latter usage of any help in understanding how the mathematical procedures might be generalised.[64] However, the intuition that lay behind Descartes' original attempt to devise a universal method was that there must be a way of presenting at least some questions such that it is immediately clear, simply from reflection upon the question, whether the information contained is true or false. For example, it is not clear from the formula $2 + 2 = 4$ that 2 and 2, when added together, do actually equal 4: we need to understand the symbols, operators, and the nature of the operations. But, when we represent numbers as line lengths or dots, we grasp the truth of the proposition immediately. It is immediately clear from putting one pair of dots, :, next to another pair of dots, :, that what we obtain is ::. There is no room for mistake or confusion.[65] Could there be something analogous to this in the non-mathematical case? In the 1630s, Descartes discovers that there can be, although he finds only one instance of it, the *cogito*. The *cogito* acts as a paradigm case of cognitive grasp: once we grasp the thought, we grasp that it could not but be true. Somehow – we shall be looking at exactly how in the next chapter – all thought must be modelled upon the type of cognitive grasp afforded by the *cogito*. Here we have something that achieves at least one aspect of what universal method was supposed to achieve, the provision of a means of making the conceptual content of a proposition so transparent that in grasping it we immediately grasp its truth or falsity.

In this sense, Descartes' epistemologised metaphysics, which uses hyperbolic doubt to generate metaphysical foundations for knowledge, stands in for, or replaces, a method of discovery. That is to say, it stands

---

[63] AT VII. 155–6.

[64] See my 'The Sources of Descartes' Procedure of Deductive Demonstration in Metaphysics and Natural Philosophy', in John Cottingham, ed., *Reason, Will, and Sensation* (Oxford, 1994).

[65] I am leaving to one side here Wittgensteinian sceptical doubts about rule-following, which hinge on the observation that rules do not fix their own application: the dot addition is a little more secure against such doubts than the use of numerals is, but in the long run nothing is immune to this form of scepticism (see Saul Kripke, *Wittgenstein on Rules and Private Language* (Oxford, 1982)).

in for at least part of what is included under the rubric of 'logic' in the Scholastic textbook tradition. And its deductive structure meets the same requirements of presentation as the textbook tradition, at least in general outline, for no one in the textbook tradition actually managed to present anything like a comprehensive system syllogistically, and the best that could be achieved was some kind of deductive rigour.

Given the nature of his metaphysics, Descartes does not strictly need to set out a separate method of discovery/presentation. So the *Principia* lacks an introductory book on 'logic'. But his earlier work in natural philosophy indicates that he does not need a metaphysics in order to do natural philosophy. Is the separate treatment of metaphysics really necessary to the project? I have mentioned that Gassendi collapsed metaphysics into natural philosophy. Something like this had, in effect, been the approach of Descartes and Beeckman in their collaboration in the early 1620s,[66] and in the early 1630s, when Descartes was working on *Le Monde*.[67] Moreover, it was the approach followed by Descartes' Dutch disciple Regius, who was sent *Le Monde* in 1641, and who developed its naturalistic approach, eschewing the idea of a need for separate metaphysical foundations, much to the annoyance of Descartes.[68] It is of note that it was also the approach of the standard authoritative exposition of Cartesian natural philosophy in the second half of the seventeenth century, namely Rohault's *Traité de Physique* (1671).

Gassendi thought that metaphysics and theology could be pursued by means of natural philosophy because he had a teleological understanding of nature as manifesting God's intentions. Descartes completely rejects this view. Indeed, in Part IV of the *Principia*, he gives an account of the formation of the Earth which wholly excludes any considerations of design, something which, more than anything else, evoked a hostile response to Descartes in England in the second half of the seventeenth century.[69] Moreover, Descartes' God is both completely inscrutable and completely transcendent,[70] and natural philosophy could never be the kind of guide to theology that it was for Gassendi and seventeenth-century English natural philosophers.

---

[66] See Gaukroger and Schuster, 'The Hydrostatic Paradox and the Origins of Cartesian Dynamics'.

[67] See my *Descartes, An Intellectual Biography*, ch. 7.

[68] See Theo Verbeek, 'The Invention of Nature: Descartes and Regius', in Stephen Gaukroger et al. eds., *Descartes' Natural Philosophy* (London, 2000), 149–67. On the details of Regius' natural philosophy see Paul Mouy, *Le Développement de la physique cartésienne, 1646–1712* (Paris, 1934), 73–85.

[69] See Peter Harrison, 'The Influence of Cartesian Cosmology in England', in Stephen Gaukroger, John Schuster, and John Sutton, eds., *Descartes' Natural Philosophy* (London, 2000), 168–92.

[70] See Gaukroger, *Descartes, A Intellectual Biography*, 203–10.

Descartes' view of the relation between metaphysics and natural philosophy is, in this sense, closer to the Scholastic view than Gassendi's. To
the extent to which there is an intimate relation between metaphysics
and natural philosophy, metaphysics provides a grounding for natural
philosophy, not the other way around. But, in that case, one might ask
whether any price is paid in *Le Monde* for foregoing such grounding. As
far as substantive natural–philosophical doctrine is concerned, there is
little in Parts II and III of the *Principia* that is not already in *Le Monde*, and
what there is that is new – with the possible exception (depending on
one's interpretation of it) of the doctrine of the reciprocity of motion –
is entirely compatible with *Le Monde*.

The metaphysics of Part I of the *Principia* is a legitimatory enterprise. Its
aim is to provide a foundation for the natural philosophy which follows,
a natural philosophy which has manifestly not been thought through on
the basis of a sceptically driven foundationalist metaphysics, but which
has been worked out quite independently. This is evident from *Le Monde*,
but this is not to say that *Le Monde* is metaphysics-free, for it harbours a
number of fundamental considerations about the nature of space, matter,
motion, and the nature of God's activity in the natural world that are certainly 'metaphysical' in one legitimate sense of that term. Nevertheless,
these have quite a different role from that played by metaphysical considerations in Gassendi's project, and, for example, from that played by
Henry More's attempt to move from his critical reflections on Descartes'
concept of space and matter to a conception of what God must be like.[71]
Descartes never thinks of natural philosophy as a basis for natural theology, implicitly rejecting Gassendi's 'royal road'.

The metaphysics underlying the natural philosophy of *Le Monde* is
deeply embedded in that natural philosophy, and works hand in hand
with it to an extent that separation is difficult if not impossible. In Parts I
and II of the *Principia*, Descartes makes the metaphysics underlying his
natural philosophy explicit and reworks it into a vocabulary borrowed
from the Scholastic textbook tradition. This involves two things. First, to
make this metaphysics explicit he must separate it out from the natural
philosophy. In some respects this separation is unnatural and forced,
whereas in other respects it is useful in drawing out otherwise hid-
den consequences that need to be scrutinised. Second, the 'descriptive'
metaphysics underlying the natural philosophy must be matched both

---

[71] See the discussion in Alexandre Koyré, *From the Closed World to the Infinite Universe* (Baltimore, 1957),
110–54.

to the legitimatory metaphysics of the early sections of Part I, and to the contingencies of the Aristotelian vocabulary of substances, modes, and accidents. However, Descartes often construes this vocabulary in quite novel ways, and he is able to subject it to a thorough reform. Above all, he very skilfully transforms a theologically driven metaphysics into an epistemologically driven one, effectively altering the whole purpose of the exercise. It is to the legitimatory metaphysics of Part I that we now turn.

CHAPTER 3

Principia, *Part I: The principles of knowledge*

Part I of the *Principia* covers much the same material that Descartes had already set out in the *Meditationes*, and Descartes tells one correspondent that 'it is only an abridgement of what I wrote in the *Meditationes*'.[1] The *Meditationes*, however, gives every impression of being self-contained, whereas Part I of the *Principia* is only one of six Parts of the project as initially envisaged, and effectively forms an introduction to what follows by providing a metaphysical basis for the natural philosophy that is developed there. In understanding the role of Part I in the larger project, it will be helpful to begin by mapping out the dangers, as we will have to steer a path through the Charybdis of treating the remainder of the *Principia* as an appendage to Part I, and the Scylla of treating Part I as a redundant introduction to the remainder.

If the *Meditationes* is as self-contained as it appears, we must ask what the purpose of the *Principia* is. Certainly, on one widespread reading of the *Meditationes*, the real novelty and originality of Descartes' project consist in his showing, by means of a project of radical doubt, the need for foundations for knowledge, and then providing these foundations, so that we might reconstruct anew the world that Meditation I called into doubt. In other words, the project consists in the attempt to establish that our grounds for believing the world has the properties it has are insecure, and then going on to show that these grounds can be replaced by something secure if, in subjecting our beliefs to intense sceptical doubt, we find something that is resistant to such doubt, so that we can then proceed to build knowledge up on the basis of this. It is worth noting that such an understanding of Descartes' project would accord with the Aristotelian doctrine of *regressus*, pursued in detail in the sixteenth century,

---

[1] Descartes to Chanut, 26 February 1649; AT v. 291. He adds that 'there is no need to take time off to read the *Meditationes* in order to understand it'.

whereby, in order to escape the apparent circularity in establishing basic causal principles from the observation of a range of effects and then deducing these effects from the basic principles, it is argued that the kind of knowledge of effects one has at the beginning of this process is different from the kind of knowledge one has at the end. The former is knowledge *that* something is the case, whereas the latter is knowledge *why* it is the case, that to say, it is causal knowledge, which brings with it an explanation of the phenomenon observed. If this were the kind of thing that Descartes were doing, Parts II and following of the *Principia* would simply provide a rebuilding of the pre-doubt world on new foundations, the pathbreaking work having been done in showing just what foundations are needed and what form they must take.

It is important to understand from the outset that this is not what Descartes is doing. The need to build the world on new foundations derives from the fact that Descartes wants to construct a completely new world, or rather he wants to show that a new world he has already constructed in natural–philosophical terms in *Le Monde* can be legitimated in metaphysical terms. The world that the *Meditationes* and *Principia* begin with is completely different from the world that we end up with in sketch form in Meditation VI, and which is set out in detail from Part II of the *Principia* onwards. *Regressus* is inherently conservative in that it takes the world as it is given in sensation as inherently veridical and asks for the causal processes underlying this world. Such an approach could not be further from Descartes' aims, which are very radical, invoking a picture of the cosmos that has none of the sensory qualities ascribed to the world on the traditional account: indeed, it is exactly the same radically mechanist account of the cosmos that he arrived at, by quite different means, in *Le Monde*. Descartes' own view of the relative standing of the *Meditationes* – and by implication Part I of the *Principia* – is made very clear in his remark to Burman in 1648:

A point to note is that you should not devote so much effort to the *Meditationes* and to metaphysical questions, or give them elaborate treatment in commentaries and the like. Still less should one do what some try to do, and dig more deeply into these questions than the author did: he has dealt with them all quite deeply enough. It is sufficient to have grasped them once in a general way, and then to remember the conclusion. Otherwise they draw the mind too far away from physical and observable things, and make it unfit to study them. Yet it is just these physical studies that it is most desirable for men to pursue, since they would yield abundant benefits for life.[2]

---

[2] AT v. 165.

Here, far from the *Meditationes* being the core of the exercise, it is treated
as merely an introduction to the real work.

This being the case, we can ask why we need Part I at all. In one sense,
the chronology of Descartes' writings shows that we do not need it. *Le
Monde* and *L'Homme* had been written without the benefit of the foundationalist metaphysics of the *Meditationes*, and those parts of the *Principia*
that go beyond *Le Monde*, such as the laws of collision and the doctrine
of the reciprocity of motion, in no way depend upon this metaphysics.
But Descartes' own view was that the metaphysics of Part I was in fact
an essential and inseparable part of the project. This is made very clear
in his dispute with Regius, to whom he had sent a copy of at least parts
of *Le Monde* and *L'Homme*. Regius, previously Descartes' disciple, had set
out his own account of a Cartesian natural philosophy on the basis of his
reading of *Le Monde* and *L'Homme* in his *Fundamenta physices* (1646), and
Descartes attacked Regius in his *Notæ in Programma*,[3] which appeared at
the beginning of 1648.[4] The main thrust of the response was that, because Regius' work lacks metaphysical grounding, of the kind that the
Principia provides, it is subject to all manner of confusions.

In other words, while Descartes' natural philosophy may stand on its
own for some purposes, for others it needs to be incorporated into a metaphysical system. What these 'other' purposes are is a difficult question.
It goes without saying that they include the task of metaphysical legitimation of Descartes' natural philosophy, that is, the attempt to show
that his natural philosophy follows from basic metaphysical principles
which no one can doubt, adherents of Scholastic thought included (he
had tested the mettle of his Scholastic contemporaries in their Replies
to the *Meditationes* and found nothing to concern him). But there are
also more specific questions that are worked through in some detail in
a metaphysical way which bear directly on his natural–philosophical
concerns, such as the nature of the division between mind and body,
and the causal relation between God and nature. The question of God's
immutability had been raised in *Le Monde*, but, far from introducing metaphysical considerations there, what it did was to show why theological
and metaphysical questions are not relevant to natural philosophy, because the constancy of God's action means that nature runs smoothly, so
smoothly that discussion of the source of this constancy does not further

---

3 AT vIIIB. 341–69.
4 See Theo Verbeek, 'Le contexte historique des *Notæ in Programma Quoddam*', in Theo Verbeek,
 ed., *Descartes et Regius* (Amsterdam, 1993), 1–34; and 'The Invention of Nature: Descartes and
 Regius'.

the natural–philosophical project. By contrast, the treatment of God in the *Principia* does have consequences for Descartes' understanding of natural philosophy, and his metaphysical treatment of the mind/body relation has consequences, for example, for his understanding of physical processes, animal cognition, and the nature of human psychology and ethics. Other specific questions are more difficult to decide, and we will be better placed to confront them as they arise.

Finally, there is also the general question of the systematic structure of the *Principia*, grounded in metaphysics as it is, providing various degrees of certainty for the particular claims of the later Parts. The idea that Descartes somehow arrived at, or would ever claim to have arrived at, his substantive and specific empirical claims about the physical world by deducing them from the *cogito* or the nature of God is ridiculous. By the end of Book IV of the *Principia*, he has offered accounts of such phenomena as the distances of the planets from the sun, the material constitution of the sun, the motion of comets, the colours of the rainbow, sunspots, solidity and fluidity, why the moon moves faster than the earth, the nature of transparency, the rarefaction and condensation of matter, why air and water flow from east to west, the nature of the earth's interior, the nature of quicksilver, the nature of bitumen and sulphur, why the water in certain wells is brackish, the nature of glass, magnetism, and static electricity. It would be credulous in the extreme to claim that these phenomena could be deduced from metaphysical principles of any kind, and Descartes never claimed he had done this.

The closest he comes to a general claim about deducing things from first principles is in article 64 of Part II, where he tells us that he does 'not accept or desire in physics any principles other than those accepted in geometry or abstract mathematics[5]; because all the phenomena of nature are explained thereby, and demonstrations concerning them which are certain can be given'. In elucidation he writes:

For I frankly admit that I know of no material substance other than that which is divisible, has shape, and can move in every possible way, and this the geometers call quantity and take as the object of their demonstrations. Moreover, our concern is exclusively with the division, shape and motions of this substance, and nothing concerning these can be accepted as true unless it be deduced from indubitably true common notions with such certainty that it can be regarded as a mathematical demonstration. And because all natural phenomena can be

---

[5] 'Abstract mathematics', i.e. geometry, arithmetic, and algebra, as opposed to practical mathematics, which includes areas such as astronomy, harmonics, statics etc.

explained in this way, as one can judge from what follows, I believe that no other physical principles should be accepted or even desired. (Part II art. 64)

Note two things about this statement. First, the natural philosophy is deduced from physical principles, not metaphysical ones. All *scientia*-style – i.e. textbook – presentations of natural philosophy use first principles. Descartes is telling us that his first principles are those of mechanism: they postulate an inert, homogeneous matter which moves in particular ways and nothing else, for nothing else is needed to obtain his results. Moreover, this enables him to pursue natural philosophy quantitatively, as Kepler, Galileo, Beeckman and others were doing. In other words, what Descartes is drawing attention to is not the fact that he is making deductions from first principles, since this is unremarkable, but the content of those first principles, which marks his project out starkly from those of Scholastic textbooks.

Second, Descartes is not saying that deduction is a means of *discovery* of results in natural philosophy. The method he advocates for discovery in natural philosophy, as is clear from *La Dioptrique* and his treatment of the rainbow in *Les Meteores*, which, as we saw in chapter 1, he singles out as the example of his method in the letter to Antoine Vatier of 22 February 1638, is to start from problem-solving, and his 'method' is designed to facilitate such problem-solving. The problems have to be posed in quantitative terms, and there are a number of constraints on what form an acceptable solution takes: one cannot posit 'occult qualities', one must seek 'simple natures', and so on. The solution is then tested experimentally to determine how well it holds up compared with other possible explanations meeting the same constraints which also appear to account for the facts. Finally, the solution is incorporated into a system of natural philosophy, and the principal aim of the *Principia* is to set out this natural philosophy in detail. The *Principia* is a textbook, it sets out a *scientia*, and the aim of textbooks is not to show one how the empirical results were arrived at – for that one needs to go to *La Dioptrique*, or Discourse VIII of *Les Meteores*, or the various letters and other unpublished writings on mechanics and optics – but to set them out in a systematic way.

A textbook gives one a systematic overview of the subject, presenting its ultimate foundations, and showing how the parts of the subject are connected. Ultimately, the empirically verified results have to be fitted into this system, but these empirical results themselves are not shown to be true or false by their incorporation within this system: they are shown to be true or false purely in observational and experimental terms. Nevertheless, by being placed within a systematic structure such as that provided by the *Principia*, the degree of certainty of results can be established or reinforced: fundamental truths can be separated from ones having a significant degree of contingency, and the degree of dependence of truths can be established.[6] This is what *scientia* consisted in for Scholastic authors, and it is what Descartes is offering.

DOUBT AND KNOWLEDGE

It will be helpful to begin by setting out Descartes' strategy. In the first 30 articles of Part I, Descartes begins by taking us through various forms of sceptical doubt and ends up in article 30 showing how 'the doubts previously listed are removed'. This is the point at which we can start on the positive part of the project, but we can now make the start only on Descartes' terms, and these terms are much more restrictive than they might initially appear. In other words, making the start at article 30 is a very different enterprise from making a start at article 1. What in article 30 removes 'the doubts previously listed' is the application of the doctrine of clear and distinct ideas. This is the doctrine that generates the basic features of Descartes' epistemologically driven metaphysical programme, and what is distinctive and novel about it is that it reverses the traditional procedure whereby, when we inquire into the nature of something, we first establish its existence and then ask what properties or features it has. Descartes' use of the principle of clear and distinct ideas forces us to proceed in the opposite direction. We can only ask whether something exists once we have a clear and distinct conception of what it is that we are asking about, for only then do we have a proper grasp of the problem. Consequently, we must ask about the nature of something before we can proceed to ask whether something having that nature exists. Descartes uses the problems raised by scepticism to establish this as the only reliable procedure by which to establish the reality of things. Showing us how this works in the case of God, a case particularly – and possibly uniquely – suited to this kind of approach because of the vast and relatively unconstrained range of things one could mean by God, he then proceeds to use it to establish the nature of the division between mind and body, and, most contentiously of all, to provide a metaphysical entry into

---

[6] It is worth noting in this context just how modest Descartes is in arts. 205 and 206 of Part IV about just what degree of certainty is achievable.

natural philosophy completely different from anything in the history of the subject. He requires us to move from our conception of the physical world to the actual existence of the physical world, but to do this we must have a clear and distinct conception of the physical world. Trading on the case of clarity and distinctness in mathematics, he constrains what is going to count as a clear and distinct idea of the physical world in such a way that the only conception able to emerge that indisputably meets the criterion of clarity and distinctness is a mechanist one.

Descartes uses the criterion in the first place to isolate the physical world from God and from mind, showing that both of these are quite distinct from the physical world, and thereby pointing us in the direction of a physical world that lacks certain distinctive properties that we associate with the supernatural and the mental: it is completely regular and deterministic in its behaviour, it does not contain any of the 'souls' traditionally postulated to account for vital or other functions, it does not initiate activity but merely conserves a pre-given amount of activity, causation occurs only by means of physical contact, and so on. Then the criterion is used in quite a different way, to identify candidates for existence, and here Descartes argues that the only kind of physical world whose existence I can intelligibly inquire about is one I can conceive clearly and distinctly, and that the only way in which we can satisfy this criterion is by thinking about the world in quantitative terms – that is, in terms of an inert matter whose only property is spatial extension – and characterising it in a purely geometrical way. We thereby arrive at a mechanistic account of the universe as the only possible option. And that is the point of the first part of the exercise. Once this has been established, we can then move on to establishing some of the features of this physical world in Part II.

The key moves in this strategy are the use of sceptical doubt to force open the question of what our starting point should be, and to establish clear and distinct ideas as the only possible starting point. In the Scholastic textbook tradition, virtually the first thing that is introduced is the distinction between matter and form, matter being simply the substratum in which the activity of the relevant form is manifested, and it is the activity of forms that physics investigates. Descartes' natural philosophy has no place for forms, but he cannot engage this question effectively straight away, so instead of starting with the basic metaphysics of matter he postpones discussion to articles 51–6, by which time he is safely on his own territory. He begins instead with the search for a criterion by which the veridicality of our thoughts or beliefs can be secured, using hyperbolic

doubt to systematically reject various sensory and other cognitive criteria, and to establish clear and distinct ideas as the only criterion able to
secure veridicality.

Traditionally one might have expected a treatise of this kind to begin
by establishing common ground, but Descartes begins by moving in the
opposite direction. Any potential common ground is undermined by hyperbolic doubt – this is the primary reason for introducing hyperbolic
doubt – and it is distinctive both in the form of doubt involved, which
is epistemological rather than epistemic (it concerns knowledge claims
rather than beliefs), and in the fact that it is hyperbolic, because it raises
problems not about things that are intrinsically doubtful but about matters of which we can be certain. On the first question, traditional forms of
scepticism, such as that of the ancient Pyrrhonists, were directed against
beliefs: the argument was basically that no belief we hold is any more
justified than the opposite belief because beliefs are always relative to
a whole range of variable and contingent factors. Sensory beliefs, for
example, are relative to the state of the thing perceived, to the medium
in which it was perceived, and to the state of the perceiver, and no state
could be singled out as being objective or even optimal. As a consequence
we were not entitled to any of our beliefs.[7] Descartes' scepticism is different from this. He does not ask us to abandon our beliefs, just the claim
that any of these beliefs constitutes knowledge (until it is firmly based).
Second, Descartes asks us to doubt things which we may well continue
to believe, and with good reason, such as the propositions that two and
two equal four, or that there is an external world. We can be justified in
acting upon these beliefs, we may even be unable to conceive of what it
would be like for those beliefs to be false (this is particularly the case with
mathematical beliefs), but our not being able to conceive how something
could be false does not mean it cannot be false. God's powers are such
that he could deceive me into thinking there was a physical world when
in fact there was not one, by manipulating my cognitive states (art. 5).
More generally, what we can or cannot conceive is not a constraint on
God's powers: just because we could not conceive the radii of a circle
being of unequal lengths does not mean that it was not possible for God
to make them of unequal lengths.[8]

We might think of this doctrine as hyperrealism: how things are is
independent not only of what evidence we could have concerning them,

[7] See my 'The Ten Modes of Aenesidemus and the Myth of Ancient Scepticism', *British Journal for
the History of Philosophy* 3 (1995), 371–87.
[8] This is the example used in Descartes to Mersenne, 27 May 1630; AT I. 152.

but even of how it is possible for us to conceive of them being. It is this hyperrealism that provides the conceptual space for hyperbolic doubt. This
might seem to generate a problem for Descartes' doctrine that we must
have a clear and distinct grasp of the properties of something before we
can inquire into the existence of whatever it is that has those properties.
For, if how things are is independent of how it is possible for us to conceive of them, what is the point of starting from our conceptions and then
trying to establish whether anything corresponds to these conceptions?
Descartes' point is that we can, in fact, make a connection between our
conception of things and how things really are, but on two conditions.
First, we must conceive of them clearly and distinctly, and, second, God
must guarantee that whatever we conceive clearly and distinctly is true.
If it is God who has provided us with the capacity to make clear and
distinct judgements in the first place, then, given the nature of God, there
would be no point us having this capacity unless it did, in fact, enable us
to grasp things as they really are. Descartes' point is that it is impossible
for us to grasp how things are simply by relying on human resources,
and this is why clear and distinct grasp requires a divine guarantee.

We saw in chapter 1 that Descartes believed from an early stage, initially in a mathematical context, that there must be a way of presenting
at least some questions such that it is immediately clear, simply from
reflection upon the question, whether the information contained is true
or false. We also saw that he devised a way of representing numbers as
line lengths such that arithmetical operations performed upon these line
lengths could be made completely transparent: once we grasp the operation we grasp its truth or falsity. The *cogito* affords a non-mathematical
example of such grasp: the one thing we are unable to doubt is that we
are doubting, or, more generally, thinking, since doubting is a form of
thinking. The very act of doubting reveals to me something that I cannot
doubt, namely that I am thinking, and this is how the *cogito* stops the
regress of doubt. It is able to do this because it is a clear and distinct
grasp, just as my grasp of $2 + 2 = 4$, represented by bringing together
two line lengths of two units each and placing them end to end, is such
that I cannot be mistaken. But, between the 1620s, when his concern
was with the representation of arithmetical operations, and the metaphysical concerns of the 1630s onwards, there has been a development
in Descartes' thought that changes the nature and significance of the
doctrine of clear and distinct ideas.[9] While he was concerned with the

---

[9] On the complex history of the development of Descartes' doctrine of clear and distinct ideas see
my *Descartes, An Intellectual Biography*, esp. chs. 4 and 8.

mathematical case, the clarity and distinctness with which I grasped a proposition was constitutive of the truth (or falsity) of the proposition. A genuinely clear and distinct grasp revealed everything about the truth or falsity of the proposition. Hyperrealism undermines this: it opens up the possibility that we can have a clear and distinct grasp of something and yet still be mistaken. When this occurs, we are faced with hyperbolic doubt. This being the case, what does our feeling that we cannot possibly be mistaken in grasping the *cogito* derive from, and what justification can we provide for this? Descartes trades on our intuitions about our degree of certainty in this case and asks what could possibly legitimate it. The only answer is a divine guarantee. And once we have been provided with this, then, as the title of article 13 announces, 'the knowledge of remaining things depends on a knowledge of God'.

ESSENCE AND EXISTENCE

Descartes explicitly applies the 'essence before existence' doctrine to God, implying that others had not always been clear about what is at issue, and he criticises 'those theologians who, following ordinary logic, ask whether God exists before asking what His nature is'.[10] But what is more interesting is the fact that he makes it into a general doctrine. In the replies to the first set of Objections to the *Meditationes*, he writes: 'according to the rules of true logic we must never ask whether something exists unless we already know what it is'.[11] There may look to be a sleight of hand here. It is hard to deny that, in asking for the existence of something, we must be familiar with enough features of the thing to enable us to identify it, for if we cannot identify it then obviously we cannot ask whether *it* exists, but that does not mean that we must have a complete and full understanding of the thing before we can ask whether it exists. There is surely a difference between having enough information to identify something and grasping its essential qualities.[12]

---

[10] Descartes to Mersenne, 11 December 1640; AT III. 273. I do not think any theologians literally operated in this way, but as Jorge Secada (*Descartes' Metaphysics* (Cambridge, 2000), 8) points out, late Scholastic authors were generally committed to 'existence before essence' as a general thesis. The Coimbra commentator Fonseca writes: 'first we show that a thing exists, next what it is' (*Institutionum dialecticarum libri octo* (Lisbon, 1564) VII. 40); and Suárez tells us that 'the question "what is it?" presupposes the question "is it"?' (*Metaphysicorum disputationum tomi dui*, 2 vols. (Cologne, 1614), XXIX.2.1).

[11] AT III. 273.

[12] Aquinas makes the point that if we have 'no account' of something we cannot ask whether it exists, but that does not mean we can only ask about its existence when we have its 'essential definition'. See the discussion in Secada, *Descartes' Metaphysics* (the Aquinas passage is cited on p. 10).

Descartes seems to run the two together. Nevertheless, while in the usual case there is a gap between the two, we cannot rule out the possibility that there may be exceptional cases in which we do not have criteria of identity before we have at least some kind of grasp of the essence of the thing in question. Descartes treats the cases of his fundamental substances – God, the mind, and the physical world – like this.

The way in which the essence before existence approach is used differs somewhat in the three cases, however. In the case of God, there may well be agreement that the task is to establish the existence of something whose essence we have set out carefully. In the case of the arguments for the nature of the mind and its difference from the body, Descartes sees the question in one respect in the reverse: we clearly know the existence of the mind, and this means we must somehow already understand its essence clearly. He replies to Gassendi:

> I am surprised that you should say here that all my considerations about the wax demonstrate that I distinctly know that I exist, but not that I know what I am or what my nature is: for the one cannot be demonstrated without the other.[13]

Nevertheless, this does not mean that the inferential direction is from existence to essence, but rather that, when we grasp the existence of something, we must have already grasped its essential properties. For Descartes, our knowledge of the self – that is, our mind – comes not through a grasp of its existence but through the grasp of its properties. As he points out article 11,

> it is very well known through the natural light [of reason] that no properties or qualities belong to nothingness; and accordingly, whenever we perceive some properties or qualities, we must necessarily find a thing or substance to which they belong there; and that the more properties or qualities we perceive in the thing or substance, the more clearly we know it. However, it is obvious that we perceive more properties or qualities in the mind than in any other thing, since absolutely nothing can cause us to know something other than our mind, without at the same time bringing us with even more certainty to the knowledge of our mind itself.

In other words, our knowledge of existence is inferential: we are aware of certain properties and qualities, and we infer the existence of something having those properties. In the case of the mind, however, the properties we are aware of are sufficiently clear and distinct for us to be sure that

---

[13] AT VII. 359.

they are essential properties, so in making the inference back to the bearer of those properties, we are grasping the existence of something whose essence we have specified in advance. Note also that, unlike the cases of God and the physical world, the mind is distinctive in that we cannot but approach it through clear and distinct ideas.

The case of the physical world is different again. Here, we do not move from defined or agreed essential qualities to the existence of something having those qualities, but from a set of constraints on how we should conceive of the physical world to the existence of a physical world that meets those constraints. In using this approach to open up questions about the nature of the physical world, Descartes has some justification in believing that what he is offering is so different from the usual account that there are no identifying features which are both substantial and uncontentious. The model of the cosmos he is rejecting, for example, depends crucially upon a range of judgements made on the basis of deeply entrenched theories and observations which Descartes simply does not accept, for reasons he will spell out in Parts II and III. The issue becomes that of what constraints we should accept in asking not just whether the physical world exists, but what kind of thing the physical world is. The only criterion that has come through the tests of hyperbolic doubt unscathed is that by which we accept something only if it can be conceived by us clearly and distinctly. The arguments for the existence of God show us what kind of God exists; the arguments for the existence of mind show us the essential properties of the mind; the arguments for the existence of the physical world will show us what kind of physical world exists.

The discussion of God in articles 14–30 is, then, not about the existence of God per se, but about his nature. God is needed to guarantee the veridicality of the faculty of clear and distinct ideas that he has provided us with, but for this he would have to be a good god. But God surely is a good god. If he were not, he would not be God at all. Here we come to the question of just what is at stake in Descartes' arguments in articles 14–29, which are concerned ostensibly with God's existence. A feature of arguments for the existence of God per se is that God is ill-defined. Zeus is a god for the Greeks, the totality of existing things is for Spinoza, but neither the pagan Zeus nor Spinoza's *deus sive natura* are God for Christians. Arguments for the existence of God, unlike arguments for the existence of the external world, are generally speaking arguments for the existence of something that has very specific but very disputed qualities, many of which may be defined extra-philosophically,

and which cannot be necessarily captured or demonstrated philosophically. Seventeenth-century Christianity was no exception: one begins
with a reasonably specific understanding of what God is, and then shows
that this thing exists. The defining features of what one wants to establish the existence of are always going to be closer to essential features in
an era in which what was at issue was not the existence of God, which
was not in contention, but what kind of God there was: these disputes
had shifted since the Middle Ages from disputes between Christians and
non-Christians (particularly Muslims), to disputes between Catholics and
Protestants, and between various sects or movements within these con-
fessions. Remember that Descartes' contemporaries were not atheists,
and he was writing for a Christian audience fully convinced of the existence of a broadly Christian God. His aim is not to convince someone
who does not believe in the existence of God that God exists, but rather
to establish something about the nature of God.

One key issue in sixteenth- and seventeenth-century philosophical
disputes was the question of God's transcendence. There had been a
move amongst both Neoplatonists and more naturalistically inclined
Aristotelians in the Renaissance to invest the natural realm with so many
powers that God became incorporated into nature to varying degrees.
Mersenne had developed a form of mechanism to combat this development, which he saw as leading to pantheism and other heretical doctrines,
and to restore the transcendence of God.[14] Realising that Scholasticism
was unable to deal decisively with the threat because Aristotelian forms
were in some cases the source of it, he stripped nature of Aristotelian
forms and potentialities, as well as more radical kinds of natural activity,
thereby forcing a strict separation between God's supernatural activity and the inertness of the natural realm, the latter having the great
advantage that it made nature much easier to quantify.

Transcendence is the most important thing that Descartes' proofs for
the existence of God set out to establish, and this is above all true of
the ontological proof. The ontological proof is different from traditional
proofs of the existence of God such as those offered by Aquinas, in that
these typically deduce God's existence from some feature of creation:
from the harmony in nature, from the necessity for a chain of causation
to begin somewhere, from the apparent goal-directedness of natural processes, and so on. In this way, our approach to God is always through

---

[14] See my *Descartes, An Intellectual Biography*, 146–52, and, for a detailed account, see Robert Lenoble, *Mersenne ou la naissance du mécanisme*, 2nd edn (Paris, 1971).

something other than himself: we can show his existence only if we think of him as the creator of the physical world, for example. The ontological argument, by contrast, treats God quite independently of anything he might have done. It is not part of the essential nature of God that he created the world, and the ontological proof is designed, in Descartes' hands, to capture something about the essential nature of God. Moreover, the ontological argument invites us to reflect on a clear and distinct idea and to draw out its consequences without any reference to empirical questions. The argument works by reflecting on the nature of God as something that has every perfection (this is in effect proposed as a clear and distinct idea of God), and asking whether something could have every perfection if it did not exist, for surely it is more perfect to exist than not to exist, so something with every perfection must exist. The problems with the argument are notorious: first, as Aquinas pointed out (thinking of Anselm's version), the argument assumes that God has every perfection, but classical Greek philosophers, for example, would not have thought of God in this way; second, it is not possible for something literally to have every perfection (perfectly round and perfectly square, perfectly good and perfectly bad, etc.); third, the argument depends, as Aquinas also pointed out, on the assumption that existence is a property, whereas existence seems more like a precondition for something having a property than a property itself; and, finally, even if we could accommodate all these points, all the argument would show would be that *if* there existed something with every perfection, then the existence of this something would be necessary, which is very far from showing that in fact there does exist something whose existence is necessary. But, of course, this last point is irrelevant if the audience does accept that God exists, as Descartes' audience did, for what is then demonstrated is, first, the transcendence of this God, and, second, his necessary existence. God's transcendence and perfection are then reinforced in the next argument (arts. 17–18), which is designed to show that God's perfections are transcendent perfections, and could not possibly be an extrapolation from human perfections, but also that we can grasp these perfections because of their simplicity.

In order to align this transcendent perfect God fully with that of Christianity, it remains to be shown that he also a creator, and here Descartes treats us to one of his most ingenious arguments. The idea underlying it is that cause and effect must be simultaneous, because if events are not temporally proximate they cannot affect one another; this being the case, only something present can be the cause of something present. My

existence is present, so we can ask what the cause of my present existence is, and the answer cannot be something past, such as the fact that
I existed a few minutes ago. It must be something present, but what? I
do not have the power to put myself into existence, so the cause of my
present existence must be something outside of me, and God is really the
only candidate.[15]

The upshot of the arguments for the existence of God is that God is
transcendent, perfect, and the creator of everything: and these are qualities God must have if he is to be God, not qualities which we discover as
a matter of fact he has. The ontological argument in particular trades on
the idea that essence precedes existence in the case of God. And there
is certainly a case to be made that for something to be God, i.e. to 'genuinely' be God, it would have to have a particular set of characteristics.
Another quality God must have is 'goodness'. Descartes' intended audience would of course have agreed with him that God was good, in the
sense of morally good, but what is at issue for Descartes' God is not so
much freedom from moral deceit as freedom from epistemological deceit. How could Descartes establish this? One possibility is to point out
that, since God has given us our cognitive capacities, and since he has
given them to us in order that we might know the world he has created,
these capacities yield a truthful account of what the world is like. It was
traditionally accepted that nature (for Aristotle) or God (for his Christian
followers) had provided us with the cognitive organs we have in order
that we might know the structure of the world. In this sense it would have
been assumed by Descartes' readers that God is free from cognitive deceit. The traditional understanding of this doctrine, however, had been
that God had guaranteed the veridicality of our sense organs. Descartes
rejects this account of our sense organs, arguing that sensation, when
unchecked, does in fact mislead us, and misleads us systematically, about
the nature of the world, and that we should not assume that the reason we
have sense organs is so that they might reveal its basic structure to us. As

[15] There are many questions we might want to raise about this demonstration, not least why present
existence needs to be caused in the first place: surely it is coming into existence and going out
of existence that need explanation, not remaining in existence. One common objection is that
this argument for God's existence from the nature of causation implies that no earlier event can
bring about a later one, but this does not, in fact, follow. Descartes believed that bodies remain
in inertial states, such as rectilinear motion, without external causes, and it is because of this
that later events can result from earlier ones, even though they are not in temporal proximity:
as a result of a collision, for example, the inertial state of a body may be caused to change, but
it will remain in this changed inertial state at all later times unless it enters into another causal
interaction. What is not clear is how Descartes can allow this in the case of physical inertial states
without allowing it in the case of existence per se.

he puts it in Meditation VI: 'the proper purpose of sensory perceptions given me by nature is simply to inform the mind of what is beneficial or harmful for the mind/body composite'.[16] Descartes is not denying that our senses are reliable per se, only that they are unreliable, at least by themselves, as guides to how the world is.

If sensation is ruled out, we need to ask what part of our cognitive life is reliable as a guide to how the world is. The answer lies in a form of reflective judgement about our perceptions and beliefs, which is no less natural than sensation (although, as we shall see later, it is lacking in animals, and this is one of the things that marks out animal perception from human perception), but which, unlike sensation, is concerned with veridicality. God does not guarantee the veridicality of sensation, because its function is not to inform us of the nature of the world, but he does guarantee the veridicality of clear and distinct ideas, because the function of these is to inform us about the world (as well as about purely intellectual matters, like mathematics and metaphysics). We might think of clear and distinct ideas as the epistemological analogue of conscience, as something that God has given us in order to guide us in cognitive matters, just as he has given us conscience to guide us in moral matters. The fact that he has given us these faculties for these purposes settles any question of whether they might deceive us.[17]

CLARITY AND DISTINCTNESS

If God has endowed us with a faculty of clear and distinct perception, and guaranteed that faculty, we need some account of how it is possible for human error to occur. The account that Descartes provides is in effect a reworking of the classical Augustinian account of sin. On the Augustinian view, God, although he is omniscient and omnipotent, is also perfect, so he cannot be the cause of error. But nor can sin simply be privation of goodness, for it is something that has distinctive properties of its own. In response to this dilemma, Augustine postulates a faculty of free will, whereby the responsibility for the existence of evil can be borne by humans.[18] Similarly in Descartes' account of error. Error is neither

---

[16] AT VII. 83.

[17] It is worth noting here that we can substitute 'nature' for 'God' in these arguments (thereby effectively taking them back to their original Aristotelian version), or even, with a little adjustment, 'evolution' (thereby placing them in the realm of modern evolutionary epistemology), to obtain a more general assessment of their force.

[18] On the background to this complex question see Albrecht Dihle, *The Theory of the Will in Classical Antiquity* (Berkeley, 1982).

God's doing nor simply the absence of truth, it is something for which we must take responsibility.

To explain how error comes about, Descartes invokes two 'modes of thinking', namely the 'perception of the intellect' and 'the operation of the will' (art. 32). The former is not the source of error, for we may perceive something unclearly or indistinctly, but it is only when we make a judgement on the basis of an unclear perception that error arises. This is perhaps clearest in his account of colour. For Descartes, our perception of size and figure is different from our perception of such phenomena as colour and pain. We ascribe each of these to objects (to a part of our body in the case of pain), but on very different grounds. In the case of the first two, the ascription is on the basis of a clear and distinct idea, in the case of the latter it is not. When we say that we perceive colours in objects, for example, this is just to say that we perceive something in the objects whose nature we do not know, by means of a clear, vivid sensation which we call the sensation of colour (art. 70). In fact, colours are not in objects on Descartes' account, but this does not mean that we make a mistake when we see colours as being in objects, only when, on the basis of this, we judge that they are in objects. Such a judgement is the work of the will, and Descartes proceeds to defend the traditional view that free will is the highest human perfection (art. 37), freedom that is manifest to us in the process of doubt itself (art. 39). Descartes avoids the traditional problem of the irreconcilability of God's omnipotence and the existence of free will simply by reminding us of God's transcendence, and of the fact that just because we cannot grasp something does not mean that it does not occur (art. 41). The same argument had been put forward earlier in the case of our knowledge of empirical and mathematical questions, but access had finally been allowed to these through the faculty of clear and distinct ideas. Descartes' view in the case of free will, however, seems to be that we have not been granted clear and distinct perception in this case, so there is no point pursuing the question of reconciling free will and God's foreknowledge further.

As regards the sources of error, Descartes lists four at the end of Part I (arts. 71–4). The first two relate to our inability to distinguish those things which are properly mental from those that are properly physical, for example in the ascription of qualities of sensations, such as colours, to physical objects. Descartes' argument is that we naturally make these misascriptions in childhood and then they pass into adulthood with us because they have been so deeply engrained. We shall return to the mind/body distinction later. The third source of error is lack of attention and concentration, with the result that we rely upon common opinons. This is a theme that runs through Descartes' writings from the *Regulae* onwards, and the notion of attention is central to the psychology of clear and distinct perception. Fourth, Descartes tells us that 'we attach our concepts to words which do not accurately correspond to things' (art. 74). The lack of correspondence between words and things was a common seventeenth-century complaint,[19] and Descartes had earlier mused on the possibility of a language in which natural correspondences could be established, but he had not considered the project realistic.[20]

Our only guarantee of freedom from error is to assent solely to what we perceive clearly and distinctly (art. 43). Now one of the sticking points of Descartes' account lies in the question of just what a clear and distinct perception consists in. Indeed, this problem appeared to many of Descartes' contemporaries and sucessors alike to be the weakest point in his whole argument. While Malebranche, in his distinction between ideas and sensations, and Spinoza, in his account of 'adequate' ideas, will set out from a version of the Cartesian doctrine, neither of them developed it in a Cartesian way, and other philosophers just ignored it. The difficulty with the doctrine turned on the fact that we are seemingly free to choose what we consider ourselves to perceive clearly and distinctly. As Gassendi pointed out in his comments on the *Meditationes*, what one person claims to have conceived clearly and distinctly, another regards as confused and obscure, and there seems to be no way of deciding such issues, with the result that the criterion is useless.[21]

We can trace the genealogy of Descartes' doctrine of clear and distinct ideas back to its roots in the rhetorical–psychological theories of the Roman rhetorical writers, especially Quintilian.[22] Quintilian was concerned with the qualities of the 'image', with the search for and presentation of images that are distinctive in their vividness and particularity, above all with the question of what features or qualities they must have if they are to be employed effectively in convincing an audience. Whether one is an orator at court or an actor on stage, Quintilian tells us, our aim is to engage the emotions of the audience, and perhaps to get it to behave in a particular way as a result, and what one needs in order to do this

---

[19] See James Knowlson, *Universal Language Schemes in England and France, 1600–1800* (Toronto, 1975), and M. M. Slaughter, *Universal Language and Scientific Taxonomy in the Seventeenth Century* (Cambridge, 1982).

[20] AT I. 80–2.

[21] See, for example, Gassendi's point about how different people have different clear and distinct ideas on the taste of a water melon, depending on one's age, state of health etc., AT VII. 278–9.

[22] See my *Descartes, An Intellectual Biography*, 115–24.

is to employ images that have the quality of *evidentia* – vivid illustration. The core of Quintilian's account is that unless we are already convinced by our own images, we will not be in a position to use them to convince others. So self-conviction is a prerequisite for the conviction of others. And self-conviction, like the conviction of one's audience, depends on the qualities of the image, amongst which must figure clarity and vividness. Note that in this version of the doctrine of clear and distinct ideas, there is no problem in recognising a clear and distinct idea. Whether an idea is clear and distinct is manifested in its application: the degree to which it moves us, or moves our audience, is a sign of its clarity and distinctness.

In taking up this model of self-conviction, Descartes transforms it from a rhetorical doctrine, in which we amplify some emotion or belief by presenting that belief clearly and distinctly to ourselves, into a cognitive doctrine, in which we assess the truth or falsity of an idea by presenting it to ourselves clearly and distinctly. The first version of this new cognitive doctrine is evident in the *Regulae*, in Rule 3 for example, where we are told that what we must seek is something we can clearly and evidently intuit, and that the mind that is 'clear and attentive' will be able to achieve this. The early *Regulae* draws its model of knowledge almost exclusively from mathematics, and the doctrine of clear and distinct ideas is applied to the case of mathematics in what becomes a paradigmatic way. We have already looked at an example of this in the case of arithmetical operations.[23] The idea is that, by representing arithmetical operations in terms of operations on line lengths, we grasp the validity of the operation in a clear and distinct way. Here, again, the clarity and distinctness of the idea is manifested in its application. At the end of the 1620s, however, Descartes abandons this kind of clear and distinct grasp as a general model and gradually shifts to a metaphysical conception whereby clarity and distinctness, which now requires a divine guarantee, is manifested paradigmatically in the *cogito*. Now even if one were to allow that the kind of grasp we have in the *cogito* is the same kind of immediate awareness that we had earlier in the mathematical cases, there is a major difference. The similarity between each of the mathematical cases could be established by the employment of a definite, straightforward procedure, namely representation of the problem in terms of line lengths: and it broke down exactly where this procedure broke down. But, in the case of the *cogito*, there is no procedure at all for deciding whether any similarity holds, and all we have to go on is the phenomenology of the experience, so that

---

[23] For an example of the presentation of geometrical operations in a clear and distinct way (algebraically), see ibid., 175–6.

clarity and distinctness ultimately become, at worst, little more than a matter of individual psychology.

Indeed, the *cogito* itself may be at least part of the cause of the problem in this respect. It is supposed to be a paradigm instance of clear and distinct grasp, and thereby a model for the rest of knowledge. But is it even knowledge at all? The Scholastics thought of knowledge in causal or explanatory terms: knowing about something meant knowing why it was the way it was, knowing how it got to be as it was, knowing whether and how it realised some aim or purpose or function, how its constituent parts made it the way it was, and so on. What legitimates the *cogito* is not some procedure which is simple and generates real results (as was the case in the *Regulae*), but a divine guarantee whose workings are, and will remain, a complete mystery to us. The *cogito* offers nothing causal or explanatory, it does not show us anything – in the way that the line-length representation of arithmetical operations show us how addition, subtraction, multiplication, division, and taking roots worked. So it is hardly surprising that there is no procedure that we are able to follow which will show us when we are genuinely grasping ideas in a clear and distinct way.

Now a great deal of what Descartes argues in the *Principia* is independent of the success or failure of his doctrine of clear and distinct ideas to provide the kind of guarantee offered in Part I, and indeed the bulk of its natural philosophy had already been developed without the benefit of this doctrine in *Le Monde*, but the legimatory part of the programme, in which we are led to a mechanist natural philosophy purely on the basis of reflecting on our clear and distinct ideas, looks doomed. Descartes seems to concede Gassendi's point, that what is clear and distinct for one person will not be for another, in article 50, where we are told that even 'common notions', which include 'eternal truths' such as the basic truths of mathematics and logic, while there 'is no doubt that they can be clearly and distinctly perceived', are not necessarily so perceived by everyone, and 'may be opposed by the prejudiced opinions of some men'. But there is another side to this, for Descartes' formulation suggests that there is going to be agreement on clear and distinct ideas among those who have freed themselves from such prejudices.

Everything hinges on Descartes' ability to flesh out this notion of freedom from prejudice. Neither the quality of our psychological state nor God's guarantee is enough to guide us towards clear and distinct grasp. Although the discussion of error, which we have looked at, touches on this question, it is patently unconvincing as an account of who is in a position to grasp things clearly and distinctly and who is not. It has looked up to now that clear and distinct grasp is something that is available to everyone without precondition. But in fact there are preconditions, and they are such that access to clear and distinct ideas, at least in the case of natural philosophy, is much more restricted than we might have thought. We cannot deal with this question fully until we have examined Descartes' account of the passions, which bears directly on the issue of how one goes about creating the right state of mind for knowledge acquisition, but we can at least register what is at stake here.

In *La Recherche de la vérité*, which I have indicated was probably a first experiment in setting out his natural philosophy, before he settled on the format of the *Principia*, Descartes raises the question of the kind of mentality needed to be a natural philosopher. This is a question that Francis Bacon, whose works were well known in Descartes' circle, had pursued in detail, and Bacon's model of the natural philosopher as a practical (as opposed to a merely contemplative) man who could bypass Scholastic learning and think and, above all, experiment for himself was a powerful model from the 1620s onwards.[24] *La Recherche* contrasts the *honnête homme* and the Scholastic philosopher, suggesting that the former, the man of action who is not highly educated but is honest and trustworthy in his views, is fitted, in a way that the disputatious Scholastic is not, to be trained as a Cartesian natural philosopher.[25] In the terminology of clear and distinct ideas, it is the *honnête homme* who has the capacity for grasping truths because he is able to, and inclined to, use his natural faculty of clarity and distinctness: he has been led astray less than the Scholastic. When it comes to details – for which we must wait until we have a proper understanding of cognitive and affective states in human beings – we see that as much rests on a capacity for clarity and distinctness as does on just what clarity and distinctness amount to. The ability to formulate and recognise clear and distinct ideas requires the overcoming of obstacles, and it turns out (as is clear from *La Recherche*) that, in practice, this is an exercise for which not everyone is equally equipped. If Descartes can make good his idea of the *honnête homme*, then he must have some way of checking the apparent variation in what appears clear and distinct from person to person. It might be thought that he should

---

[24] See my *Francis Bacon and the Transformation of Early-Modern Philosophy* (Cambridge, 2001). On the question of Descartes' familiarity with Bacon's works, see the references to Bacon in his correspondence: AT I. 109, 195, 251, 321; IV. 619, 632, 634, 684, 692–3; V. 258.

[25] See the discussion in Alberto Guillermo Ranea, 'A "Science for *honnêtes hommes*": *La Recherche de la Vérité* and the Deconstruction of Experimental Knowledge', in Stephen Gaukroger et al. eds., *Descartes' Natural Philosophy* (London, 2000), 313–29.

not have to do this, since hyperbolic doubt erases our beliefs to such
an extent that we each become a natural–philosophical *tabula rasa*. But
Descartes realises, practically, that people come to natural philosophy not
with a *tabula rasa* but with different sets of highly developed beliefs which
are motivated in different ways and developed to different degrees, and
it is a consequence of this that some are more fitted than others to follow
the path of instruction/enlightenment in natural philosophy. He needs
to provide an account of how one achieves clear and distinct ideas which
goes beyond the idealised procedure of hyperbolic doubt and faces up to
the psychological complexities of the 'prejudices' that one encounters.
This can only be realised, if at all, in his theory of the passions, for it is
only here that we can begin to glimpse how the *persona* of the natural
philosopher can be shaped out of that of the *honnête homme*.

THE METAPHYSICS OF SUBSTANCE

There are two things that particularly mark out the project of the *Principia*
from that of *Le Monde*. The first is the use of the doctrine of clear and
distinct ideas – the need for which had been established through the use
of hyperbolic doubt – to set out the fundamental characteristics of God,
the mind, and the physical world. The second is a system of fundamental
metaphysical categories, based terminologically on those of Scholastic
metaphysics, but whose content is filled out in a novel way. Both of
these are absent from *Le Monde*, as we have seen, but both are equally
fundamental to the way in which the legitimatory programme of the
Principia works.

The metaphysical discussion starts out badly, but in an interesting
way. Instead of offering one definition of substance, as we might reasonably have expected, Descartes offers two incompatible definitions. In
article 51 he defines substance as 'whatever exists in such a way that it
needs no other thing in order to exist'. God is a substance in this sense,
but mind and matter clearly are not. In article 52 he defines substance
as 'whatever needs only the participation of God in order to exist'. This
clearly accommodates mind and matter, but it seems to exclude God.
Descartes concludes that the term 'substance' is not univocal. Nevertheless, it might seem that there is a way in which we can adapt the second
definition to include God. As the ontological argument has shown, the
existence of God depends on nothing but God's essence. Since, given
his essence, God could not fail to exist, and since the existence of the
other substances depends not on their own essences but on the existence

of God, which depends on his essence, it may seem we could conclude that everything depends on God's essence. We seem to have a univocal sense of substance here, namely, a substance is anything that depends only on God's essence. But there are two problems with this. First, the way in which God's existence depends on his essence is completely different from the way in which our existence depends on his essence: God's essence is such that his existence is necessary, but it is not such that our existence is necessary. The univocal definition achieves a univocal sense of substance only at the cost of making the notion of dependence equivocal. Second, while the univocal definition precludes the properties (modes, qualities, and attributes) of matter and mind being substances, because they depend upon material and spiritual substances for their existence, it does not exclude the properties of God, since these depend only on God. Hence, on the univocal definition the properties of God would be substances in their own right, which is impossible.

Such equivocation on the fundamental notion of substance in a Scholastic textbook would be unthinkable. The central issue of the relation between natural philosophy and a theologically driven metaphysics is at stake in these questions in the textbook tradition. Developing and refining a notion of substance that includes both created and uncreated substance, both finite and infinite substance, that fixes the priorities between metaphysics and natural philosophy, that reconciles their competing claims in a metaphysically regulated synthesis, is, more than anything else, the point of the exercise. Not so for Descartes. What Descartes is concerned with in the *Principia* is not reconciling a theologically driven metaphysics and natural philosophy, but using the categories of traditional metaphysics to formulate the fundamentals of his natural philosophy. In fact the real work is not done by the notion of substance at all, but by the epistemological doctrine of clear and distinct ideas. This is why it does not matter that we need two completely different definitions of substance just to identify the three substances. What matters, as article 54 makes clear, is that 'we have clear and distinct notions of thinking and corporeal substance, and similarly of God'. Three different clear and distinct notions give us three different things, no matter what the details of the definitions of substance: 'we perceive [the three substances] to be distinct from one another from the sole fact that we can clearly and distinctly understand one without the other' (art. 60).

This does not mean that the metaphysical conceptions of substance play no role, however. The second definition of substance is the crucial one in developing basic metaphysical categories in articles 53 to 65, since what is at issue here is the distinction between a substance and the various kinds of properties it has, and the distinction between mind and matter in terms of their characteristic properties. Descartes' account of substances works at several levels: first, the distinction between attributes, qualities, and modes; second, the distinction between those attributes and modes that are in the thing and those that are merely a way of thinking about the thing (universals); third, the three kinds of distinctions between things, namely real, modal, and rational.

His general classification of the properties of substance (art. 56) is a threefold one:

> We understand by *modes* here exactly the same as what we mean by *attributes* or *qualities* elsewhere. We talk of *modes* when we consider the substance as being affected by these things. When the modification enables us to identify the substance as being of a particular kind, we use the term *quality*. When we are simply thinking of them in a more general way, as being inherent in a substance, we call them *attributes*.

This is not the most helpful presentation of the distinction, but from the way in which he goes on to use it in the remainder of the *Principia*, and other passages in which which it is discussed, it is clear that the crucial distinction is that between attributes and modes.[26] This distinction, at least, is relatively clear cut: attributes are those properties of something without which it would cease to be what it is, whereas the modes of something are those of its properties that can vary without changing the nature of the thing. Attributes include such things as existence and duration, but also the distinguishing features of substances, such as the attributes of extension and thought: if a body were to become unextended it would no longer be a body, for example, just as if a mind were to stop thinking it would cease to be a mind. Modes of substances include such things as a body's being in a particular state of motion or rest, or a mind's having particular memories or thoughts. God, being unchangeable, has only attributes, not modes.

The distinction between attributes and modes to some degree mirrors the Scholastic distinction between essential and non-essential accidents or forms, a crucial part of the Aristotelian doctrine of form and the Scholastic metaphysics based upon it.[27] Substance is something that exists in its own right, whereas accidents or forms are properties, and properties cannot have an independent existence: this was a fundamental

---

[26] See Descartes to ***, 1645 or 1646; AT IV. 348–50, where the issue is discussed in terms of attributes and modes, with qualities not even mentioned. One possible candidate for a quality of material substance is impenetrability: see my *Descartes, An Intellectual Biography*, 366–7.

[27] See the detailed discussion of late Scholastic metaphysics in Part I of Dennis Des Chene, *Physiologia: Natural Philosophy in Late Aristotelian and Cartesian Thought* (Ithaca, 1996).

disagreement between Aristotle and Plato, who wanted to grant forms an independent existence. They exist not in their own right but in substance. But we must distinguish between those forms or attributes that provide something with its identity, make it what it is, and those that are non-essential. Descartes' distinction works in a different way. On the Scholastic doctrine, essential and non-essential accidents are both equally accidents and both are immediately related to substance. But Descartes' modes, unlike non-essential accidents, are not immediately related to substance: their relation to substance is mediated through attributes. Extension is the principal attribute of corporeal substance and the modes of corporeal substance are ways of being extended. Despite the fact that what modal state something is in is contingent in a way that its attributes are not, modes depend on the essence of substance because they depend on the attributes of substance. Shape, for example, is a mode of corporeal bodies, and whatever shape a corporeal body has is dependent on the fact that it is extended. Moreover, its particular extension must be manifested in some shape. Similarly, being in some mental state is a mode of the mind, and whatever mental state a mind is in is dependent on the fact that the mind is characterised by the attribute of thinking, where this attribute must be manifested in some mental state. For the present, we can say that modes are the particular ways in which the attributes of substance exist or are manifested.[28] We shall have occasion to return to the question of what more precisely Descartes means by modes when we come to his account of motion in the next chapter.

The Scholastics distinguished not only between essential and non-essential accidents, but between first- and second-level substances and their accidents. The issue here turns on the standing of universals. Plato's view had been that what makes something what it is is the fact that it shares in or instantiates a form or universal. Aristotle rejected this account, arguing that what makes something what it is must be something inherent in that thing. In the most straightforward case, one common to Scholastic philosophers, what makes Socrates, for example, a man is his immortal soul, not his sharing in some universal property of being human. His immortal soul is his substantial form. But the predicate 'is human' is said truly of Socrates, Plato, and Aristotle, because the substantial form of 'humanness' informs the individuals referred to.[29]

---

[28] See the discussion in Daniel Garber, *Descartes' Metaphysical Physics* (Chicago, 1992), 63–70.
[29] See the discussion in Des Chene, *Physiologia*, 76–80. I have simplified radically here. Des Chene, ibid., ch. 3, gives a blow-by-blow account.

'Humanness' here is the abstraction from the substantial form and is sometimes called a 'second substance'. Similarly with non-essential accidents. 'White' can be truly predicated of Socrates because Socrates has the non-essential accident of being white, but it can also be truly predicated of Socrates, Plato, and Aristotle because they share something, namely they are all white.

Descartes denies any independent reality to these 'second' substances and accidents. They are, for him, merely modes under which we consider things. Duration, for example, is not the physical endurance or persistence of the thing in time, but merely 'a mode under which we conceive of that thing as long as it continues to exist'. Similarly, order and number are not in the things ordered or numbered, but are merely 'modes under which we consider these things' (art. 55). Generally, 'number and all universals are only modes of thinking' (art. 58) for 'when number is not being considered in any created things, but only in the abstract or in general, it is merely a mode of thought; as are all the other things which we call *universals*'. Universals arise, Descartes explains (art. 59), when we use the one idea to represent things that are similar to one another. We give this idea a name, and in doing this it becomes a universal. Such universals are then divided into smaller groupings. So, for example, we have an idea of a figure bounded by three sides, which provides us with a *genus*, and within this genus we note that some triangles have one right angle: this is a *difference* which yields a *species* of right-angled triangles, which all have the *property* that the square of the hypotenuse is equal to the sum of the squares of the other two sides. Finally, we can imagine some of these triangles to be moved whereas others are not moved, and this is an *accident* in them.

For a metaphysical realist – someone who holds that there exist, as well as individual things, universals which are independent of those things – divisions in nature reflect divisions among universals. If we reject the idea that universals are anything more than generic names, as Descartes does, some other account of natural divisions needs to be supplied.[30] This is exactly what Descartes sets out to provide in his account of real, modal, and rational differences. Real distinctions (art. 60) are exclusively distinctions between substances: the distinction between my mind and my body, between my mind and the minds of others, and between my body and the parts of my body, and between my body and the bodies of

---

[30] On the complex medieval disputes on the questions of substances and their individuation, see Jorge Gracia, *Individuation in Scholasticism: the Later Middle Ages and the Counter-Reformation, 1150–1650* (Albany, N.Y., 1994).

others, for example, are all real distinctions. The basis of such distinctions is always the clarity and distinctness of our grasp of the differences we are concerned with. But 'real' distinctions between one body and another and one mind and another are problematic for Descartes, and were a source of intense dispute for his successors such as Cordemoy, Spinoza, and Leibniz. Leibniz, returning to late Scholastic notions, offered the doctrine that a substance had to have both a principle of unity, which made it into an individual thing, and a principle of identity, which made it the same thing over time. To secure this, Leibniz argued, we need to reintroduce the notion of substantial forms, rightly expelled by Descartes and others from natural philosophy proper, but vital to the metaphysical underpinnings of natural philosophy, for without these there would be no basis for treating material things as substances in a strict sense, since they would lack both unity and identity.[31] This was a radical proposal which neither Descartes nor his followers would have been likely to embrace, but the problems were deep ones. We shall look at the question of how bodies can be distinct from one another in the next chapter, for Descartes does offer some account of this in Book II of the *Principia*, although there is no agreement on just what his account is. The problem of distinguishing minds from one another in terms of a 'real' distinction is even more serious, but receives no discussion at all. Embodied minds can be distinguished from one another in that they have different sensations, memories etc., but, even with continuity of consciousness, what makes them the same mind over time? Indeed, why do different memories and sensations form a basis for distinguishing minds from one another? As one of Descartes' correspondents pointed out, in connection with the establishment of the idea of the self as *res cogitans* in the *Meditationes*, 'you do not know whether it is you yourself who think or whether the world soul in you does the thinking, as the Platonists believe'.[32] What is at issue is actually the Averroist doctrine (subsequently assimilated by sixteenth-century Platonists, and quite compatible with some forms of Neoplatonism) that there can only be one intellect in the universe, because intellect, unlike matter, is not the kind of thing that can be divided up. The problems in this respect are exacerbated when we turn to disembodied mind, which has no sensations or memories properly speaking. Descartes' metaphysics has no resources by which to establish

---

[31] See, for example, Leibniz, *Discours de metaphysique*, XII: *Die philosophische Schriften von G. W. Leibniz*, ed. C. I. Gerhardt, 7 vols. (Berlin, 1875–90), IV. 436. See also Leibniz to Arnauld, April 1678, *Die philosophische Schriften*, II. 96.

[32] *** to Descartes [July 1641]; AT III. 403.

the unity and identity of individual minds and, particularly in the case of disembodied minds, his criterion of clear and distinct ideas can have no purchase either.

The next kind of distinctions are modal ones (art. 61), which hold in two types of case: between a mode and the substance of which it is a mode, and between two different modes of the same substance. In the first case, the difference between a substance and a mode of that substance is clear from the fact that we can conceive of a substance without that mode, but not vice versa. In the second, the difference is evident from the fact that 'we can recognise one mode without the other and vice versa, but we can recognise neither without the substance to which they belong'. We can recognise the squareness and the motion of a rock independently of one another, for example, but we cannot recognise either of them without recognising the substance to which they belong. The distinction between the modes of two different substances is a real and not a modal difference, however, because we cannot grasp the modes clearly without grasping the substances of which they are the modes. Finally, rational distinctions (art. 62) hold between a substance and something that must be attributed to it if we are to comprehend it, that is, if we are to form a clear and distinct grasp of it. So, for example, 'because any substance ceases to be if it ceases to endure, substance is distinguished from its duration only in the reason'.

The first application of these distinctions – which will be especially important throughout the *Principia* – is to the question of the nature of mind and body. The distinction between these two substances is known in two ways. The first is via their attributes, as thinking and extended substances, and this is the way 'in which they are most clearly and distinctly understood' (art. 63). The second is via their modes, as when we think of a body having various shapes but retaining the same volume. Descartes then makes the crucial move (art. 65):

We shall best understand the many different modes of thought, such as understanding, imagining, remembering, willing, etc., and also the diverse modes of extension or those pertaining to extension, such as all figures, and situation and movements of parts, if we regard them only as modes of the things in which they are.

Descartes adds that we are to understand motion in the first instance as something modal, that is, as local motion, without considering the forces responsible for motion, as in Aristotelian natural philosophy. We shall look at just what this approach commits us to in the next chapter.

Part I of the *Principia* offers us very little in the way of elucidation of the nature of mind and matter, but two things are evident from the identification of substances with their attributes and modes. The first is that mind and body are separate substances with completely different sets of properties. One thing this means is that there is no grey area between the two, there are no blurred boundaries. This has implications for both Descartes' treatment of matter and his treatment of mind. It means, for example, that the kinds of conscious and intrinsically goal-directed activity we associate with mind are absent from matter. What exactly this amounts to is complex, and I shall argue in chapter 7 that it does not preclude sentience in mindless animals, provided this can be explained purely in terms of the activity of completely inert matter. Second, it means that neither matter nor mind admits of degrees. There are no different kinds of matter, of the sort offered in traditional theories of the elements for example; nor are there different degrees of mental functioning, as in traditional accounts of higher and lower faculties.

CHAPTER 4

Principia, *Part II: The principles of material objects*

MATTER THEORY AND MECHANICS

Part II of the *Principia* deals with the foundational principles of Descartes' physical theory, which take the form of a synthesis of matter theory and mechanics.[1] Descartes pushed this enterprise further than any of his contemporaries, and his cosmology, which we shall be looking at in the next chapter, is the first to present a full model of the universe that integrates mechanical and matter–theoretic considerations. Such an integration was extremely problematic, and there are questions about whether it is even possible. Mechanics deals with physical processes in terms of the motions undergone by bodies and the nature of the forces responsible for these motions. Matter theory deals with how the physical behaviour of a body is determined by what it is made of, and in the seventeenth century it typically achieves this in a corpuscularian fashion, by investigating how

---

[1] Descartes' project does not distinguish mechanics and matter theory, although I hope to show in this chapter that the conceptual basis for the distinction is there in Descartes' work, as it was in the work of his contemporaries such as Beeckman and Galileo. Two things should be noted in this connection. First, by 'mechanics' I mean a group of disciplines – statics, kinematics, dynamics – at least the first two of which would have been included by Descartes under the term 'physico-mathematics' rather than under the rubric of 'mechanics'. Descartes uses the latter term to refer to simple machines and their operation, a topic not touched upon in work intended for publication but developed in letters: see Alan Gabbey, 'Newton's "Mathematical Principles of Natural Philosophy": A Treatise on "Mechanics"?', in P. M. Harman and Alan Shapiro, eds., *The Investigation of Difficult Things* (Cambridge, 1992), 305–22; Alan Gabbey, 'Descartes' Physics and Descartes' Mechanics: Chicken and Egg?', in Stephen Voss, ed., *Essays on the Philosophy and Science of René Descartes* (New York, 1993), 311–23; and Daniel Garber, 'A Different Descartes: Descartes and the Programme for a Mathematical Physics in his Correspondence', in Stephen Gaukroger et al. eds., *Descartes' Natural Philosophy* (London, 2000), 113–30. Second, the meaning of the term 'mechanics' as I am using it is an eighteenth-century one, established above all by Euler, but two of the practices it picks out, statics and kinematics, were well established in the work of Stevin and Galileo, for example. For a detailed account of how Descartes tries to rethink the traditional mechanical discipline of statics in terms of his own natural philosophy (in turn developed primarily in terms of matter theory), and some general considerations on the relations between the traditional disciplines of practical mathematics and natural philosophy, see Gaukroger and Schuster, 'The Hydrostatic Paradox and the Origins of Cartesian Dynamics'.

the nature and arrangement of the constituent parts of a body determine its behaviour. Mechanical and matter–theoretic approaches to physical theory are very different; they engage fundamentally different kinds of considerations, and on the face of it offer explanations of different phenomena. We do not explain how levers, inclined planes, screws, and pulleys work in terms of matter theory. Correlatively, it is far from clear that the appropriate form of explanation of the phenomena of burning, fermentation, and differences between fluids and solids is in terms of mechanics.

Traditionally, matter theory had been constitutive of natural philosophy, and it was generally assumed from the pre-Socratics up to the seventeenth century that the key to understanding physical processes lay in understanding the nature of matter and its behaviour, whether this understanding took the form of a theory about how matter is regulated by external immaterial principles, internal immaterial principles, or by the behaviour of the internal material constituents of macroscopic bodies. The traditional disciplines of practical mathematics included such areas as geometrical optics, positional astronomy, harmonics, and statics, the latter being the only area of mechanics that had been developed in antiquity. Statics, along with the other disciplines, was considered very much as a branch of mathematics, which meant – on the prevailing Aristotelian conception – that it dealt with abstractions and hypotheses rather than with physical reality. In other words, it was not part of natural philosophy; it was not something that one would use to explore the nature of the physical world.

Around the beginning of the seventeenth century, however, there was an attempt to draw on the traditional disciplines of practical mathematics and to incorporate these into natural philosophy. In particular, mathematical astronomy had traditionally been considered able to provide mathematical models of the cosmos, but had not been considered to be in a position to establish the physical reality of any of them. Galileo had pushed hard for the incorporation of mathematical astronomy into natural philosophy, and had sought to rid it of the merely hypothetical standing that it had had up to that point.[2] The kind of account of celestial motion he offered was very different from that we find in Aristotle, or in sixteenth-century Scholastic writers on cosmology and astronomy. Galileo attempted to develop a mechanical theory, above all a dynamics,

---

[2] For details see Mario Biagioli, *Galileo Courtier: the Practice of Science in the Culture of Absolutism* (Chicago, 1993).

that made natural–philosophical sense of Copernicanism, in the way that Aristotelian natural philosophy had been used to ground and make physical sense of the Ptolemaic system. The epitome of the purely mechanical approach fostered in Galileo was Newton's *Principia*, where celestial bodies were represented as dimensionless mass points moving in an otherwise empty space under the influence of mechanically defined forces. Newton never thought this was the whole story, however, above all because the nature of gravitational force was left wholly unexplained in the mechanical account, and he believed that matter theory – in the form of a systematised alchemy, which for Newton combined speculative and empirical considerations in a more satisfactory way than other versions of matter theory – would reveal the source and nature of gravity deep inside matter.

By the eighteenth century, there were various axiomatic systems of mechanics on the model of Newton's *Principia* – above all in the work of Euler, d'Alembert, and Lagrange[3] – in which an attempt was made to explain the properties of matter in purely mechanical terms, that is to say, in which matter theory was reduced to mechanics by building up the macroscopic properties of matter from idealised microscopic constituents that were construed wholly in mechanical terms. Euler, for example, starts with a kinematic analysis of motion, and then gradually progresses to the dynamics of isolated mass-points, proceeds next to rigid bodies, which he builds up out of the mass-points he has just analysed, then considers flexible bodies as a dynamic modification of rigid bodies, then elastic bodies as a dynamic modification of flexible bodies, and finally fluids, as a dynamic modification of elastic bodies, developing his increasingly complex physical and mathematical tools as he goes on.[4] This was not even remotely an option for seventeenth-century natural philosophers, and it was not something they aspired to (with the possible exception of Hobbes, who was in any case the least able to achieve it). Rather, the goal of those at the forefront of developments in a mechanistic natural philosophy in the seventeenth century was the synthesis of mechanics and matter theory. How this goal was to be realised, however, was a

---

3 Leonhard Euler, *Mechanica sive motus scientia analytice exposita*, 2 vols. (St Petersburg, 1738–40); Jean le Rond d'Alembert, *Traité de Dynamique* (Paris, 1743); Louis de Lagrange, *Méchanique analytique* (Paris, 1788). See Michel Blay, *La Naissance de la mécanique analytique* (Paris, 1992).

4 Euler, *Mechanica*. See the contributions of Clifford Truesdell to *Leonhardi Euleri opera omnia*: 'The Rational Mechanics of Flexible or Elastic Bodies, 1638–1788', series 2, vol. 11, section 2 (Zurich, 1960); 'Rational Fluid Mechanics, 1687–1765', series 2, vol. 12 (Zurich, 1954); and Stephen Gaukroger, 'The Metaphysics of Impenetrability: Euler's Conception of Force', *British Journal for the History of Science* 15 (1982), 132–54.

deeply problematic question. It was clear to Descartes that a mechanics alone was lacking in many respects, and from his very earliest exercises in hydrostatics in 1619, he had attempted to flesh out mathematically rigorous demonstrations concerning the pressure exerted by fluids on the bottom of their containers with an account of how the constituent material parts of the fluid behave such that the result is the mathematically characterisable macroscopic phenomenon.[5]

The matter theory with which seventeenth-century natural philosophers attempted to reconcile mechanics was not, in the main, Aristotelian matter theory,[6] but rather various forms of corpuscularianism. While Descartes' account is corpuscularian in some respects, it is quite different from the atomist models being advocated by Hobbes, Gassendi, and others. In particular, it works not with small corpuscles of matter moving freely in a void, but with variously shaped regions of matter moving in a dense fluid medium, where there is complete homogeneity between the moving regions and the medium through which they move. The very fact that the bits of matter that move through the medium are completely homogeneous with that medium indicates that it is mechanics rather than matter theory that is doing the work here, for the difference between solids and the fluids through which they move is not something that can be captured in terms of matter theory, since the matter making up solids and fluids is not only exactly the same, it is also of exactly the same density and consistency. Any differences between solids and fluids must be explained mechanically.

In turning to the question of why Descartes conceives of the cosmos as comprising parcels of matter moving through, or being carried along by, dense fluids in the first place, we need to ask whether this is motivated by considerations from mechanics, matter theory, or metaphysics. Descartes offers a number of metaphysical arguments against the possibility of a void in the *Principia*, but his treatment of mechanical problems in terms of the behaviour of matter in a fluid medium, as opposed to a void, predates any discussion of such metaphysical considerations, and indeed can be traced back to his earliest work on mechanics. Descartes developed his natural–philosophical vocabulary in the context of statics and above all hydrostatics, where the behaviour of bodies is analysed in terms of their interaction with the surrounding medium: more generally, mechanics

---

[5] See Gaukroger and Schuster, 'The Hydrostatic Paradox and the Origins of Cartesian Dynamics'.
[6] There were some such attempts, which worked through Aristotle's notion of the 'subordinate sciences': see Peter Dear, *Discipline and Experience: the Mathematical Way in the Scientific Revolution* (Chicago, 1995).

for Descartes is a theory about how bodies behave under a system of mechanical constraints.[7] We shall see evidence of this in this chapter, when we look at Descartes' laws of motion, where a statical model plays a crucial role, and in the next chapter when we look at his account of solar systems, where models drawn from hydrostatics play a crucial role.

MATERIAL EXTENSION

The first 22 articles of Part II of the *Principia* set out the theory of material extension. Descartes begins with a defence of his theory of matter – a theory in which extension or space turns out to be identical with matter – that is designed to be fundamental to his mechanics. The discussion turns on the doctrine of clear and distinct ideas in three ways.

First, we use our clear and distinct ideas of God, mind, and matter to show that these are distinct. However, the mind and the body are 'united', in that sensations, for example, clearly derive from the body and are not self-induced by the mind. Descartes puts off discussion of this question, and it is the proper subject of the projected Parts V and VI, so we shall come back to it in chapters 7 and 8. Second, Descartes reminds us of the inability of our senses to deliver clear and distinct ideas about the nature of matter. The senses, he tells us, 'do not teach what really exists in things, but only what can harm or benefit the union of the mind and the body' (art. 3). Consequently, we must 'lay aside those prejudices that derive from the senses' and this means rejecting the idea that the nature of body consists in sensory qualities such as 'weight, hardness, or colour'. Third, we must start our exploration of the nature of matter from our clear and distinct idea of it.

Our clear and distinct idea of matter tells us that the nature of body 'consists in extension alone'. A crucial part of the criterion of clarity and distinctness here is whether we can imagine a substance to lack some quality. Descartes argues that we can imagine a body lacking hardness, colour, weight, and other sensory qualities, but we cannot imagine it lacking extension. He gives the example of hardness: we can imagine bodies always receding from us as we approach them, so that we were never able to touch them, but we do not think that such bodies thereby fail to be bodies, so we can imagine bodies without hardness (art. 4). What is at issue here becomes clear in article 7, when, discussing rarefaction

---

[7] See my 'The Foundational Role of Statics and Hydrostatics in Descartes' Natural Philosophy'.

and air, he remarks that 'there is no reason why we should believe that all bodies that exist must affect our senses'.

What does it mean to say that the nature of body 'consists in extension alone'? In article 13 we are told:

> The terms 'place' and 'space', then, do not signify anything different from the body which is said to be in a place. They merely refer to its size, shape, and position relative to other bodies. To determine position, we have to look at various other bodies which we regard as immobile; and in relation to different bodies we may say that the same thing is both changing and not changing its place at the same time.

To understand Descartes' concern here, we need to grasp the wider context of thought about the nature of space. The idea that space, something whose properties were generally conceived to be purely geometrical (that is to say, intellectual rather than physical), and which was causally inert, could be a substance in its own right, was a great source of concern to many in the seventeenth century. The problems were compounded by the fact that if one made space a substance it was difficult to see how one could avoid making it ontologically prior to its material content, for space could exist without matter (there could be empty space) but matter could not exist without space.

One doctrine to which Descartes is opposed is the Aristotelian doctrine of place. On this doctrine, a body's place carries dynamical implications that mere spatial location never could. The Aristotelian notion of place is intended to designate something absolute. A thing is not in a particular place with respect to some other thing, it is in a particular place *per se*. The cosmos has an absolute directional structure. Left and right, and backwards and forwards, are absolute directions defined in terms of the (absolute) motion of the stars,[8] but the crucial directions are up and down, for these form the basis for Aristotle's doctrine of natural place, which determines the motions of different kinds of substance.[9] In the absence of external constraint, for example, fire will tend to move upwards and heavy bodies will tend to move downwards. Place shapes the dynamic behaviour of the body. The rationale behind this lies in Aristotle's general approach to the problem of change, which he characterises in terms of a variation in properties or qualities of the thing undergoing the change. Local motion is a change in respect of place, and like all forms of change, it can be specified in terms of a *terminus a quo* and a *terminus*

---

[8] *De Caelo*, 285b16–17 and 287b22–288a12.
[9] The main discussion is in Book Δ of the *Physics*.

ad quem, where in this case the termini are contraries. The *terminus ad quem* provides the process with an end or goal which it realises: without it, there is no process, no motion, at all. Aristotle's concern is with a general theory of change, which includes everything from processes whose termini are contradictories, such as generation and corruption, to those whose termini are contraries, such as change of shape. The doctrine of place, with its absolute directions, is crucial to the Aristotelian doctrine of dynamics: why things move is central to how they move.

Descartes' response to this doctrine is threefold. First, he separates questions of why things move from how they move. 'We shall understand motion best', he tells us in Part I article 65, 'if we think only of local motion and do not enquire into the force by which it is produced', and indeed he proceeds in Part II by discussing the nature of motion without reference to cause, turning only in article 36 to the discussion of causation. This is a distinctive way of proceeding in early modern natural philosophy, to be found in different forms in Galileo, Beeckman, Hobbes, Gassendi, and others, and indeed it yields dividends,[10] but there is no defence of it offered. The only argument we find in this connection is the claim in *Le Monde* that the Aristotelian conception yields a definition of motion that is unintelligible.[11] This is disingenuous, however, for an intelligible account of the Aristotelian understanding of local motion can be given, and in any case Descartes' own definition of motion in *Le Monde,* as bodies passing from one place to another and occupying all the spaces in between,[12] turns out to be not so straightforward once 'place' and 'body' have been defined.

The difficulties turn on the fact that 'place', 'space', and 'body' are interdefined in Descartes, as they are, albeit it in a very different way, in Aristotle. This brings us to the second and third features of Descartes' response to the Aristotelian conception. The second is that he argues that place and body are the same thing; the third that he abandons the doctrine of absolute direction. These are difficult and much disputed questions, and it will be helpful to have some idea of the reaction of

---

[10] On the origins of Descartes' distinctive approach in this respect, see Gaukroger and Schuster, 'The Hydrostatic Paradox and the Origins of Cartesian Dynamics'.

[11] Quoting the definition of motion given in *Physics* 210b10, he writes: 'They themselves admit that the nature of their motion is very little understood. And trying to make it more intelligible, they have still not been able to explain it more clearly than in these terms: *Motus est actus entis in potentia, prout in potentia est.* These terms are so obscure to me that I am compelled to leave them in Latin because I cannot interpret them. (And in fact the words "motion is the act of a being which is in potency, in so far as it is in potency" are no clearer for being in the vernacular.)', AT XI. 39.

[12] AT XI. 40.

other seventeenth-century natural philosophers to the Aristotelian notion before we turn to Descartes' response.

The range of non-Scholastic views on space is well represented in
English natural philosophy in the seventeenth century. At the beginning
of that century, we find William Gilbert attacking the Aristotelian notion
of place, whereby a body's behaviour is determined by the fact that it will
move towards its natural place, for example (earthy bodies downwards,
fire upwards). Gilbert objects on the grounds that the location of a body
cannot have a causal effect. 'Position is nothing', he writes, 'it does not
exist; all power resides in bodies themselves'.[13] Hobbes goes further in
chapter 7 of his *De Corpore*,[14] the composition of which began around
the time Descartes was working on the *Principia*. He denies the reality
of space: it is not a substance that acts as a container for bodies, for
bodies are complete in themselves and need no such container. Space
is just a subjective frame of reference, not real in its own right. It is
our awareness of body 'simply' – i.e. of body having no other attribute
except that it is located somewhere. But, although body certainly exists
outside our minds, the space which body occupies is a purely mental
construction. Space is a 'phantasm', a mental abstraction, an imaginary
extension – it is the system of co-ordinates or external locations which the
mind constructs out of its experience of real extended things. *Real* space
is space inherent in body. In other words, real space is corporeality itself:
'so that a body is to imaginary space what a thing is to the knowledge of
that thing, for our knowledge of existing things is that imagination which
is produced by the action of these things on our senses, and therefore
imaginary space, which is the imagination of body, is the same as our
knowledge of existing body'. Space is, in short, 'privation of body'. The
meaning of privation depends in the first place on our knowledge of body,
and refers only to the possibility of body coming into being. Considered
by itself, privation of body is a 'figment' or 'empty imagination'.

At the same time that Hobbes was working on *De Corpore*, Henry More
was beginning to reflect on the nature of space in a wholly different way,

[13] William Gilbert, *De mundo nostro sublunari nova* (Amsterdam, 1651), Book II, ch. 8, p. 144; quoted in
Milic Capek, *The Philosophical Impact of Contemporary Physics* (New York, 1961), 29. Francis Bacon
echoes this, rejecting the idea that heavy bodies naturally move downwards and light ones
upwards because 'there is no local motion which is not excited either by the parts of the body
moved, or by the adjacent bodies, or by those contiguous or proximate to it, or at least by those
which lie within its sphere of activity' (*The Works of Francis Bacon*, ed. James Spedding, Robert
Leslie Ellis, and Douglas Denon Heath, 14 vols. (London, 1857–74), V. 202).
[14] Thomas Hobbes, *The English Works of Thomas Hobbes*, ed., Sir William Molesworth, 11 vols.
(London, 1839–1845) I. 91–4.

treating it as a spirit, and ultimately as divine extension.[15] More agrees with Descartes that space is something extended, and extension cannot be an extension of nothing: distance between two bodies is real or, at the very least, a relation which has a real basis. But he denies that void space is nothing. It is, on the contrary, a completely real entity. Because space is extended, More argues, it must be a real attribute of a real subject, since there cannot be attributes without subjects. Descartes was right in looking for substance to support extension, he argues, but he was wrong in finding it in matter, for it is found not only in matter but also where no matter is present. Indeed, he says, we cannot but conceive of 'a certain immobile extension' which always has and always will exist, and he identifies this extension with spirit: and not *a* spirit, but the spirit, i.e. God. Space is not only something real, it is something divine.

Finally, on Newton's account of matter, influenced by More and set out in the unfinished *De gravitatione*,[16] it is something like a force, rather than extension, that characterises matter. He puts forward a hypothetical reconstruction of God's creation of matter. First, God makes some region of space impervious to already existing bodies; that is to say he creates an impenetrable region of space. Impenetrability now becomes the essence of matter. (It is worth noting that Descartes had in a sense thought that impenetrability is the essence of matter, because extension is the essence of matter, and whatever is extended is impenetrable, and whatever is impenetrable is extended.[17]) Second, having established this region of impenetrability, he allows it to move, according to certain laws. Third, this mobile impenetrable region is opaque, and hence such regions are perceptible. And because it is impenetrable, it is tangible. It is a body. For the existence of such bodies, Newton tells us, 'nothing is required but extension and the action of the divine will'. Extension and body are radically distinct: 'extension is eternal, infinite, uncreated, uniform throughout, not in the least mobile, nor capable of inducing change of motion in bodies or change of thought in the mind; whereas body is opposite in every respect'. The conception of impenetrability as the essence of matter – that is, thinking of the difference between occupied and unoccupied

---

[15] As well as the works collected in *A Collection of Several Philosophical Writings* (London, 1712), see also his *Enchiridium metaphysicum* (London, 1671). See the discussion in Koyré, *From the Closed World to the Infinite Universe*, ch. 6.

[16] 'De Gravitatione et aequipondio fluidorum'. Text and translation in A. Rupert Hall and Marie Boas Hall, eds., *Unpublished Scientific Papers of Isaac Newton* (Cambridge, 1962), 89–156.

[17] See Descartes to More, 15 April 1649; AT V. 341–2; also Reply to Sixth Set of Objections to the *Meditationes*; AT VII. 442. See also Descartes to More, 5 February 1649; AT V. 269, on the problem of why extension should be given preference over impenetrability if they are coextensive.

regions of space in terms of differences between impenetrable and penetrable regions of space – was developed separately in the eighteenth century in the pioneers of 'rational mechanics', Euler and d'Alembert,[18] and was to prove one of the mainstays of classical mechanics.

One thing a broader consideration of seventeenth-century conceptions of space highlights is the fact that space and place are bound up with conceptions of matter not just in the Aristotelian conception but in its seventeenth-century competitors. Descartes is offering none of these, but, before we turn finally to look at just what he is offering, we need to say a word about his claim that 'to determine position, we have to look at various other bodies which we regard as immobile'. In the wake of the *Principia*, various protracted and fundamental disputes broke out over the existence of absolute space, on the question of whether spatial locations, and changes in spatial location, are absolute or relative. These were provoked by the revision of Descartes' rules of collision by Huygens, by Newton's defence of absolute space, and particularly by the dispute between Leibniz and Clarke over the existence of absolute space, coming to a head in Mach and then finally in Einstein.[19] It is far from clear that this is the context in which we should read Descartes' remarks about the relativity of motion, even though it may well have been these remarks that initially stimulated Newton, for example, to think about the question of absolute space.

Descartes rejects notions of 'place' and 'space' equally, identifying both with 'body' and then telling us that 'to determine position, we have to look at various other bodies which we regard as immobile'. One difference we are perhaps inclined to point to is that place is directional whereas space is not: Newton's absolute space does not have directions such as up and down. What is absolute about it is that, of the many co-ordinate systems that can be mapped on to it, one of these is unique (if undiscoverable), in that it genuinely distinguishes bodies at rest from bodies not at rest, whatever their motion, whether inertial or not. There is no reason to think that this kind of conception is what Descartes is arguing against. If we think of the cosmological systems that were in contention at the time

---

[18] On Euler see my 'The Metaphysics of Impenetrability'. D'Alembert begins his 'Definitions and Preliminary Notions' with the statement that: 'If two regions of extension which are similar and equal to one another are *impenetrable* . . . each of these two regions of extension will be what is called *body*' (*Traité de Dynamique*, 1).

[19] Mach thought that directionality was a feature of the distribution of matter in the universe rather than a feature of space, while Einstein revised the notion of space radically, a result of which was that space could causally interact with matter, which transformed the whole question of directionality.

that Descartes was writing, then the one that operates with something we might unambiguously label 'space' as opposed to Aristotelian 'place' is the Epicurean system.[20] But despite being a space of infinite extent, and having no absolute framework of the Aristotelian kind, Epicurean space is manifestly directional. The atoms all fall in the same direction because of their weight, which acts downwards, and indeed this is why the Epicurean 'swerve' is introduced, for without some deviation from this primitive atomic rain, no worlds would be formed.[21]

Since by far the most likely contender for the notion of space that Descartes has in mind is the Epicurean one, when he rejects 'place and space' he is not rejecting a directional notion of space and a non-directional one, but two directional ones, which suggests his target is the idea that space has an intrinsic directionality. This would, naturally, also make much more sense of the fact that he groups them together, and then argues for the relativity of motion. The argument for the relativity of motion is Descartes' way of establishing the universe has no intrinsic directionality. Of course, there are other conceptions which do not involve intrinsic spatial directionality – Newton's for example – but it is important that we distinguish between what reasons there might be to accept Descartes' rejection of intrinsic directionality and what the arguments for his alternative are. What he rejects is something that Newton would equally have rejected, had the intrinsic directionality of space still been an issue at the time he was writing. But it was not still an issue, and Newton is not proposing an alternative solution to the problem of intrinsic directionality – direction of motion is simply a function of gravitation and inertia for Newton. Rather, the issue for Newton was the absolute nature of motion, something that Descartes' solution to the original problem had denied.

THE NATURE OF MOTION

If we see the problem that Descartes is concerned with as being, in the first instance, one of directionality rather than being that of whether space is absolute or not, then we can grasp the rationale behind his solution. To determine (purely kinematically) whether a body is moving or not, and

---

[20] On the revival of atomism and Descartes' reaction to it, see Garber, *Descartes' Metaphysical Physics*, ch. 5. Garber (p. 120) quickly passes over the question of the direction of atoms.
[21] See Lucretius, *De Rerum Natura*, Book II, 216–93. Lucretius was widely read in sixteenth- and seventeenth-century France; see Simone Fraisse, *L'Influence de Lucrèce en France au Seizième Siècle* (Paris, 1962).

at what rate, we need to be able to impose some reference point against which the motion can be judged to have taken place. If space itself has no intrinsic directions, and if the reference point cannot be fixed by a global system of co-ordinates – Cartesian material extension is of 'indefinite' extent, which means there is no centre, or boundaries that we can use as reference points – then this reference point is going to be conventional and relative. Consider the image Descartes presents in article 31:

Each body has only one motion of its own, for it is understood to move away from only one set of bodies, which are contiguous with it and at rest. But it can also share in countless other motions, namely in the cases where it is a part of other bodies which have other motions. For example, someone walking on a ship has a watch in his pocket: the wheels of the watch have only one motion of their own, but they also share in another motion because they are in contact with the walking man, and they and he form the one body. They also share in additional motions in virtue of being on a ship which is being tossed on the waves, in virtue of being in contact with the sea itself, and lastly, in virtue of their contact with the whole Earth, if indeed the whole Earth is in motion. Now all the motions really will exist in the motion of the watch, but we cannot easily comprehend all these motions at the one time, nor even know what they are.

The image is one that fits the Cartesian cosmos well: it is indefinite in extent – which for these purposes is the same as its being infinite – and it can be thought of as comprising an indefinite number of interlocking parts, along the lines of a system of interlocking gears of varying sizes which contain no empty spaces between them, and which in effect go on to infinity. If we think of the cosmos as an indefinitely extended system of interlocking gears with what is in effect an infinitely complex system of motions and counter-motions, it will indeed be natural to think of the motions of gears relative to one another.

The reference point against which we judge motion has to be local on Descartes' account, and indeed takes the form of identifying a body that we take as stationary, and determining motions in respect to that body. Descartes outlines how the latter might work in article 13:

To determine position, we have to look at various other bodies which we regard as immobile; and in relation to different bodies we may say that the same thing is both changing and not changing its place at the same time. For example, when a ship is under way, a person seated in the stern always remains in one place as far as the parts of the ship are concerned, for he maintains the same situation in relation to them. But this same person is constantly changing his place as far as the shores are concerned, since he is constantly moving away from some and towards others. Furthermore, if we think the Earth moves, and travels from west to east exactly as far as the ship progresses from the east towards the west, we shall again say that the person seated in the stern does not change his place, because we are now determining his place in relation to certain fixed points in the heavens. Finally, if we think that there are no truly motionless points to be found in the universe (a supposition we will show below to be probable) we shall conclude that nothing has a permanent place, except as determined by our thought.

This is undeniably a problematic definition, generating anomalies and uncertainties, and standing in need of considerable refinement, and perhaps significant revision. Before we can assess these, however, we need to take note of an issue that shapes the whole question, namely whether the refinement or revision can be pursued in a satisfactory way in purely kinematic terms, or whether it can be guided or fleshed out dynamically. In the light of this, the best way to proceed will be to look, in turn, at why Descartes is apparently so committed to leaving dynamical considerations out of his account of motion, at what his modifications to the kinematic account achieve, and at whether his account does after all have a dynamical basis.

In article 25 Descartes defines motion as 'the transference of one part of matter or of one body from the vicinity of those bodies immediately contiguous with it and considered as at rest, into the vicinity of others'. This definition is proposed as an alternative to that 'of common usage', whereby motion is identified with 'the force (*vis*) or action (*actio*) that brings about the transference', and he opposes this latter view

to show that motion is always in the moving body, as opposed to the body that brings about the motion. The two are not normally distinguished with sufficient care; and I want to make it clear that the motion of something that moves is, like the lack of motion that is in a thing at rest, a mere mode of that thing and not itself a subsistent thing, just as shape is a mere mode of a thing that has shape.

In other words, *contra* the Aristotelian view, a body in motion does not have some *extra* quality (an amount of speed) that a body at rest lacks, any more than a round body has an *extra* quality (an amount of roundness) that a square one lacks: they just have different qualities. What is perplexing is that Descartes treats these as contrary qualities, telling us that 'rest and motion are different modes of body' (art. 27), and 'rest is the contrary of motion' (art. 37). What we might expect him to have said is that a body is in a particular modal state with respect to motion, which can take any number of values, one of which is zero, which is the value it takes when the body is at rest. The trouble is that moving bodies and bodies at rest do not behave in the same way in Descartes' account of collision. Rule 3 (art. 48) describes the outcome of the collision of two equal bodies moving at different speeds, and Rule 6 (art. 51) that of the collision of two bodies one of which is at rest, and the outcomes are quite different. Again, Rule 4 (art. 49) describes the impact of a moving smaller body with a stationary larger one, and Rule 5 (art. 50) describes the impact of a stationary smaller body with a larger moving one, and the outcomes are quite different.

Because one of Descartes' main concerns is to deny the Aristotelian doctrine that the motion of (terrestrial) bodies is something that naturally comes to an end, he talks of rest being the opposite of motion. This claim, along with the claim that 'nothing moves by virtue of its own nature toward its opposite or own destruction', can then be joined as premises in his argument that bodies in motion will remain in that state (art. 37). Now when he talks of bodies 'always remaining in the same state', it is clear from the context that this covers changes of speed, as well as moving bodies coming to a stop: bodies have no more reason to alter speed than they do to stop, and this is central to his understanding of inertial states. In article 44, he tells us that motions at the same speed are never contrary to one another: the contrary opposition is that 'between motion and rest, or even between rapidity of motion and slowness of motion', which looks like he is treating differences in speed on a par with difference between speed and rest, except that he then adds – 'that is, to the extent that this slowness partakes of the nature of rest'. This qualification just does not make sense: a slowly moving body is still a moving body, and if, as Descartes maintains, rest and motion are contrary qualities, if rest is the opposite of motion, then a slow motion is partaking of its contrary, or even worse, 'of the nature of' its contrary.

There seem to be two different conceptions of the relation between motion and rest here. One of these is the idea of rest being a limiting case of motion, and this conception is surely the appropriate one in the case of the first law of nature, that 'each thing, as far as is in its power, always remains in the same state' (art. 37). What we are given here is a description of the behaviour of a body when it is not interacting with any other bodies (a situation that never arises in practice in a Cartesian universe). The second conception is one on which motion and rest are taken generically as different and contrary modes of a body. This conception is operative primarily when Descartes talks about interaction between bodies, as in collision. Now one thing that is difficult to avoid, when dealing with collisions, is forces. And, as we shall see, when he comes to elaborate on his conception of motion in terms of the idea of reciprocity, dynamical models lurk not far beneath the surface. Descartes has developed his dynamical vocabulary in statics and hydrostatics, and has worked it through in physical optics (the *Principia* version of which will come in Part III), and statics and hydrostatics do very much lend themselves to a sharp distinction of kind between rest and motion, which correspond to equilibrium and departure from equilibrium respectively.

More generally, what I want to suggest is that there are two layers beneath Descartes' account of motion. First, at the deepest layer there are two competing models underlying his approach to motion, a kinematic one which does not make a sharp distinction between motion and rest but treats the latter as a limiting case of the former, and a dynamically motivated one which does make a sharp distinction, because of the roots of this dynamics in statics and hydrostatics. These are very much below the surface at this stage, coming to the surface only in the attempt to construe different inertial states in terms of an otherwise incoherent 'partaking of' or mixing of rest and motion. They become a little more manifest in the discussion of the rules of collision, however, and then in Descartes' cosmology (Part III). The second layer, which works at the level of providing some guidance as to when motion occurs, also has two competing models, and these are again a kinematic and a dynamic one, but they both derive from the dynamic model at the first layer.

The first layer represents two fundamentally different physical conceptions of the relation between rest and motion, driven by a difference between statical and kinematic conceptions of the nature of rest: as an equilibrium state and as a limiting case respectively. The second layer, by contrast, is premised on a particular dynamical reading of the nature of motion, the distinction arising, I shall argue, because the dynamical concepts used to formulate the distinction are inadequate for Descartes' presentational purposes, and he has to translate them into kinematic terms. Whereas the first layer works in terms of two different ways of thinking through the distinction between motion and rest, the second works in terms of how we identify what motion something has in terms which invoke nothing more than geometry and kinematics. The great complexity of the sections on motion, and the atypical but manifest irreconcilability of the different parts of his account, result, I believe, from the fact that these layers overlap at crucial junctures: in particular, whether something can be said to be moving or not is clearly going to become tied up with how one makes the distinction between motion and rest. But I think we make a reasonably clear separation between them, and above all between what drives them, for they are really directed towards different concerns.

Let us turn then to the second-level questions, a prime example of which is Descartes' sharp distinction between his own highly geometrical definition of motion in terms of transference, and the 'vulgar' dynamic definition in terms of 'the force or action that brings about the transference'. 'We are not concerned here', he tells us in article 27, 'with the action which is understood to be in whatever initiates or stops the motion of a body, but only with the body's transference, or absence of transference, namely rest'. In other words, he wants a definition of motion that makes no reference to force or action, and more generally he wants to pursue his natural philosophy without making reference to force or action. In that case, we might expect talk of force to be absent from the *Principia*, but it is not: force (*vis*) appears 290 times in the text, and the related terms action (*actio*) and striving (*conatus*) appear 59 and 8 times respectively.[22] It is as if Descartes cannot avoid dynamical terminology, despite his attempt to construe motion in a purely kinematic way. This is not surprising. The physical theory that he developed in the 1620s, which came to fruition in *Le Monde*, was certainly worked through in terms of notions of force, as I have indicated. Fitted out anew for the *Principia*, this physical theory is taken out of the dynamical context of *Le Monde* and subjected to a set of constraints that are dictated less by the requirements of late Scholastic natural philosophy as by the requirements of 'clarity and distinctness' that Descartes himself imposes upon his exposition. These latter requirements are designed, among other things, to set standards which only his natural philosophy can attain, thereby showing the superiority of his natural philosophy over others, particularly that of the late Scholastics. Second, note that Descartes is not saying that he is showing us how to develop a physical theory for ourselves: he is holding up his own natural philosophy, suitably translated into his own reformulated Scholastic vocabulary, and attempting to show that it meets certain very stringent criteria of adequacy. The best way to think through the problems he is concerned with may be to work with dynamical concepts, but that will not show the legitimacy of the system or what that legitimacy consists in. So what we are presented with is a rewriting of his natural philosophy in terms so clear and distinct that, simply by reflecting on what he says, it will become clear that his system is the true one.

Descartes tried much the same procedure in the 1620s, attempting to show, in the later *Regulae*, that mathematical operations could be represented in a way that their truth or falsity was manifest: what one needed

---

[22] See the alphabetical entries in Franco Aurelio Meschini, *Indice dei Principia Philosophiæ di René Descartes* (Florence, 1996).

to do was to represent them clearly and distinctly in terms of operations on line lengths. As I indicated in chapter 1, this project failed, as Descartes was unable to represent more complex algebraic operations in these terms. So, too, in the *Principia*, the rewriting of his physical theory in clear and distinct terms (where a very geometrical conception of motion has taken over the role that line lengths had, as the paradigm of clarity and distinctness), does not work either. Because the *Principia* rewriting of physical theory is far more extensive than the *Regulae* rewriting of algebra, it intrudes into the physical theory far more deeply, yielding something which has the ability to profoundly redirect physical theory. On the other hand, because we are provided with significant detail in the *Principia*, it is easier to identify just where things start to come apart.

What Descartes wants, ideally, is a purely kinematic, geometrically defined, conception of motion. There are a number of purely kinematic refinements that Descartes makes to the definition offered in article 13, and these do go some way to remedying some of the difficulties. A crucial ingredient in this refinement is the definition of the position of a body in terms of its 'external space' in article 15, which

can be taken to be the surface which most closely surrounds what is in that place. It should be noted here that 'surface' does not mean any part of the surrounding body, but merely the boundary between the surrounding and the surrounded bodies, which is just a mode. Or to put it another way, we understand by 'surface' the common surface which is not a part of one body more than of the other, and which is considered to be the same so long as it has the same size and shape. For even if the whole surrounding body, with its surface, is changed, we do not on that account judge that the surrounded body changes its place if it maintains the same situation among those external bodies which we consider to be at rest.

The definition of position in terms of contiguous bodies underlies Descartes' attempts to avoid the impression given in article 13 that ascription of motion to a body might depend upon the arbitrary choice of a reference body. After all, as he puts it in article 24, 'the same thing can at a given time be said both to change its place and not to change its place, and so the same thing can be said to be moved and not to be moved'. This is dealt with in article 28 by means of the notion of contiguous bodies:

I have also added that the transference is *effected from the vicinity of those bodies contiguous to it into the vicinity of others*, and not from one place to another; because, as has been explained above, 'place' can be considered in several ways, depending on our conception. However, when we take motion to be the transference of a body from the vicinity of those contiguous to it, we cannot attribute to that moving body more than one motion at any given time; because at any given time, only a certain number of bodies can be contiguous to it.

Then in article 29, he adds a crucial refinement, the reciprocity of translation:

Finally, I have stated that this transference is effected from the vicinity, not of any contiguous bodies, but only those which we consider to be at rest. For the transference is reciprocal; and we cannot conceive of a body AB being transported from the vicinity of the body CD without also understanding that the body CD is transported from the vicinity of the body AB, and that exactly the same force and action is required for the one transference as for the other. Thus if we wish to attribute to nature a motion which is absolutely its own, without referring it to anything else, then when two immediately contiguous bodies are transported, one in one direction and the other in another, and are thereby separated from each other, we should say there is as much motion in one as in the other. However, this is a significant departure from the usual way of speaking, for we are on the Earth and think it to be at rest, and the fact that we see those of its parts that are touching other smaller bodies being transported from the vicinity of those bodies does not cause us to conclude that the Earth is moved.

Finally, in article 30 he gives us the final piece in the kinematic solution to the motion of bodies: a body moves only if it moves as a whole. To illustrate this he sets out an ingenious example. We let EFGH be the Earth (Fig. 4.1), and on its surface are the two bodies AB and CD, 'AB being transported from E toward F at the same time as the body CD is transported from H toward G'. Now the parts of the Earth contiguous to AB

are transported from B to A, and the action employed in this transference must be neither different in nature nor weaker in the parts of the Earth than in the

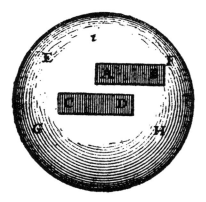

Figure 4.1

body AB; we do not on that account understand that the Earth moves from B toward A, or from the [East] toward the [West].

Why, given the reciprocity of motion, do we not say the Earth moves equally? There are basically two reasons. First, a body is in motion if its whole surface, and not merely a portion of its surface, moves relative to its neighbourhood: this allows AB and CD to move, but not the Earth. Second, AB and CD can move in relation to the Earth but the Earth cannot move in relation to them, for it would have to move in two contradictory directions, East and West, at the same time. The only way to keep the kinematics consistent is to deny that the larger body is in motion.

This appears to give us a kinematic criterion by which to decide which bodies are really in motion, but it does so at the cost of making the key notion of reciprocity of motion wholly obscure: on the one hand, the Earth is moving because of the principle of reciprocity of motion, but, on the other hand, it cannot be moving, for the motion it would have would be an impossible one. The question comes to a head in Descartes' correspondence with More. More questions Descartes' account of reciprocity of motion. Commenting on article 29, he suggests we let AB be a tower and CD be a westerly wind blowing through its window.[23] Can we just as easily treat the air as being at rest and the tower as moving towards the West?, asks More. Descartes replies by trying to bring out what is at issue by changing the example. He asks More to imagine two men trying to free a grounded boat, one pushing the boat from the shore, the other sitting in the boat and pushing against the shore:

> If the force exerted by the men is identical, the effort (*conatus*) of the man on the shore contributes to the boat's motion no less than that of the man in the boat, who is transferred along with it. Therefore it is obvious that the action by which the boat recedes from the shore is equally in the shore as in the boat.[24]

It would be natural to assume that Descartes has changed the example because he has found one that fits his case better. But, in fact, what the new example seems to show is that it is the boat, and not the shore, that is really moving. So by parity of reasoning, it is the wind, not the tower, that is really moving. Even more interesting is how he achieves

[23] More to Descartes, 5 March 1649; AT v. 312.
[24] Descartes to More, 15 April 1649; AT v. 346.

this result. Remember that in article 27 Descartes has informed us that
'we are not concerned here with the action which is understood to be
in whatever initiates or stops the motion of a body, but only with the
body's transference'. But it is precisely action (*actio*), and two other dynamical concepts, force (*vis*) and effort (*conatus*), that do the work in the
example he uses. What it establishes is the reciprocity of the force responsible for the motion of the boat, but not the reciprocity of the motion
of the boat and the motion of the shore. It looks as if what Descartes
has tried to do is to translate a notion of dynamic reciprocity directly
into kinematic terms, for his only way of trying to clear up a confused
kinematic account is to revert to the dynamic one that is, in fact, its
source.

   This raises the question of the extent to which dynamics underlies
Descartes' approach to kinematics in the 1640s. He had relied upon and
explicitly defended a number of dynamical notions in his earlier writings,
and he had thought of motion above all in terms of the dynamical notion
of *actio*. *Actio* is a term of the art deriving from his 1618/19 writings on
hydrostatics,[25] and it forms the backbone of his optics.[26] In *Le Monde*,
not only does he constantly refer to the action of light to designate a
form of transmission without transference,[27] but the action of a body
is designated as the (rectilinear) motion it would have undergone in the
absence of external constraints, and which remains in the body moving
in a circular path in the form of a tendency to motion.[28] *La Dioptrique*
is full of talk about action, as we might expect, and Descartes refers to
light as 'a certain motion, or a very quick and lively action',[29] and in the
Meteores he refers to the 'action or movement' that constitutes the true
nature of light.[30] In 1638, Morin takes Descartes up on this, accusing
him of equivocating between the cause – action – and effect – motion.[31]
Indeed action does seem to have an equivocal standing between motion,
tendency to motion (which might perhaps be construed as a component
into which a motion can be resolved, as in the discussion of motion in a
sling[32]), and a force, as when he talks about actions being balanced.[33] But,
in response, Descartes simply offers a definition of motion as 'the action

---

[25] See Gaukroger and Schuster, 'The Hydrostatic Paradox and the Origins of Cartesian Dynamics'.
[26] See, for example, John Schuster, 'Descartes *Opticien*: The Construction of the Law of Refraction and the Manufacture of its Physical Rationales, 1618–29', in Stephen Gaukroger et al. eds., *Descartes' Natural Philosophy* (London, 2000), 258–312.
[27] E.g. AT XI. 4–5, 29–30, 53, 83.   [28] AT XI. 44.   [29] AT VI. 84.   [30] AT VI. 331.
[31] Morin to Descartes 12 August 1638; AT II. 291.
[32] AT XI. 85–6, developing 45–6.   [33] AT XI. 79.

by which the parts of [luminous bodies] change their place'.[34] This is equivocal: 'the action by which' could simply mean that 'motion' and 'the action of changing place' are just two terms for the same thing, or it could mean that there is something underlying the motion, causing it, namely an action or force, of which motion is the effect. What is doing the work is the latter notion, but this is not something he is going to be able to spell out in clear and distinct terms, so the strategy in the *Principia* will be this: having already done the work, and developed his physical theory in terms of an underlying dynamics, he attempts to rewrite the already developed physical theory in terms of a new, more stringent, more economical vocabulary, which has recourse only to geometrically definable notions.

One might be tempted here to think of dynamics as being part of Descartes' method of discovery, and of kinematics as being his method of presentation. Distinctions between discovery and presentation are very important in Descartes, and there is indeed a sense in which kinematics is his method of presentation, as we have just seen. But discovery is a much more complex issue. In his first formative work in hydrostatics, Descartes started with a macroscopic geometrical representation of a problem and developed a micro-mechanical model of it in order to provide an account of the physical causes behind the phenomenon. Similarly, in his optics, using dynamical concepts such as the idea of *actio*, developed in hydro-statics, he starts from geometrical optics and sets out to understand why light behaves in particular geometrically defined ways by looking at the physical constitution and behaviour of luminous matter. In both cases, there is a move from a clear geometrical representation of the problem to a far less precise, but much more probing, attempt to think the problem through in terms of the underlying physical processes. Dynamics has certainly been a crucial part of Descartes' discovery process, but it has not been constitutive of it: a dynamical fleshing out of geometrically construed problems and solutions always involved a very complex interaction – in effect a balancing act – between the different kinds of resource available to him.[35] What we get in the *Principia* is not a restatement of the original geometrically defined problems, nor a translation of the dynamic material back into the original geometrical form of the problem, but something quite new: a translation of fundamental physical results,

---

[34] Descartes to Morin, 12 September 1638; AT II. 364.
[35] I explored these questions in *Descartes, An Intellectual Biography*, especially in chs. 4–6. For a much more detailed account of the formative case of hydrostatics, see Gaukroger and Schuster, 'The Hydrostatic Paradox and the Origins of Cartesian Dynamics'. On the case of optics, see Schuster, 'Descartes *Opticien*'.

which have been thought through in dynamical terms, into a system shaped by constraints formulated to legitimate his natural philosophy.

THE FIRST TWO LAWS OF MOTION

The operational core of Part II of the *Principia* consists of a conservation principle and three 'laws of nature', appended to the third of which are seven 'rules' describing the behaviour of bodies in collision. The latter are new to the *Principia*, whereas the conservation law and the laws of motion are to be found in *Le Monde*, as we saw in chapter 1.

A quantitative theory is impossible without conservation laws. If the total amount of motion or force in a system (or at least something which has force or motion as a component) is not fixed, if the total amount of motion or force can increase or decrease for example, then calculation of exchanges of force or motion is not possible.[36] Aristotle, whose natural philosophy was qualitative, saw no need for conservation of motion. Motion – or at least terrestrial motion – was a process that a body underwent in order to achieve some end, such as reaching its natural place, and once this end was achieved the motion simply ceased. Forces, motions, and even causes could come into and go out of existence: Aristotle thinks of causes, for example, as eventually dying away.[37] This accords well with ordinary experience, where motions come to an end sooner or later, and causes die away: the ripples caused by a stone thrown into the water, for example, gradually die away and the water returns to its previous state. Cartesian natural philosophy, by contrast, if it is to be quantitative, needs a conservation law.

The title of article 36 tells us that God is the primary cause of motion and that he always maintains an equal quantity of it in the universe. Descartes talks of the same amount of 'motion and rest' being conserved in the universe as a whole, distributed differently in different parts of the universe at different times. One might initially think that what is conserved is the total amount of speed in the universe, but we must remember that motion is a mode of a body, and so not something separate from it. The amount of motion in the universe is a function not just of

---

[36] This is only to say that at least some quantity must be conserved, it does not mean that total closure of the system is necessary. Newton, for example, has conservation of momentum, but not conservation of energy, and allows that motion can be lost in hard-body collisions, whereas Leibniz argues that the system must be completely closed and that both must be conserved. For details see Wilson L. Scott, *The Conflict between Atomism and Conservation Theory, 1644–1860* (London, 1970). By the middle of the nineteenth century, total closure had become a general desideratum.

[37] See Richard Sorabji, *Necessity, Cause and Blame: Perspectives on Aristotle's Theory* (London, 1980).

speed but of the size/volume/mass of matter having that speed, in other words the extent of the universe over which that speed is distributed, so that 'we must think that when one part of matter moves twice as fast as another which is twice as large, there is as much motion in the smaller as in the larger'. What Descartes considers to be conserved is size times speed, understood as a scalar quantity. In fact, this is just one of many things that might be conserved on the basis of the argument given: all we can really conclude is that something involving some power of speed or velocity is conserved. Why this particular version should have been chosen is not indicated, but the answer is not difficult to find. The statics of simple machines provides a model in the law of the lever, where conserved force is equal to weight times instantaneous displacement. Descartes sets out the principle to Mersenne, telling him that

if you have a balance in equilibrium and you place on it the smallest weight that is able to make it turn, then it will turn very slowly, whereas if you put twice this weight on it, it will turn more than twice as fast. And in contrast, if you take a fan in your hand, without your having to use any force except that needed to support it, you can raise and lower it with the same speed that it would fall by itself in the air if you let it go; but to raise and lower it twice as fast, you have to employ the same force, which will be more than double the other, since that one was nil.[38]

It is clear what Descartes has done: he has simply translated from the statical case to the kinematic one, leaving weight much as it is and transforming instantaneous displacement into speed.[39]

The immutability of God which underlies the conservation of 'motion' (size times speed) is manifested in the form of laws of nature which are 'the secondary and particular causes of the various motions that we notice in individual bodies' (art. 37). The first of these laws of nature specifies what form the conservation of motion takes. Just as bodies retain their shape, so they retain their state of rest if they are at rest, and their state of motion if they are in motion. More generally, in absence of external causes a body will retain its state of motion or rest. The rationale behind this is that given in article 37: 'rest is the opposite of motion, and nothing moves by virtue of its own nature toward its opposite or its own destruction'. In the case of remaining in the same state of motion (i.e. maintaining the same speed), as opposed to just remaining in motion, his rationale depends on the idea

---

[38] Descartes to Mersenne, 2 February 1643; AT III. 614.
[39] See Richard S. Westfall, *Force in Newton's Physics: The Science of Dynamics in the Seventeenth Century* (London, 1971), 75.

that different states of motion depend on different amounts of motion and rest, for this is the only way change of speed can be accommodated.

The first law, by itself, tells us nothing about the direction of motion, because it deals with scalar quantities. But motion is always motion in a particular direction (even if relatively defined). When we looked at modes in the previous chapter, we noted that extension is the principal attribute of corporeal substance, and the modes of corporeal substance are ways of being extended: the particular extension must be manifested in some shape, in some state of rest or motion, and so on for all the modes. Such modes – we can call them first-order modes – are the particular ways in which the attributes of substance exist or are manifested.[40] In the case of motion, however, there is also a second-order mode, a mode that qualifies the mode of motion, and this is 'determination'.[41] While shape and state of motion/rest are properties – modes – in terms of which the attributes of substances must be expressed, determination is a second-order mode in terms of which the first-order mode of motion must be expressed.

The first law of nature is designed to establish that first-order modes do not change without an external cause. The second law is designed to establish that the second-order modes do not change without an external cause, where the only second-order mode that Descartes mentions is determination, which is a directional quantity.[42] The law tells us that 'everything that moves is determined in the individual instants which can be specified as it moves, to continue its motion in a given direction along a straight line, and never along a curved line' (art. 39). This completes the account of an isolated body, and Descartes is constantly at pains to point out that in nature we will never actually find such behaviour, because the motion of bodies always ceases in the terrestrial realm owing to a number of causes, many of which we may be unaware of, and their motion is never rectilinear because in a plenum more complex looped motions are required for the translation of bodies.

The transition to the kinds of principles that have a more direct applicability to the phenomena Descartes sets out to explain – and the origin and structure of solar systems will be paramount among these, as we shall see in the next chapter – begins in the second part of the discussion of the second law. The title of article 39, which sets out the second law, tells us

---

[40] I am indebted here to the discussion in Peter McLaughlin, 'Force, Determination and Impact', in Stephen Gaukroger et al. eds., *Descartes' Natural Philosophy* (London, 2000), 81–112.

[41] See Descartes to Clerselier, 17 February 1645; AT IV. 185.

[42] On determination see Alan Gabbey, 'Force and Inertia in the Seventeenth Century: Descartes and Newton', in Stephen Gaukroger, ed., *Descartes: Philosophy, Mathematics and Physics* (New York, 1980), 230–320; and McLaughlin, 'Force, Determination and Impact'.

that 'all motion is, of itself, along straight lines; and consequently, bodies that are moving in a circle always tend to move away from the centre of the circle that they are describing'. Here we get to what, for Descartes, will be the cutting edge of his cosmology: a force acting radially out from the centre, which we shall call centrifugal force. The two laws of nature that he has already provided employ minimal, non-dynamic, and relatively uncontentious premises. The principal premise is God's immutability, and he has managed to construe motion and rest in such a way that immutability rules out moving bodies coming to rest because of some internal principle, while at the same time keeping the argument very much within the framework of a Christianised Aristotelianism. On the other hand, what these laws of nature give us is, as it stands, not a great deal of use in the cosmological arguments for which Part II is really just a preparation. The introduction of centrifugal force changes all this, partly because it is a dynamic notion, and partly because of the radical use to which he will put it in his account of the origin and structure of the solar system.

The aim is to let centrifugal force ride on the relatively secure arguments establishing the first two laws. Here is how Descartes establishes the rationale for the second law in article 39 (I include the phrases added in the French version):

When the stone A is rotated in the sling EA [Fig. 4.2] and describes the circle

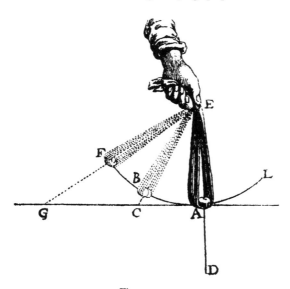

Figure 4.2

ABF, then at the instant at which it is at point A, it is inclined to move along the tangent of the circle toward C. We cannot conceive that it is inclined to any circular movement, for although it will previously come from L to A along a curved line, none of this circular motion can be understood to remain in it when it is at point A. Moreover, this is confirmed by experience, because if the stone then leaves the sling, it will continue to move, not toward B, but toward C. From this it follows that any body that is moving in a circle constantly tends to move directly away from the centre of the circle that it is describing. Indeed, our hand can even feel this while we are turning the stone in the sling, for it pulls and stretches the rope in an attempt to move away from our hand in a straight line. This consideration is of great importance, and will be so frequently used in what follows that it must be very carefully noticed here.

At first glance, this passage seems unproblematic. The stone is constrained to move in a circle, along LA, but if the constraint were removed at A, it would not continue along the curved path ABF but along a rectilinear path at a tangent to the curve at A, namely along ACG. In other words, its 'natural' or unconstrained motion is a rectilinear one.

In chapter 7 of *Le Monde*, Descartes had offered the same analysis of motion in a sling in setting out his 'rules of motion'.[43] However, in chapter 13, in elaborating on the importance of the law for his cosmology, he offered an interpretation of what happens in this case which actually depends on our analysing the motion of the stone in a completely different way. He argues that the tendency of the stone to move at a tangent (ACG) to the circular path it is following is to be analysed in terms of two components of this tendency. One is a radial tendency outwards (EAD), which I am calling centrifugal force, the other is the motion along the circular path ABF which, we are told, is in no way impeded by the sling.[44] In other words, the circular motion of the stone in the sling is not caused by any external constraint, including anything imposed by the sling: the body naturally follows this path. And in kinematic terms, this means that this circular motion is an inertial motion![45] Descartes is thinking of a body being held in a stable circular path in terms of forces that act outwards from the centre being exactly balanced by forces that act inwards from the periphery, and the notion of equilibrium seems quite appropriate here. The trouble is that this statical model, which is what Descartes appeals to when he wants to think through a problem dynamically,

---

[43] AT XI. 45–7.   [44] AT XI. 85–7.
[45] See the perceptive account in Westfall, *Force in Newton's Physics*, 78–82.

directly contradicts what has seemed, with the 'benefit' of hindsight, to be a crucial kinematic result, namely the principle of rectilinear inertia. His statical model leads him to accept a notion of what is effectively circular equilibrium. It is crucial here that we identify the different contributions of statics and kinematics to his account if we are to understand just what is going on in this account. The principle of rectilinear inertia tells us that in the absence of 'external' forces a body will continue in a state of rest or uniform rectilinear motion. The principle of circular equilibrium tells us that a body in circular motion is in a state of dynamic equilibrium, it is dynamically balanced, and in the absence of 'external' forces will continue in that state. This is a problematic principle – as Newton realised (and stated in his third law of motion), every body is dynamically balanced – but it is not the principle itself that generates the problems in Descartes' account. Rather, these problems arise from the fact that Descartes describes rectilinear motion and circular motion by reference to what turn out to be conflicting principles. But because these conflicting principles derive from different models, which draw attention to different aspects of the situation and pick out different things as requiring explanation, the conflict is not so apparent, at least to Descartes, who seems to move between equilibrium and inertia as if they were the same thing.

At first sight, he seems to have resolved this problem in the *Principia*, for, in the absence of any analysis along the lines of that given in chapter 13 of *Le Monde*, the natural interpretation of the stone in the sling is the one whereby the circular motion is the constrained one, and the natural motion is the rectilinear motion at a tangent to the circle. But again the problems begin when Descartes moves into a cosmological context, for what he wants from the case of the motion of a body in a sling is not something that this analysis can provide. The trouble is that for his cosmology he needs a radial tendency outwards from the centre (EAD). This becomes clear when, in Part III, he tries to use his laws of motion in a cosmological context: article 58 of Part III explains 'how bodies that are rotated strive to move away from the centre of their motion', and 'that all the matter of the heavens strives similarly to move away from certain centres' (Part III art. 60), illustrating this, in Part III article 58, by the motion of an ant crawling along the length of a rotating rod:

So that it may be clearly understood [that rotating bodies strive to move away from the centre of their motion], let us compare the motion by which this stone when at A would go towards C – if it were impeded by no other force – with the motion by which an ant, starting at the same point A, would also be moved towards C. We are assuming [Fig. 4.3] EY to be a rod on which the ant would

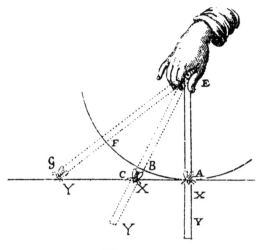

Figure 4.3

be walking in a straight line from A toward Y, while the rod was being rotated around centre E, and its point A would thus describe the circle ABF. We are also assuming the rotation of the rod to be in such a proportion to the motion of the ant, that the ant would be at point X when the rod was at C, at point Y when the rod was at G, and so on. Thus the ant itself would always be on the straight line ACG.

To reinforce the point, he uses the example of a ball placed in a hollow tube: as the tube is rotated from one of its ends, the ball moves outwards from the centre (Part III art. 59). Of course, as Descartes realises, once the ball leaves the tube – once the constraints on the motion of the ball are removed – the ball will not continue along the direction AY but will be projected at a tangent to the circle. But the point is that, in the cosmological context, the constraints are never removed because the universe is packed with homogeneous matter, so that light, for example, will always be transmitted radially outwards from a centrally rotating sun. Cartesian optics and cosmology depend crucially upon the existence of a force acting radially outwards. When, in article 39, he tells us that 'our hand can even feel this while we are turning the stone in the sling, for it pulls and stretches the rope in an attempt to move away from our hand in a straight line', the stone is not pulling the rope at a tangent but radially outwards. The presentation of the second law in the *Principia* certainly looks more consistent than that of *Le Monde*, but in fact it is just that the difficulties are buried more deeply in the *Principia*. *Le Monde* in effect offered two analyses, one in chapter 7 which was consonant with Descartes' kinematic definition of motion, and a different one in chapter 13 which was consonant with his attempt to develop a dynamical account instrumental in his cosmology. His analysis of the motion of the stone in a sling in *Le Monde* is fundamentally flawed, and the main casualty is what I have called centrifugal force. There is simply no force acting radially outwards from the centre. His elementary kinematics cannot establish that there is, and his more elaborate dynamical model, derived from statics, takes us in a completely inappropriate direction. This problem has not disappeared in the *Principia*, it is just less evident. But, in the final analysis, the same transition has to be made there: it is the pulling on the string that is identified as being of 'great importance, and will be so frequently used in what follows that it must be very carefully noticed here'. The pulling on the string is what illustrates the tendency in all rotating bodies 'to move away from the centre of the circle that they are describing'. Yet this pulling on the string has no basis in his kinematics.

THE THIRD LAW OF MOTION

The first and second laws deal with isolated bodies, telling us, respectively, in what way their first-order and second-order modes are conserved. The third law, and the rules of collision appended to it, tell us what happens when two of these bodies meet, in an idealised case. The main features of this case are that there is no other matter present (so that we can think of them as travelling in a void), and that the only collisions are in a straight line in two dimensions. Above all, however, the bodies are considered to be perfectly hard – that is, are not deformed in collision – and it is central to Descartes' account that behaviour of bodies in collision must be explained fully in terms of the conservation of motion: the ball rebounds simply because its motion, as an absolute quantity, persists.[46] To think of the rebound as being caused by elasticity would be to introduce, at a fundamental explanatory level, a poorly understood (and, for Descartes, unquantifiable) force which could never meet his stringent requirements of clarity and distinctness.

---

[46] See A. I. Sabra, *Theories of Light from Descartes to Newton* (Cambridge, 1981), 82.

The third law employs a dynamic language right from the start, and even the title of article 40 gives us an indication of the 'contest' model that underpins Descartes' understanding of collision:

> The third law: that a body upon coming into contact with a stronger one, loses none of its motion; but that, upon coming into contact with a weaker one, it loses as much as it transfers to that weaker body.

Elaborating on the law, Descartes talks of the weaker body having 'less force to continue to move in a straight line than the other has to resist it'. We are given no definition of what this force is, and we have to try to work out from context, or from passages elsewhere in his writings, just what notion, or notions, he is employing.

In demonstrating the third law, Descartes makes crucial use of the distinction between the first-order mode, motion, and the second-order mode, determination. The motion of a body can remain intact, he tells us, while its determination changes. Indeed, there is a fundamental distinction to be made between motion and determination. Motion is simple and, in virtue of this simplicity, will continue unless destroyed by an external cause. Determination, on the other hand, is not simple:

> In an encounter with an unyielding body, there certainly appears to be a cause that prevents the motion of the body that strikes the other from maintaining its determination in the same direction. However, there is no cause that would remove or decrease the motion itself since motion is not contrary to motion. From which it follows that motion must not be diminished. (art. 41)

What Descartes has in mind here is the case of light rays being reflected from a surface, which he models on a tennis ball being reflected from a surface.[47] The case is described in *La Dioptrique*.[48] Fig 4.4 shows a tennis ball travelling from A to B, bouncing off a reflecting surface CBE, and being reflected to F in the same time it takes to travel from A to B. The impact of the ball at B Descartes treats as the collision of two perfectly inelastic bodies, in which the ball retains its speed but changes direction. The rationale behind this is that if the force of motion, or speed, and direction of motion were the same thing, then the ball would first have to stop before it changed direction, and if it stopped a new cause would be needed for it to move again. But there is no such new cause available: therefore, its force or speed is not affected in the impact, only

---

[47] Descartes is, of course, thinking of real tennis, where the balls are highly inelastic, as opposed to lawn tennis, which was a mid-nineteenth-century development which introduced elastic balls.
[48] AT vi. 93–6.

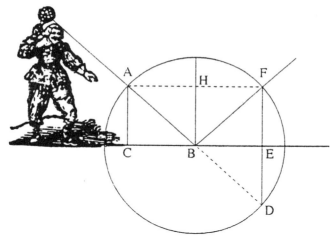

Figure 4.4

the direction of its motion, which is changed. If we make Descartes'
distinction between speed and determination, then we can understand
how the speed might be conserved, while direction is altered. Determination is, unlike speed, a composite mode and therefore not preserved
in the way that speed is. The speed of the ball before being reflected is
represented by the line AB, and after reflection by a line of the same
length BF. The line AB also represents the determination of the ball,
since determination is after all a mode of the motion,[49] and it can be
resolved into two orthogonal lines AH and AC. Article 32 explains how
single motions may be regarded as multiple, and in the present case the
two orthogonal components are AC, which is directly opposed to the
surface CBE, and AH, which is parallel to the surface so not involved in
the collision. Because determination AH is not involved in the collision
that results in the reflection, it is preserved, remaining a component of
the determination of the reflected ball. Since the ball arrives at F from
B in the same time it took to travel from A to B – AB and BF represent
the same speeds – the orthogonal components of BF will be HF and EF.
In other words, AC has been replaced by EF, which, simply in virtue

---

[49] Note also that, like motion, it is a magnitude: Descartes writes to Clerselier on 17 February
that, in collision, a body can pass to another more than half its speed and 'more than half its
determination': AT IV. 186. In the end, however, it seems that determination turns out to resist
any completely consistent reading; see McLaughlin, 'Force, Determination and Impact' for the
best statement of the difficulties, and a realistic solution to them.

of resolving the motion into its orthogonal components, must have the opposite direction.

The third law covers collision, so there must be some form of opposition between bodies. Motions of equal speed are never opposed to another, but 'the determination of a body to move in a given direction' is opposed to 'a body in its path which is either at rest or moving in a contrary manner' (art. 44). This opposition is set out in terms of opposing forces in article 43:

Each thing strives, as far as is in its power, to remain in the same state, in accordance with the first law stated above. From this it follows that a body that is joined to another has some force to resist being separated from it, while a body that is separate has some force to remain separate. A body at rest has some force to remain at rest, and consequently to resist everything which might change it; while a moving body has some force to continue its motion, that is, to continue to move at the same speed and in the same direction. Furthermore, this force must be measured not only by the size of the body in which this force exists, and by the extent of the surface which separates this body from those around it, but also by the speed and nature of its motion, and by the different ways in which bodies come into contact with one another.

Note here that we have both a force of a moving body to resist change of state, that is, to continue in its directed motion, and a force of a body at rest to resist change of state. Now the ontological standing of forces in the *Principia* has been the subject of much controversy, some writers denying that forces exist at all, and maintaining that all we have at the most fundamental level is matter in motion,[50] while others have argued that forces are inherent in bodies.[51] As we have seen, Descartes does talk about forces, and indeed talks of bodies having more force the larger they are or the quicker they move. I have suggested above that Descartes cannot get by without the language of forces, and we have seen that, in his earlier writings, questions such as the behaviour of fluids and the propagation of light (both questions that will be crucial for Part III) are explicitly thought through in dynamic terms. In the *Principia*, Descartes attempts to reformulate his natural philosophy in 'clear and distinct' terms, and this does impose severe constraints on what kinds of notions he can employ. But, even within these constraints, he seems to find some

---

[50] Advocates of this view include E. J. Dijksterhuis, *The Mechanisation of the World Picture* (New York, 1961), 403–18; Eric J. Aiton, *The Vortex Theory of Planetary Motions* (London, 1972), 4; and Garber, *Descartes' Metaphysical Physics*, passim.

[51] Advocates of this view include Martial Gueroult, 'The Metaphysics and Physics of Force in Descartes', in Stephen Gaukroger, ed., *Descartes: Philosophy, Mathematics and Physics* (New York, 1980), 196–229; and Gabbey, 'Force and Inertia in the Seventeenth Century'.

place for force. In a letter to Regius, for example, he writes, in a sketch of a reply to Voetius intended for publication:

> It would certainly be absurd for those who believe in substantial forms to say that these forms are themselves the immediate principle of their actions; but it cannot be absurd to say this if one does not regard such forms as distinct from active qualities. Now we do not deny active qualities, but we say only that they should not be regarded as having any degree of reality greater than that of modes, for to regard them so is to conceive of them as substances.[52]

Sometimes, certain forces cannot be accommodated at all, elasticity being a prime example. As we have seen, Descartes is adamant that collision be described in terms of the behaviour of inelastic bodies. In that way it can all be done in terms of conservation of motion,[53] avoiding recourse to dynamic notions like elasticity. Here we have a case where it is not simply a question of moving from a perfectly functional dynamic notion to a more geometrical, kinematic one, but where the physical theory is shaped by the constraints of clarity and distinctness. But, at the other extreme, there are cases where his geometrical, kinematic formulation of physical interactions is really just unintelligible unless we grasp the dynamical model that lies behind it. This is the case with Rule 4 of the rules of collision, which are intended to flesh out the third law by describing non-oblique impacts between idealised inelastic bodies. Most of the rules are problematic in one way or another, and Huygens managed to derive a set of correct rules for elastic collision on the hypothesis that Rule 1, which describes the impact of two bodies of equal size and speed, holds for elastic but not inelastic collisions, and then abandoning all the others, deriving the new rules from his reconstrual of this first of Descartes' rules.[54] Some of the rules suffer simply from the fact that motion is a scalar quantity for Descartes, and equal motions in opposite directions cannot be registered by differences in sign: this is a problem

---

[52] Descartes to Regius, January 1642; AT III. 503.
[53] Unfortunately if one works with the correct rules for inelastic collision then motion is not conserved. Beeckman had arrived at correct rules by 1618 and Descartes was probably familiar with these, but could not accept the consequence of the continuous decrease in the quantity of motion: see Aiton, *The Vortex Theory of Planetary Motions*, 39. The existence and behaviour of perfectly hard bodies was intensely debated for more than a century after the appearance of Descartes' *Principia*: see Scott, *The Conflict between Atomism and Conservation Theory*, as well as the review of this book by Alan Gabbey in *Studies in History and Philosophy of Science* 4 (1973), 373–85.
[54] There are good accounts of Huygens' work in Alan Gabbey, 'Huygens and Mechanics', in H. J. M. Bos, ed., *Studies on Christiaan Huygens* (Lisse, 1980), 166–99; Westfall, *Force in Newton's Physics*, ch. 4; and Julian B. Barbour, *Absolute or Relative Motion? Volume 1: The Discovery of Dynamics* (Cambridge, 1989), ch. 9.

in Rule 2 (art. 47), which describes the collision of two bodies of unequal sizes but equal speeds, and Rule 3 (art. 48), which describes the
collision of two bodies of equal sizes but unequal speeds. The problem
with Rules 4 and 5 is quite different however. Rule 4 (art. 49) tells us
that when a smaller moving body encounters a larger stationary one,
it rebounds with its original speed, leaving the larger body unaffected.
Rule 5 (art. 50) tells us that when a larger moving body encounters a
smaller stationary one, then both proceed in the direction of the motion
after impact with a speed equal to the product of the size of the larger
body times the velocity of the larger body, divided by the sum of the two
sizes.

   This is peculiar for a number of reasons. Rule 4 specifies that a smaller
body can never move a larger one, no matter what its speed, and no matter how slight the difference in size. It is quite contrary to our empirical
experience (to the extent that we can extrapolate to the case of perfectly
inelastic bodies) that a rapidly moving body which was very marginally
smaller than a larger stationary body, would simply rebound on impact
with it, having failed to affect the larger body at all, and leaving it in the
same stationary state as it was before impact. Descartes seems to recognise this, telling us in article 53 (French version) that 'experience seems
to contradict the rules I have just explained', and telling us explicitly in
the introduction to Rule 4 that it may not hold when the body is surrounded by air or some other fluid. More importantly, given Descartes'
definition of motion, which body is moving and which is stationary is a
matter of determining the appropriate reference point, and it would be
very easy to find a reference point from which the larger body would be
the moving body and the smaller body the stationary one, but then we
would be in the situation described by Rule 5, which provides a completely different outcome. Of course, we could argue that the outcome
of the collision will retrospectively tell us which of the bodies was moving
and which was stationary (leaving to one side the fact that there are also
going to be reference points that indicate that both bodies are moving),
but this will require us to conceive of motion in a far more absolute way
than that sanctioned by the kinematic criteria that Descartes provides.
Kinematically, the two rules are inconsistent.

   It is not too difficult to understand why Descartes should have insisted
on Rule 4, for it underpins his optics, and it is perhaps his realisation that
it is needed for his optics that led him to change his mind on this question,
for five years earlier he had written to Mersenne on two occasions allowing that a smaller moving body can dislodge a larger stationary one, and

even indicating how the resultant speed is determined.[55] In seeking to explain why light rays, which follow rectilinear paths, behave in particular geometrically defined ways when they are reflected or refracted, he models light micro-mechanically. In reflection, for example, light corpuscles strike a larger body and are reflected from its surface. Kinematically specified laws of collision, of the kind Descartes provides, should be enough to describe the various kinds of interaction possible here, and in this way should underpin an explanation of why light behaves in particular geometrically defined ways when it encounters a reflecting surface, or when it moves from one optical medium to another. The linchpins of this treatment are his accounts of reflection and refraction, and we can confine our attention to the former, which we have already looked at in trying to elucidate the notion of determination. Descartes starts from the idea that when a light ray strikes a reflecting surface obliquely, the angle of incidence equals the angle of reflection. To show why this happens, he resolves the ray into components, and he distinguishes the speed of the ray and its determination. In fleshing out the geometry of the situation in physical terms, Descartes simply has to imagine the light ray being composed of minute corpuscles and striking a larger body. Now, if such a body were to be moved by a light corpuscle, then of course the light corpuscle would have to transfer some of its motion to the larger body, in which case it would be retarded, and not only its direction but also its speed would be affected. And, if this happened, the angle of reflection would not then equal the angle of incidence: rather, the situation would be more like refraction, where a change in the speed of the light ray causes the bending of the ray. The kinematics have got to match what we know about the geometry of reflection, and the geometry of reflection does not deal with approximations: geometrical optics is just a particular interpretation of geometry, which is the paradigm of exactness. In providing a physical model for the geometrical behaviour of light rays, this exactness, which is of the essence of geometry, cannot be lost. If the geometrical analysis of the behaviour of light shows that the angle of incidence equals the angle of reflection, it equals it exactly, whether the light is striking a raindrop or the ocean. And, if that is the case, the light corpuscle cannot move the body from whose surface it is reflected.

This explains why Rule 4 is so important for Descartes, but it does not explain what he thinks makes Rule 4 correct. If one looks to Descartes for a rationale of the law, what one finds is a physical claim – that a smaller

---

[55] Descartes to Mersenne, 25 December 1639; AT II. 627 and 28 October 1640; AT III. 210–11.

moving body colliding with a larger stationary one cannot affect the state of the larger body – filled out in quasi-Scholastic natural–philosophical terms. There are two important premises in Descartes' treatment. The first is that rest has as much reality as does motion: rest is not simply a 'privation' of motion as the Scholastics had argued. The second is that rest and motion are opposed to one another: they are modal contraries. We must therefore think of the interaction of the bodies in terms of the smaller having a particular quantity of motion, and the larger having a particular quantity of rest. These are opposing states, so the bodies will be in dynamic opposition, and Rule 4 therefore describes a contest, as it were, between a larger body at rest and a smaller body in motion. The bodies exercise a force to resist changes of their states, and the magnitude of this force Descartes considers to be a function of their size. A body in motion cannot, for that reason alone, have more force than one at rest; nor can greater speed confer greater force upon it. Either of these would undermine the ontological equivalence of rest and motion that Descartes wants to defend. Now, bearing this in mind, we can ask what happens when the smaller moving body collides with a larger stationary one. Clearly they cannot both remain in the same state in collision, so there will have to be a change of state. And, since the smaller or 'weaker' body can hardly change the state of the larger or 'stronger' one, it is the smaller one that has its state changed (the direction of its motion is reversed), the larger body remaining unaffected in the process.

This account explains why it has to be an all-or-nothing matter. We might be tempted to ask why the smaller body should not move the larger one if the smaller body had sufficient speed, or if the difference in size were very marginal. The answer to the first question is that the ontological equivalence of motion and rest makes the speed of the smaller body irrelevant to the outcome of the collision. The answer to the second is that, because of the irrelevance of speed, the only remaining factor is size. Still, it does seem somewhat peculiar that the outcome would be the same irrespective of whether the difference in size were very significant, or whether the two bodies were almost exactly the same size. The peculiarity is removed immediately once we think of the situation in terms of statics, however. Think of the bodies as occupying the two pans of an (idealised frictionless) beam balance. The arm will always be tipped down on the side of the heavier, no matter how slight the difference in weight. That this is indeed the reasoning behind Descartes' account is made clear in a letter to Hobbes in which Descartes responds to Hobbes' claim that the extent to which a body is moved is proportional to the force exerted on it, so that even the smallest force will move a body to some extent. Descartes replies:

His assumption that *what does not yield to the smallest force cannot be moved by any force at all* has no semblance of truth. Does anyone think that a weight of 100 pounds in a balance would yield to a weight of one pound placed in the other pan of the scale simply because it yields to a weight of 200 pounds?[56]

What Rule 4 seems to do is to reduce the question to one of statics, by removing considerations of speed. And the means by which it does this is through the principle of the ontological equivalence of motion and rest. Descartes' statement of this equivalence has often been seen as an important move in the direction of a proper understanding of the principle of inertia, as a step on the road from seeing rest simply as a privation of motion, to treating rest and uniform rectilinear motion as being dynamically on the same footing, as being states that require no force for their maintenance. This may well have been the route followed in Newton, and he may well have been directed along this route by reading Descartes.[57] But it is not so clear that this captures the direction of Descartes' own thinking here. Quite the contrary, the principle of the ontological equivalence of motion and rest, which in a physical context such as the rules of collision amounts to a dynamical equivalence, is in fact a step in a completely different direction for Descartes. The ontological or dynamical equivalence of motion and rest means that what holds for rest holds for motion. Statics tells us about the behaviour of bodies at rest: perhaps it can be built upon to deal with bodies in motion, if motion can somehow be seen to be a variation on rest (a departure from an equilibrium state). If, like Descartes, one has developed one's principal dynamical concepts in the context of statics, one is going to be forced into this kind of manoeuvre at times, and, far from what is involved here being a translation of dynamical concepts into kinematic terms, what we seem to have is the pursuit of a dynamics for which there is no kinematic rationale.

What comes out in Descartes' presentation of the laws of nature and the rules of collision is the complexity of the layering of physical theory in the *Principia*. The dynamic underpinnings of the project are clearer if, as I have tried to show, we compare the presentation of doctrines in the *Principia* with earlier, more explicitly dynamical formulations of the same doctrine, and if we bear in mind that the presentation of everything

---

[56] Descartes to Mersenne for Hobbes, [21 January 1641]; AT III. 287.
[57] See Gabbey, 'Force and Inertia in the Seventeenth Century', 267ff.

in clear and distinct terms is how the *Principia* operates, and that this inevitably requires translation of dynamically formulated doctrines into different terms. But these dynamic underpinnings occasionally erupt onto the surface of the *Principia* as well, and Rule 4 and the doctrine of centrifugal force – one of which hinges on the beam balance, the other on the idea of forces in equilibrium – are important evidence of this, all the more important as they lie at the foundations of Cartesian optics and Cartesian cosmology respectively.

THE MECHANISATION OF MATTER THEORY:
SOLIDS AND FLUIDS

Rule 4, in the French version,[58] adds a crucial qualification to his statement of the Rule, namely that it holds only if the larger stationary body 'has, not only no apparent motion, but also is not surrounded by air or some other fluid (which makes the hard bodies immersed in such a fluid very easily movable, as I shall show)' (art. 49). Immediately after setting out the rules, Descartes makes a general qualification about their applicability, in article 53. 'Experience often seems to contradict the rules I have just explained', he tells us. What are described in the rules of collision are the interactions of bodies separated from one another, but

because there cannot be any bodies in the world that are thus separated from all others, and because we seldom encounter bodies that are perfectly solid, it is very difficult to perform the calculation to determine to what extent the motion of each body may be changed by collisions with others. Before we can judge whether these rules do or do not hold here, we must simultaneously calculate the effects of all those bodies that surround the bodies in question and which affect their motion. But these effects differ greatly, depending on whether the surrounding bodies are solid or fluid, and therefore it is necessary that we should enquire immediately into the difference between fluid and solid bodies.

There are in fact two kinds of revision or elaboration needed before the applicability of the rules of collision can be seriously assessed. The first kind of questions is purely mechanical. The rules have described only one kind of collision, and once we consider fully the range of possible collisions in a three-dimensional space, it is clear that Descartes has covered only a small range of possible types of collision. Moreover, the

---

[58] Descartes himself was responsible for the revisions to the French version, and he writes to Mersenne to tell him that if he sees Picot, the French translator, he should tell him that his revisions have been delayed because he has had difficulty finding the time 'in which to clarify my laws of motion', Descartes to Mersenne, 20 April 1646; AT IV. 396.

surface area of the colliding bodies is crucial, above all the area of contact, which means that the shape of the body has to be taken into account. Even in the idealised form that they are given, there is a strong case to be made that the rules apply to cubes rather than spheres,[59] and, in the context of the cosmology, the situation is even more complicated, as the surface area of the constituents of stars affects their degree of agitation:

for although the quantity of second-element matter in all the corpuscles that occupy a given amount of space is the same, whether they are small or large, the smaller ones have less force because they have more surface area in proportion to the quantity of their matter, and therefore can be drawn off course and turned aside in other directions more easily than larger ones. (Part III art. 125)

It is, however, a second set of questions that Descartes is concerned with here, and these are not purely mechanical questions, but rather questions about the relations between mechanics and matter theory. In particular, they concern the extent to which matter theory can be mechanised. Descartes has provided us with a number of basic laws regulating the behaviour of perfectly hard bodies either completely isolated from one another or acting upon one another in pairs in the absence of any surrounding matter. But bodies in Descartes' cosmos are neither perfectly hard nor do they exist in isolation from one another. Somehow, Descartes needs to capture the internal material constitution of bodies and the material constitution of their immediate environment, in terms which remain mechanical. At the very least, he has to provide a bridge between the mechanics of Part II, and the questions of cosmology, chemistry and physics, and physiology which occupy Parts III, IV, and V respectively, and which had traditionally been dealt with in terms of a matter theory that, for all intents and purposes, had no connection with mechanics.

Cartesian cosmology, as we saw when we looked at *Le Monde* in chapter 1, works primarily in terms of bodies being transported by fluids in which they are embedded. Unlike the classical mechanics that we associate with Galileo and Newton, where the basic model is one in which bodies move through a vacuum, and where the medium is introduced primarily as a source of resistance to motion,[60] Descartes, because his approach is modelled on hydrostatics, thinks of the medium not as

---

[59] See McLaughlin, 'Force, Determination and Impact', and Peter Damerow et al., *Exploring the Limits of Preclassical Mechanics* (New York, 1992), 96–103.
[60] See the second half of the 'First Day' of Galileo Galilei, *Two New Sciences* (Madison, 1974), 65–108; and Book II of Newton's *Principia* (Berkeley, 1999).

resisting the motion but as being largely constitutive of it. It is because the medium behaves in the way it does that the body behaves in the way it does: just as bodies immersed in fluids behave in the way they do because of their immersion in the fluid, where the properties of the fluid are at least as fundamental as those of the body, and need to be understood before we can identify what the relevant properties of the body are going to be.[61] For this reason, the standing of Descartes' laws of motion and collision rules is different from that of the basic laws of Newton's natural philosophy. They do not provide the skeleton which can be progressively fleshed out, but rather just one ingredient in a more complex picture. Galileo, in his treatment of falling bodies, can just treat the air as a source of resistance, separating out different types of resistance, such as buoyancy effect and friction, without being in any way obliged to look at the material constitution of air, far less to offer a mechanistic account of its constituents, if his account is to be successful. Descartes, by contrast, is obliged to give details of why the fluids in which bodies move behave in the way they do, and, if his explanation of this is not in terms of his basic mechanical principles, then his project has failed. As the last article of Part II puts it: 'I do not accept or desire in physics any other principles than in geometry or abstract mathematics, because all the phenomena of nature are explained thereby' (art. 64).

Descartes' account takes the form of a theory of the difference between fluid and solid bodies in which they, and their distinctive properties, are distinguished purely on a mechanical basis. The basic phenomenological difference between solids and fluids for Descartes lies in the fact that fluids will offer no resistance to bodies entering them, whereas solids will, and he puts this down to the parts of fluid bodies moving whereas those of solid bodies are stationary:

those which are moving do not prevent the places they are leaving of their own accord being occupied by others, whereas those that are at rest cannot be driven out of their places without some external force which causes this change. From this we may conclude that those bodies that are divided into very small parts which are agitated by a variety of independent motions are fluid, while those bodies whose parts are all contiguous and at rest are solid. (art. 54)

The parts of the solid body are joined together, we are told, simply by the fact that they are at rest with respect to one another (art. 55), although,

---

[61] See Gaukroger, 'The Foundational Role of Statics and Hydrostatics in Descartes' Natural Philosophy'.

if this is the case, it is unclear in what sense they are genuine, as opposed to purely notional, *parts* of the body in the first place.

Although they are the same thing – material extension – the motion of fluids and solids is different. Descartes takes the fact that air and water can act upon solid bodies so as to break them down (as in rusting and dissolving), as evidence of the rapid motion of the constituent parts of fluids, since 'no physical action of that kind can occur without the parts moving' (art. 56). Descartes' cosmology, however, will rely upon the fact that the fluids cause, rather than offer resistance to, the motion of bodies embedded in them, so it is crucial that the motion of the constituent parts of fluids does not impede the motion of solid bodies in any way, as we might initially have expected. As for a body at rest embedded in a fluid, Descartes maintains that the parts of the fluid, which are in constant motion, act upon the stationary body equally from all sides, so that the net effect is zero, and the body remains at rest. In the case of a moving body, however, the moving parts of the fluid help or reinforce the motion, allowing a large body to be moved by a small force (Fig. 4.5):

Let us first suppose that the solid body B is not yet in the fluid FD, but that the particles *aeioa* of the fluid arranged in the form of a ring, are moving circularly in the order of the symbols *aei*, and that others *auyao* are moving similarly in

Figure 4.5

the order of the symbols *ouy*. For in order for any body to be fluid, its particles must move in various ways, as we have said. If the solid body B is at rest in this fluid FD, between *a* and *o*, what will happen? The particles *aeio* will certainly be prevented by B from moving *o* toward *a* to complete the circle of their movement; and similarly the particles *ouya* will be prevented from continuing from *a* toward *o*. Those coming from *i* toward *o* will drive B toward C, while those coming from *y* toward *a* will drive it back equally toward F. As a result, these particles alone will have no force to move B, but will be driven back from *o* toward *u*, and from *a* toward *e*; and one circulation will be formed from two, following the order of the symbols *aeiouya*. Thus the collision with body B will not in any way affect the [quantity of] motion of these particles, but will only change their determination, so that the lines they move along will not be as straight, or as nearly straight, as those they would have followed had they not struck B. Finally, if some external force intervenes, driving B toward C, then this force, however slight, joined to that by which the particles of the fluid coming from *i* toward *o* also drive B toward C, will overcome that by which the particles coming from *y* toward *a* drive B back in the opposite direction. They will therefore be enough to change their determination and cause them to travel in the order of the symbols *ayuo* to the extent required so that the movement of body B not be impeded, because when two bodies are determined to move in directly opposite directions, the body having the greater force must change the determination of the other. (art. 57)

The fluid will impede the body if it is moving faster than the particles of the fluid (art. 58) but, within limits, the body may also acquire motion from the fluid (arts. 59 and 60). A solid body immersed in a fluid will be carried along by the fluid (art. 61) and indeed by Descartes' definition of motion must not be considered to be moving, because there is no transference with respect to contiguous bodies (art. 62). In other words, the speed of a body in a fluid will depend to a large extent upon the speed of the parts of the fluid, and this is going to be a crucial result for Descartes' cosmology, as it will be the main ingredient in the explanation of why planets remain in stable orbits.

CHAPTER 5

Principia, *Part III: The visible universe*

At the beginning of Part III, Descartes describes his project as that of explaining 'all the phenomena of nature' by means of the principles already set out in Part II, beginning with 'those phenomena that are the most universal and on which the rest depend' (art. 1). In connection with the realisation of this project, Descartes sets out two fundamental principles. The first is that we must not assume we know the ends for which God created the world (art. 2), and, in particular, we cannot assume that God created the world for human ends: 'it is in no way likely that all things were made for us in the sense that God had no other purpose in creating them' (art. 3). The second principle is that many more things follow from the laws set out in Part II than are evident in our universe (art. 4): our actual world is not the only one compatible with these laws.

These principles do not state commonplaces, and they engage two fundamental questions: curiosity and teleology. The question of curiosity was a highly charged one throughout the Middle Ages and the Renaissance. Augustine had argued that since heavenly bodies were mentioned only rarely in Scripture, the study of astronomy was of very limited use in dealing with scriptural questions, and was likely to distract one, and hence the most beneficial and honourable course was to desist from astronomy altogether.[1] Throughout the Middle Ages, a contrast was drawn between curiosity, which was treated as a disrespectful and unwarranted desire to know things that were none of one's concern (Adam's eating the apple of knowledge in his desire to understand the nature of good and evil, and the dire consequences that followed from this, was the paradigm case of curiosity), and wonder, which was contemplative and respectful. This changed at the beginning of the early modern era, with curiosity, conceived of as something active and probing, being transformed into a

---

[1] Augustine, *De doctrina christiana* II. XXIX. 46, cited and discussed in Hans Blumenberg, *The Genesis of the Copernican World* (Cambridge, Mass., 1987), 31.

virtue, and wonder being correspondingly transformed into something that is characteristic of an ignoramus.[2]

The question of teleology, in particular the idea of studying the universe as a means of revealing God's purpose, is something that becomes possible in a large-scale way only once one has settled the question of the legitimacy of curiosity.[3] Descartes' attitude to teleology, which is shaped by his commitment to mechanism, is firm and uncompromising, and he does not pursue any part of his natural philosophy in terms of purposes and aims. This is not so contentious in the case of most of the cosmology of Part III, although Gassendi, as we saw in chapter 2, would certainly have disagreed with it, as would increasing numbers of British natural philosophers in the course of the seventeenth and early eighteenth centuries. But when we come to the question of the formation of the Earth, in the later sections of Part III and in Part IV, and to the formation of the foetus, in Part V, we shall see that what Descartes is advocating, namely a thoroughgoing mechanist approach in which questions of purpose and goals are absent, is extremely contentious, and was widely opposed.

CELESTIAL MOTIONS

The Copernican system required the postulation of a tract of space of unprecedented vastness between Saturn and the fixed stars to account for lack of stellar parallax. It required the postulation of undetectable diurnal and annual motions of the Earth. And it required one to postulate that ordinary terrestrial bodies were on the surface of a rapidly rotating sphere, without any apparent manifestation of the physical behaviour we associate with bodies in such a state. Before observation of the supernova of 1572, which suggested that the heavens were not as fixed as Aristotelian/Ptolemaic cosmology maintained they should be, the Copernican system had little physical plausibility, Rheticus being the only advocate of Copernicanism before that time,[4] and indeed it had only a handful of advocates before the early seventeenth century.[5]

---

[2] See Lorraine Daston and Katherine Park, *Wonders and the Order of Nature, 1150–1750* (Cambridge, Mass., 1998).

[3] On this question see Hans Blumenberg, *The Legitimacy of the Modern Age* (Cambridge, Mass., 1983), especially Part IV (pp. 229–452). Blumenberg presents a detailed and persausive argument that the legitimacy of *curiositas* is one of the defining features of modernity.

[4] For details, see Thomas S. Kuhn, *The Copernican Revolution* (Cambridge Mass., 1957), and Robert Westman, 'The Melanchthon Circle, Rheticus, and the Wittenberg Interpretation of the Copernican Theory', *Isis* 66 (1975), 165–93.

[5] See Robert Westman, 'The Astronomer's Role in the Sixteenth Century: A Preliminary Study', *History of Science* 18 (1980), 105–47.

By the seventeenth century, what exactly one was defending when one defended 'Copernicanism' was more varied than it had been in the sixteenth century, and Descartes will not defend Copernicus' own system, but a far more radical version of heliocentrism.

Descartes' discussion of the nature of the cosmos opens with questions of size and distance (arts. 5–8). He points out that observation and calculation (for example, on the basis of parallax) reveal that the Moon and the Sun are further away than they appear, that the Moon is comparatively small as far as celestial bodies go, and that the Sun is far larger than it appears; that the planets are much further away than had traditionally been imagined, and that there is every indication that the 'fixed stars' lie at an immense distance from us; and finally, that the apparent size of celestial bodies will vary depending on where we are located in the universe. So far, this is quite compatible with Copernicus' model in *De revolutionibus* (see Fig. 5.1 [6]). But then, in the course of arguing that the intensity of the light of the Sun is such that it must be a source of light, by contrast with the planets and the Moon, which merely reflect light, Descartes makes a move that Copernicus never did:

> if we consider how bright and glittering the rays of the fixed stars are, despite the fact that they are at an immense distance from us and from the Sun, we will not find it hard to accept that they are like the Sun. Thus if we were as close to one of them as we are to the Sun, that star would in all probability appear as large and luminous as the Sun. (art. 9)

One reason Copernicus did not make this move is that he believed that the Sun was the centre of the universe. He may have believed this because of a staunch adherence to the rigidity and impenetrability of celestial spheres. Certainly on one reconstruction,[7] this was what caused him to reject Ptolemy's equants in the first place, since these required rotation around an off-centre axis,[8] something physically impossible if the spheres are indeed rigid. This meant he would have had to look for an alternative mechanism, the epicycles described by thirteenth-century Arab astronomers being the best candidate, and substituting these for

---

[6] Illustration from Nicholas Copernicus, *De revolutionibus* (Nuremberg, 1543), fol. 9v.

[7] See Noel M. Swerdlow, 'The Derivation and First Draft of Copernicus' Planetary Theory: A Translation of the *Commentariolus* with Commentary', *Proceedings of the American Philosophical Society* 117 (1973), 423–512. See also his '*Pseudodoxia Copernicana*: Or, Enquiries into Very Many Received Tenets and Commonly Presumed Truths, Mostly Concerning Spheres', *Archives internationales d'histoire des sciences* 26 (1976), 108–58.

[8] Because Copernicus construed the planets as describing circular orbits, however, even in his own system the Sun had to be placed slightly off-centre, with the planets rotating around a geometrically determined 'mean sun'.

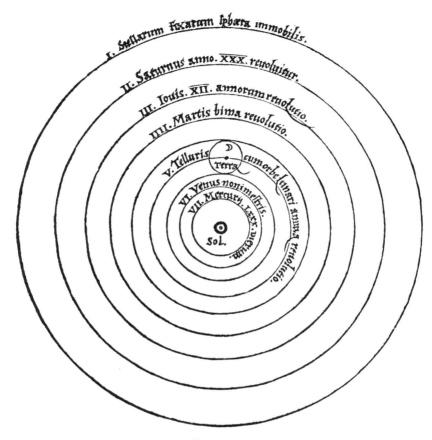

Figure 5.1

Ptolemy's equants was what pointed Copernicus in the direction of he-liocentrism. In Copernicus' cosmos, the Sun is supposed to be literally at the centre of the cosmos. But to be at the centre requires a finite space, whereas Euclidean space cannot be finite: there cannot be a non-spatial region bounding it, as philosophers since antiquity had realised.[9] A num-ber of fifteenth- and sixteenth-century natural philosophers pointed out that an infinite space cannot have a centre, and argued nevertheless for the infinity of space. Nicholas of Cusa did so in the middle of the fifteenth century, and Bruno was to restate the thesis in the 1580s, but the

[9] See Richard Sorabji, *Matter, Space, and Motion: Theories in Antiquity and Their Sequel* (London, 1988), 125–215.

question was not revisited, at least in print, until Descartes published his *Principia*,[10] although after Descartes the idea quickly became commonly accepted,[11] even though Descartes himself, as we have seen, prefers to talk of its 'indefinite' extent rather than its infinite extent.

Because it has a centre around which the planets and fixed stars revolve, Copernicus' space has an intrinsic directionality, a notion that Descartes definitively rejects, as we have seen. Descartes' cosmos has an indefinite number of planetary solar systems, each of them rotating around its own central sun, and each of these suns itself revolving on its own axis. His illustration of the system (see Fig. 5.2), where Y, f, F, S etc. are suns, leaves no doubt at all that he is advocating a multiple heliocentric system, with each sun at the centre of a vortex of rotating fluid matter which carries its planets along with it.

Descartes' defence of this system, which is the same as the system proposed in *Le Monde*, begins with the fact that our perception of the apparent rest or motion of the planets is relative to our own rest or motion, and we may be unable to tell whether, and to what degree, the cause of their apparent motion is a motion which we undergo, but of which we may be unaware, or whether it is due to a motion in what we are observing. Various astronomical hypotheses have been devised to account for the phenomena, Descartes tells us, 'without considering whether they conformed to the truth' (art. 15). The Ptolemaic system – the paradigm geocentric system – is rejected on the grounds that it fails to account for the telescopically observed phases of Venus, which are only explicable if Venus orbits the Sun. He notes that the Copernican and Tychonic systems account for the observations equally, but, whereas Copernicus has the Earth move, Tycho can see no physical rationale for this, so he attempts to devise a system in which the Earth is stationary. In fact, Descartes argues, if we adhere to his conception of motion, the Earth in Tycho's system has more motion than it does in that of Copernicus (art. 18, and in detail in arts. 38–9).

In the system Descartes proposes, we must assume that the Sun 'resembles fire in its motion and the fixed stars in its situation' (art. 21). Fire is simply the very rapid motion of the small particles of 'a very fluid and very mobile matter', for it is only if we construe it as such that we

[10] See Steven J. Dick, *Plurality of Worlds: The Origins of the Extraterrestrial Life Debate from Democritus to Kant* (Cambridge, 1982) chs. 3 and 4 on the background. For details of Bruno, see Koyré, *From the Closed World to the Infinite Universe*; Paul Henri Michel, *The Cosmology of Giordano Bruno* (Paris, 1973); Sidney Thomas Greenberg, *The Infinite in Giordano Bruno* (New York, 1978).

[11] Kuhn points out the lacuna in public defences of the infinity of the world in *The Copernican Revolution*, 289.

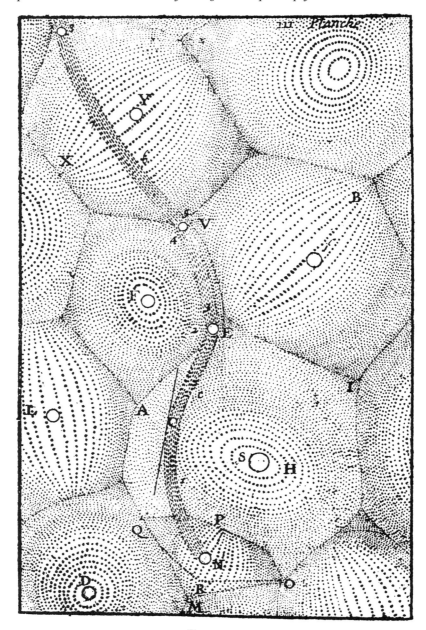

Figure 5.2

can understand (in mechanical terms) how fire is able to cause the disintegration of bodies. The parts move only in relation to one another, however, not as a whole, for the motion that constitutes fire is not that of the transportation of bodies. As for the total motion or transportation of the Sun, 'we can judge that it resembles the fixed stars in that it does not move from one place in the heaven to another'. The Sun, like each of the fixed stars, must be surrounded by a vast space: in Figure 5.2, for example, S is the Sun, while F and *f* are fixed stars, 'and we will understand that numerous others exist, above, below, and beyond the plane of this figure, scattered throughout all the dimensions of space' (art. 23).

The idea of indefinitely many local solar systems is a distinctive feature of Descartes' account – compared for example with those of Copernicus, Kepler, or Galileo – but so too, though to a lesser extent, is the idea of celestial bodies moving in a fluid, as opposed to empty space. Article 24 reads:

We must acknowledge that the matter of the heavens, like that which forms the Sun and the fixed stars, is fluid. This is an opinion that is now commonly held by all astronomers, because they see that otherwise it is almost impossible to give a satisfactory explanation of the phenomena of the planets.

That a fluid medium should have been 'commonly held by all astronomers' is possibly an exaggeration, but it is close to the truth. There had indeed been a move to interpret the crystalline spheres in fluid terms, and, with the breakdown of the sharp distinction between physical and astronomical questions, by the early decades of the seventeenth century this does seem to have been a widespread view.[12] For many it was a way of keeping the crystalline spheres in the wake of Tycho's demonstration that comets pass through the orbits of planets, which rules out shells of ice or crystal maintaining them in their orbits. The liquefaction of the crystalline spheres was a relatively painless way of rethinking the question of what kept planets and the fixed stars in their orbits, especially for those who accepted some form of geocentric theory.[13] But there was also an attraction for someone like Descartes, who wanted to account for all physical processes in terms of a physical theory that restricted physical interaction to contact action. Indeed, in Descartes' case the motivation for postulating a fluid medium is even stronger, because he

[12] See William H. Donahue, 'The Solid Planetary Spheres in Post-Copernican Natural Philosophy', in Robert S. Westman, ed., *The Copernican Achievement* (Berkeley, 1975), 244–75.

[13] Francis Bacon is a case in point: see my 'The Role of Matter Theory in Baconian and Cartesian Cosmologies', *Perspectives in Science* 8 (2000), 201–22.

has a well-developed theory of how bodies behave in fluids. By contrast, his rules of collision, which might well be used to provide a model for bodies colliding in an otherwise empty space, have no bearing on the motion of separated bodies.

PLANETARY MOTION

It is fluids, rather than the bodies embedded in them, that actually do the work in Descartes' account of planetary motion, and article 25 announces that 'the heavens carry with them all the bodies that they contain'. In particular, the fluid heavens carry the Earth along, but it is at rest with respect to this fluid and, therefore, on Descartes' kinematic definition of motion and rest, which relates them only to contiguous bodies, it is also at rest in some more absolute sense: note, however, that, whereas we have been told that the Sun 'does not move from one place to another' (art. 21), in the case of the Earth, we are told that 'the Earth is at rest in its heaven which nevertheless carries it along' (art. 26). When, in article 29, Descartes explains in what sense no motion must be attributed to the Earth, he distinguishes between the term as vulgarly understood and the precise use of the term, and concludes that in neither case can motion be attributed to the Earth. On the vulgar use of the term, people determine motion in terms of points on the Earth considered to be motionless, and in this case it would be proper to talk of the other planets as moving but not the Earth. On the precise definition, it would be wrong to conclude from the fact that the Earth 'floats in a fluid heaven whose parts are extremely mobile and that the fixed stars always remain in the same position relative to one another' that we could treat these fixed stars as motionless and use this to establish that the Earth moves, for the fixed stars are not contiguous with the Earth, and therefore cannot be used to determine motion.

Descartes' account of the motion of the Earth has seemed disingenuous to many commentators. In *Le Monde* he had set out a cosmology in which the Earth clearly moved around the Sun, but here he seems to be offering the same theory while denying, albeit in a confusingly prolix way, the single most contentious outcome of that theory, namely that the Earth moves. The most common explanation for this is that the Roman Inquisition's 1633 condemnation of Galileo, which was the reason for Descartes abandoning publication of *Le Monde*, caused him to disguise his Copernicanism: and this he did, not by revising the substantive natural philosophy of *Le Monde*, but by providing a relativist gloss on that account, thus protecting himself from possible condemnation.[14]

I do not believe that this can be the correct explanation. In the first place, Descartes' definition of motion is indeed complex but, as we have seen, we can reconstruct the motivation behind the attempt to provide something purely kinematic, and it derives primarily from his own concern with providing foundational notions which are clear and distinct. On Descartes' schema, the Earth has no power to move itself, and even if it did, it would not move in a circle, but in a straight line. It moves in a circle because it is dragged along by the surrounding fluid, something whose motion it does not affect in any way. Does this nevertheless mean it moves? That depends on what idea of motion one uses. We must remember here that the Aristotelian notion employed by Scholastic writers was not at all an intuitively clear notion, and indeed was unintelligible in some of the standard definitions, and also that, when pressed, there was no universally accepted understanding of motion. The Earth certainly moves relative to the Sun, particularly if one thinks of it in dynamic terms, as we shall see, and there is a force which Descartes associates with rotation, which acts radially out from the centre of the rotation, which is present in the Earth and which would not be present if the Earth were not revolving, but this is a revolution relative to the Sun, not relative to the fluid carrying the body:

If, in spite of this, conforming to common usage, we seem further on to attribute some motion to the Earth, it will have to be remembered that we are speaking improperly, in the way in which it is sometimes possible to say, of passengers who lie sleeping in a ship, that they nevertheless go from Calais to Dover, because the vessel takes them there. (art. 29)

The thrust of Descartes' argument is not a semantic one, however. It is that the claim that the Earth does not move has been based upon a completely misconceived understanding of motion, which in turn rests upon fundamental misconceptions about space and matter. Once these three fundamental misconceptions have been corrected, the gulf between the original context in which the claim about the Earth being at rest is made, a context which Descartes argues was a complete mess, and the kinematics of rest and motion in Cartesian natural philosophy, is so great that no real dispute about the Earth's motion is possible. All

---

[14] This has been by far the predominant view, and I defended it myself, on grounds which are no longer evident to me, in my *Descartes, An Intellectual Biography*. Dissenters, whose ranks I now join, include Garber and Des Chene.

one can do is to point to the complexities (quite genuine complexities in Descartes' account) of determining motion, and this is exactly what Descartes does.

Second, if Descartes did indeed want to disguise his 'Copernican-ism', his rejection of a universe in which the Earth is at the centre, then Figure 5.2 and the cognate figures of his cosmos scattered through-out Part III would have immediately undermined the project: could Figure 5.2, with the planets rotating around S, the Sun, possibly be con-strued as geocentric? It is clearly a picture of locally heliocentric systems. Not only that, but the way in which they are depicted suggests something physical and tangible, by contrast with the quasi-geometrical diagrams that one finds in Copernicus or Tycho Brahe. Nowhere does Descartes suggest that the whole cosmos rotates around the Earth, and, in any case, if the Sun rotated around the Earth in our solar system, wouldn't parity suggest that the suns in other solar systems rotated around one of their planets? There is no way in the world that the doctrine of the *Principia* could be taken as being ambiguous on the question of heliocentrism. Indeed, the idea of locally heliocentric systems, an idea in which our solar system has no precedence over any other, harbours far more rad-ical consequences for established natural philosophy and theology than heliocentrism – Article 34 of the 1277 Condemnation tells us explicitly that 'the first cause cannot make more than one world' – and Descartes will have no hesitation in drawing out and condoning some of these con-sequences in his discussion of the formation of the Earth later in Part III and in Part IV.

The planetary model that Descartes will operate with is set out in article 30:

Let us assume that the matter of the heavens, in which the planets are situated, revolves unceasingly, like a vortex having the Sun as its centre, and that those of its parts that are close to the Sun move more quickly than those further away, and that all planets (among which we include the Earth) always remain suspended among the same parts of this celestial matter. For by that alone, and without any other devices, all their phenomena are easily understood. Thus if some straws are floating in the eddy of a river, where the water doubles back on itself and forms a vortex as it swirls, we can see that it carries them along and makes them move in circles with it. Further, we can often see that some of these straws rotate about their own centres, and that those that are closer to the centre of the vortex that contains them complete their circle more rapidly than those that are further away from it. Finally, we see that, although these whirlpools always attempt a circular motion, they practically never describe perfect circles, but sometimes become too great in width or in length. Thus we can easily imagine that all the same things happen to the planets; and this is all we need to explain all their remaining phenomena.

The planets are carried in a vortex around the Sun, with their periods approximately proportional to their distance from the Sun, but two of the planets, the Earth and Jupiter, also have moons that Descartes is aware of (four of Jupiter's moons having been discovered by Galileo in 1609), and he explains the motion of these in terms of vortices as well, the period of the moons of Jupiter again being proportional to their distance from the centre (art. 33). He is careful to note, however, that the centres of planets will not always necessarily be in exactly the same plane, and that the orbits they describe will not always be perfectly circular (art. 34). On the first question, variation of the planets in latitude, he notes slight variations from the ecliptic (the plane of the Earth's orbit) in the planes of other planets, but points out that all these planes pass through the centre of the Sun (art. 35). On the second question, the longitudinal motion of the planets, he notes that the planets appear more distant from the Sun at particular times in their orbits (art. 36). It is possible that Descartes knew of Kepler's work on planetary orbits, since Beeckman was studying Kepler carefully from the middle of 1628 and there is some reason to think that he showed this material to Descartes at their meetings at the end of 1628 and early 1629,[15] but, if he did, there is no evidence that Descartes is referring to elliptical orbits here when he talks of orbits not being perfectly circular. It is true that in article 153 he talks of the shape of the orbit of the Moon as 'coming close to that of an ellipse', but he never extends this to the orbits of the planets, and in any case what he is referring to here is not a strict ellipse, which has two foci, but rather a shape distorted so that it resembles an ellipse, but still has a single centre. We are in the realm of a mix of mechanics and matter theory here, where contingencies, not precise mathematics, determine the shapes of orbits. Planets are always attempting to move in circular orbits, article 157 points out, 'but inasmuch as all the bodies in the universe are contiguous and act on one another, the motion of each is affected by the motions of all the others, and therefore varies in innumerable ways'.

This is evident in Descartes' dismissal of the detailed observations and calculations of Tycho and others, which placed comets between the Earth and the Sun. Descartes' view is that they must be located outside the orbit of Saturn (considered to be the outermost planet in Descartes'

---

[15] See John Schuster, *Descartes and the Scientific Revolution, 1618–1634*, 2 vols. (Ann Arbour, Mich., 1977), II. 566–79.

time), and his reasons for holding this depend not upon more detailed observations or more detailed calculations, but upon the observation that they

require this extremely vast space between the sphere of Saturn and the fixed stars in order to complete all their journeys, for these are so varied, so immense, and so dissimilar to the stability of the fixed stars and to the regular revolutions of the planets around the Sun, that they seem inexplicable by any laws of nature without this space. (art. 41)

In other words, the underlying mechanical and matter–theoretic principles of Cartesian cosmology require that they be the objects most distant from the centre of our solar system and, as we shall see when Descartes comes to discuss comets in detail (arts. 126–39), that the assumed mass or size of these objects is also determined wholly by these principles.

Descartes fully realises what is at issue here, and in effect he defends his general procedure in telling us that if what he deduces, from his basic principles or causes, 'is in exact agreement with all natural phenomena, then it seems that it would be an injustice to God to believe that the causes of the effects that are in nature and which we have thus discovered are false' (art. 43). He talks of deducing these 'in a mathematical sequence', by which he presumably means synthetically, from first principles, since there is no mathematical demonstration of any kind in the *Principia*.[16] The crucial phrase is that about an injustice to God, which is a clear signal that what is at issue is our starting out from clear and distinct principles, and proceeding in a way that preserves this clarity and distinctness: if we can do this then, as was made clear in the *Meditationes* and in Part I of the *Principia*, we will not go astray, because God has guaranteed that what we perceive clearly and distinctly is true. Nevertheless, Descartes is careful to point to the hypothetical nature of his own enterprise: *if* we start from clear and distinct principles and proceed in the appropriate way then we cannot go wrong, but, of course, not everyone is going to take Descartes' word for it that his principles actually satisfy these criteria, so he is content to have them treated as hypotheses, so long as we recognise that what he will deduce from them will 'agree entirely with the phenomena' (art. 44).

CELESTIAL MATTER AND THE TRANSMISSION OF LIGHT

One reason that these disclaimers come at this point is that Descartes is now about to present his matter theory, and this is something for

---

[16] On this question, see Garber, 'A Different Descartes', 113–30.

which he cannot plausibly claim anything more than a hypothetical status. In beginning his discussion of matter theory, he notes those basic principles which he takes himself to have established: the homogeneity and divisibility of matter, and the conservation of motion (that is, size × speed). What remains to be done is to determine the size of the parts into which this matter is divided, the speed at which they move, and the shape of the loops in which they move (art. 46). There are an infinite number of possibilities here, so Descartes proposes we make a number of assumptions on these questions, and see whether these assumptions enable us to deduce the phenomena as they appear.

The first assumption is that God divided matter into parts of a single size, the average of the various sizes of the parts of matter that now exist. Second, we assume that he introduced into the universe the same total amount of matter that it still contains. Finally, we assume that God

caused them all to begin to move with equal force, [1] each one separately around its own centre, by which means they formed a fluid body, such as I judge the heavens to be, and [2] also several together around certain other centres equidistant from each other, arranged in the universe as we see the centres of the fixed stars to be now, as well as around other more numerous points, equal in number to the planets. Thus, for example, he transported all the matter which is in the region AEI [Fig. 5.2] all together around the centre S, and, similarly, transported all the parts of matter that occupied the space AEV around the centre F, and so on, so that these parts formed as many vortices as there are now celestial bodies in the world.

Although the parts of matter in the universe cannot begin by having a spherical shape, their rotation, and the consequent breaking off of their corners, gradually wears down their shape so that they become spherical. However, not everything can be spherical in a plenum, and the broken corners and edges of the original parts of matter must fill the regions between these spheres, and in order to do this they must be extremely tiny, as well as being very active, for in the process of being broken off the original pieces they must have acquired significant speed, because they are driven by the larger parts from which they initially derive through narrow gaps, and 'we can see that by closing a bellows quite slowly, we force the air out of it quite rapidly' (art. 51). Moreover, these very small parts of matter – 'subtle matter' in Descartes' terminology – have a large surface area in proportion to their volume. Both the degree of activity and the large surface area : volume ratio turn out to be mechanically important properties, since both of these can affect the solidity of a body (art. 125). This is of great importance, since it means that once we leave the idealised context of the rules of collision, the quantity of motion that a body has is a function of more than size × speed: the degree of agitation of subtle matter is, in fact, significantly greater than the product of its size and speed.[17] Descartes has no way of quantifying the extra quantity of motion generated by these new factors, yet without them, as he realises, he cannot construct a viable cosmology.

In fact, as we saw in the discussion of *Le Monde*, it is not just cosmology but, above all, his optics that dictates what the different sizes of matter are going to be. Descartes distinguishes between three sizes of parts of matter, or 'elements' as he terms them (art. 52). The first is subtle matter, extremely fine and active, the second is the spherical globules from which subtle matter derives in the process of rubbing and grinding. A third kind is now introduced, composed of especially bulky parts. Descartes maintains that everything is composed of these three elements: 'the Sun and the fixed stars of the first, the heavens of the second, and the Earth, the planets, and the comets of the third'. Moreover, these three elements are sufficient to provide the material basis for Descartes' optics, for 'the Sun and the fixed stars emit light, the heavens transmit it, and the Earth, the comets, and the planets reflect it'.

As a significant amount of subtle matter is formed, more than is needed to fill the area between the parts of second matter, the globules (*boules*) of second matter begin to be pushed radially outwards through the action of centrifugal force, and the excess subtle matter takes its place in the more central regions, ultimately forming the Sun S and the fixed stars F and *f* (Fig. 5.2). Here we have the elements of Descartes' account of the production and transmission of light. Using the example of the stone in a sling to demonstrate the existence of a radial tendency away from the centre, he sets out to explain how the light from the disc of the Sun is passed to the eye of an observer on Earth. A globule at F (Fig. 5.3) is pushed by all those in the cone DFB but not by those outside the cone, so that if the space F were void, all those globules in the space DFB would advance to fill it (art. 62). Light is the effect of pressure in the globules, and an eye placed at F would receive impulses originating at all points between B and D, so that the whole disc of the Sun is visible. Note that this pressure is transmitted instantaneously, and there is no interference between the globules, a point that can be illustrated if we imagine a vessel

---

[17] See Edward Slowik, 'Perfect Solidity: Natural Laws and the Problem of Matter in Descartes' Universe', *History of Philosophy Quarterly* 13 (1996), 187–204.

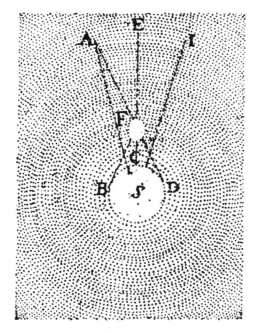

Figure 5.3

BFD containing balls of lead (Fig. 5.4), in which we make an opening at F, so that the balls descend by the force of their own weight. As soon as ball 1 moves, so, at exactly the same time do 2, 2 and 3, 3, 3, but none of the others. Moreover, it is the pressure, not the motion of the balls that does the work, and 'the force of light does not consist in any duration of motion, but only in the pressing or first preparation of motion, even

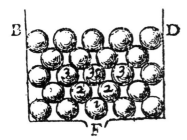 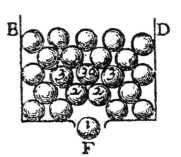

Figure 5.4

though actual motion may not result from this pressure' (art. 63). Light is, in short, a pressure caused by a tendency to centrifugal motion.

VORTEX THEORY

Descartes' cosmos is one of interlocking vortices, and like any interlocking mechanism, such as a system of gears, consideration must be given to the conditions under which the parts interact in order that the whole system does not grind to a halt because of opposed motions acting against one another. Since the system of crystalline spheres had been rejected on the grounds that such a physical structure was not compatible with the observed motion of celestial bodies, it is clearly encumbent on Descartes to show how his vortex proposal is compatible with such observed motions, particularly with the regular, continued motions of these bodies.

The first constraint on vortices is that they cannot touch at the poles, because if they did, and they were rotating in the same direction, their motions would be combined, whereas if they were rotating in opposite directions, their motions would cancel out. Consequently, what we would expect, and what is evident from the representation in Figure 5.2, is that the poles of some vortices touch the equators of others, and, where this is not possible, they at least have their poles as near as possible to the equator of contiguous vortices (arts. 65–7). The distribution of fixed stars in the sky suggests that the vortices are not all of equal size, but because of the way in which light is propagated, namely radially from the centre of a vortex, we can deduce that they must all be at the centre of vortices. While they are isolated in some respects from one another, however, there is a flow of subtle matter, on a cosmic scale, between vortices. What happens, in brief, is that subtle matter enters the vortex at the poles, moving to the centre and from there outwards towards the equator, where it meets the poles of other vortices and passes into these. In Figure 5.5, for example, the solar vortex AYBM rotates on its axis AB, while the neighbouring vortices K, O, L, and C rotate on their axes TT, YY, ZZ, and MM. The subtle matter from vortices K and L is able to enter at poles A and B, and that which is spun around axis AB will be expelled at Y and M, passing on to O and C, from where it will move to the centre of the vortex. The globules of second matter, however, being bulkier, are unable to conserve their motion in passing from the equator of one vortex to the pole of another (art. 70), and they end up being pushed out from the centre, so that a permanent reservoir of subtle matter is formed, which constantly turns on its axis. This is the Sun (art. 72).

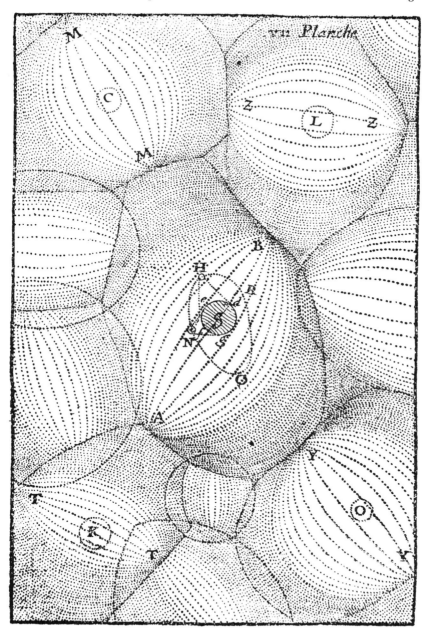

Figure 5.5

One might think that the further from the centre of the vortex a body is, the more quickly it moves; and this will indeed be an assumption in Descartes' account of the motion of comets. However, he also knew that Mercury rotates more quickly than Saturn, so speed of motion cannot be a simple function of distance from the Sun. What is needed to save the appearances here is a twofold mechanism, and Descartes had already provided this in *Le Monde*.[18] What he argued was that the closer globules of second matter are to the centre of the vortex, the smaller and faster they are. But this only holds up to the orbit of the outermost planet, Saturn. Beyond Saturn, the globules move outwards with added increments in speed (art. 82). The reason for this is that there is an artificial augmentation of the speed of the globules in the region between the Sun and Saturn, caused by the rotation of the Sun, which causes bodies contiguous to its surface to rotate more rapidly, accelerating those contiguous to these as well, but to a slightly lesser degree, and so on out to Saturn, where the effect finally peters out. The result is that, as one moves both inwards from Saturn towards the Sun, and outwards from Saturn towards the periphery, the speed of the globules increases, and it follows from this that globules nearer the Sun must be smaller than those further away, because if they were the same size they would have more centrifugal force, in which case they would be projected outwards beyond the latter (art. 85).[19]

Subtle matter is not completely uniform in size and agitation, something that Descartes puts down to the fact that it is formed from rubbings and scrapings. Some of the larger parts of this first element are able to join together, and in the process of doing this they transfer motion to the smaller parts. The former will be found predominantly flowing in a straight line from the poles to the centre of the vortex, whereas the smaller parts, because they are smaller and more agitated, are able to circulate throughout the vortex. The larger parts of the first element have to pass around the tightly packed globules of the second element, and they become twisted into grooved threads, those coming from opposite poles being twisted in opposite directions, that is, having left- and right-handed screws (art. 91), a point that is going to be important in his account of magnetism in Part IV.

Grooved particles also play a key role in the account of the formation of sunspots. Descartes' provision of two mechanisms for dealing with the fact that bodies beyond the orbit of Saturn need to increase in speed the

---

[18] AT XI. 53–6.
[19] Aiton, *The Vortex Theory of the Planetary Motions* (63 n. 78), notes that this implies that the stability of the vortex requires that the centrifugal force must not decrease with distance from the centre.

further out they lie, whereas bodies between Saturn and the Sun need to decrease in speed the further out they are from the centre, is successful as far as it goes, but there is an extra problem that Descartes had not attempted to deal with in *Le Monde*, namely that sunspots move more slowly than any of the planets, which seems to contradict the theory that the Sun rotates so rapidly it accelerates the fluid surrounding it. His response to this, the postulation of a solar atmosphere that slows down the spots and extends as far as Mercury (art. 148), adds a third mechanism on top of the other two, and has the unfortunate effect of beginning to make these mechanisms look like they are piling up merely to save the phenomena, a core criticism of the epicycles that heliocentrism was designed to eradicate. Sunspots are crucial to Descartes' account, however, as indeed they were to the physical defence of heliocentrism, being an indication both of the motion of the Sun and of the corruptibility of the heavens. The key to their formation on Descartes' account is the grooved particles of subtle matter.

These grooved particles, as we have just seen, move to the centre of the vortex. On account of their relatively small degree of agitation and their irregular surfaces, they easily lock together to form large masses at the surface of the star from which they emerge. Because of their size and small degree of agitation, they 'resist that action in which we said earlier that the force of light consists' (art. 94) and as a result they appear as a spot on the surface of the Sun. Descartes compares the process by which they are formed to the boiling of water which contains some substance which resists motion more than the water: it rises to the surface on boiling to form a scum, which, by a process of agglutination, comes to acquire the character of the third element. These spots can cover the whole surface of a star and cause it to slowly disappear, and very occasionally the fine matter in such a covered star can break to the surface so it suddenly shines brightly, as was the case, Descartes maintains, with the 'new star' (supernova) observed by Tycho Brahe in Cassiopeia in 1572 (arts. 104–114). Indeed, this account provides an explanation for why some stars can alternately appear and disappear, and why an entire vortex may occasionally be destroyed by being absorbed by other vortices.

COMETS, PLANETS, AND MOONS

Vortices are destroyed when the stars at their centre become occluded by spots. When the star remains free from spots, the vortex of which it is the centre cannot be destroyed, but if it becomes covered in spots, then how long it will last depends on how much it hinders the action of contiguous vortices. In Figure 5.2, for example, the location of vortex N is such that it impedes vortex S, and as its central star becomes more covered in spots, it will be swept up by vortex S (art. 116). A different case is that represented in Figure 5.6, where vortex C is situated between

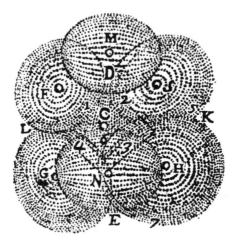

Figure 5.6

four vortices S, F, G, and H, and (above these) M and N. So long as the forces of these six surrounding vortices remain equal, vortex C cannot be completely destroyed, no matter how occluded by spots its central star is. Equilibrium between the other vortices will keep C in existence (art. 177), but the universe is a place of violent activity and nothing in it will remain in equilibrium for ever (art. 118). As the star, through occlusion, becomes less and less active, the size of the vortex diminishes until finally one of the contiguous vortices engulfs it. The imagery here is that of epidemics, and it serves to force home Descartes' very radical alternative to the incorruptible heavens of the Aristotelian/Ptolemaic picture. The Cartesian universe is one in which stars die through a natural process of formation of spots, and as a result of this whole solar systems collapse. These processes are occuring all the time, and in theory are just as likely to occur in our solar system as in any other. It scarcely needs remarking that this is hardly the theory of someone who is seeking to placate the Roman Inquisition.[20]

---

[20] The theory that ours was not the only solar system was singled out in many of the condemnations of Cartesianism. Proposition 5 of the Condemnation of the Faculty of Theology at Louvain, 1662,

When vortex N (Fig. 5.2) collapses, the agglutinated material of its former central star, which is now largely constituted of the solid matter that makes up the third element, is carried into vortex S, and it is pushed towards the centre of S by the faster moving globules at the periphery. It continues in this trajectory until it reaches a level where it has acquired a degree of agitation – which here seems to be synonymous, in kinematic language, with its degree of speed – equal to that of the surrounding globules. If this level is further out than Saturn, the body will become a comet. If it has passed beyond Saturn, however, it will become a planet.

The path of a comet is depicted in Figure 5.2. Beginning at N, it moves in the direction of C, at which it is tangential to the circle described by the globules there. Now since the comet has been led to this point by globules that are faster than those at C, the body has more force to continue in a straight line than do the surrounding bodies, so it will move along the curve C2, which passes between the circle and the straight line that is the tangent to it at C. This occurs because as soon as it has left C, it encounters matter of the second element which moves a little more quickly than that at C, and this causes the body to deviate from the straight line; its speed is increased by this matter, which causes it to deviate further, and the resultant trajectory is C2 (art. 126). Moreover, by the time it reaches E, it has enough agitation to pass into another vortex and to continue its motion, propelled in the same way by the surrounding fluid. The subsequent discussion of comets (arts. 128–39) sets out to show how this account can be accommodated to the observational information on comets, and it does this remarkably well. Comets appear and reappear without 'any rule known to us', which fits well with Descartes' account, since the comet is only visible during its period in our solar system (because, unlike stars, it does not generate light but only reflects it), during which time it describes a curved path. An explanation for the tails of comets is also offered in terms of refraction (arts. 133–9), but without any recognition that the tails always point away from the Sun.

Bodies that pass beyond the orbit of Saturn finally reach a layer where they have the same force to continue in their motion as the particles

condemns the claim that any world would have to have the same kind of matter as ours. Article 6 of the Congregation of the Priests of the Oratory, General Congregation of the Oratorians Residing in Paris, 1678, condemns the claim that 'there is no repugnance in God's creating several worlds at the same time'. Proposition 13 of the Prohibited Propositions of the Fifteenth General Congress of the Society of Jesus, 1706, condemns the claim that 'beyond the heavens, there really exists a space filled by bodies or by matter'. I take these from the extracts of condemnations given in the Appendix in Roger Ariew, John Cottingham, and Tom Sorell, *Descartes' Meditations: Background Source Materials* (Cambridge, 1998), 252–60.

of the surrounding fluid in that layer (art. 140). This force is a function
of the density of the body, and bodies of different density will revolve
at different distances from the Sun, the most dense having the largest
orbits: and indeed the explanation for the fact that the moon always
turns the same side to the Earth is given in terms of that side being less
dense than the far side. The stability of each planetary orbit is secured
through the fact that the planet is only in equilibrium in that orbit and
cannot move either away from the centre or towards it. If the planet
were to move away from the centre, it would encounter larger slower
particles which would decrease its speed and make it fall back towards the
centre, whereas if it were to move towards the centre it would encounter
smaller faster particles which would augment its force and push it from
the centre (art. 140). Once in a stable orbit, the planet would simply be
swept along by the fluid in which it was embedded. As we have seen,
in his treatment of the stone in a sling, Descartes treats the circular
motion of the stone as a natural motion, as being uncaused by anything
else (such as a tangential force), and the same holds in planetary orbits.
Accounting for the speed of the planets requires three mechanisms, as we
saw above: first, speed increases as a function of distance from the centre;
second, bodies between the centre and the orbit of Saturn are artificially
accelerated by the rotation of the Sun, an acceleration which decreases
as we move out from the centre until it finally dies out completely by the
time we reach Saturn; and, third, speed decreases between the surface
of the Sun and the orbit of Mercury due to a retarding solar atmosphere.
As for the shape of the orbit, the solar vortex is distorted by the unequal
pressures of neighbouring vortices, so that the planet does not describe
an exact circle but will describe a wider loop where the pressure is less
(art. 141). Finally, the diurnal rotation of a planet is something that it
acquires when it is first formed, and which it retains thereafter, although
there is a slight diminution in speed due to the action of the surrounding
medium (art. 140), because, unlike its orbital motion, the diurnal motion
of the Earth is not due to the motion of the fluid medium and may act
contrary to it. In his discussion of light, Descartes had indicated that
light corpuscles do not lose their rotational velocity any more than they
lose their speed,[21] and the same conditions seem to hold here.

The third kind of celestial body formed from the occluded stars of
collapsed vortices is the planetary satellites. In article 33, Descartes

---

[21] Descartes to Ciermans, 23 March 1639; AT II. 74: 'I don't know why you think the corpuscles
of celestial matter do not maintain the rotation that gives rise to colours as well as the rectilinear
motion in which light consists, for we can grasp both equally well by our reasoning.'

talks of the two planets having moons, namely Jupiter and the Earth, each being at the centre of their own vortex, which carries its satellites around with it. The implication is that planets without satellites – and no other satellites had been discovered – lacked such vortices, but it is difficult to tell how they differ from planets with satellites, since they have been formed in the same way, from occluded rotating stars. Presumably, they have rotated since they were stars, and their ejection from the centre of another vortex does not seem to impede their rotation (see Part IV art. 8). The natural reading here, I suggest, is that each planet maintains its own vortex (allowing the slight diminution due to the surrounding medium mentioned in art. 140), but that only two of them have captured bodies which subsequently revolve around the planet. Satellites are of the same material as comets and planets, however, and they have reached levels closer to the centre than Saturn, so the question arises why they do not behave like planets, finding their own layer in the fluid and being moved around the Sun by it.

Descartes suggests two possibilities as to the origins of the Earth/Moon relationship. Either the Moon moved towards the Earth before the Earth began to orbit the Sun (he considers that this is what happened in the case of Jupiter), or, more likely, the Moon, having the same density as the Earth but a greater force of agitation, had to revolve at the same distance from the centre as the Earth but more quickly. Both these possibilities are accounted for in the model that Descartes proposes (art. 149). Letting S be the Sun, and T be the Earth (see Fig. 5.7), the circle NTZ is the appropriate orbit for the two bodies. Assume the Moon travels along NTZ. Wherever it begins its motion, it will sooner or later arrive at A, close to the Earth, because it moves more quickly than the Earth. At A it will encounter resistance from the Earth's atmosphere ('air and sky'), which extends to there from T, and it will be deflected towards B, because this requires less deviation from a straight line than deflection towards D. While moving from A to B, 'all celestial matter contained in the space ABCD, which carries the Moon along, will be rotated around centre T like a vortex. This will also cause the Earth to rotate on its axis, while at the same time all these things will be transported around centre S along the circle NTZ.' Here, contrary to article 33, it sounds as if it is the motion of the Moon around ABCD that causes the vortex. It is impossible to tell which of these accounts of the origin of the vortex Descartes has in mind, possibly both: it is possible that the vortex is initially caused by the rapid rotation of a planet accelerating the fluid matter around it, and the force of this vortex is then

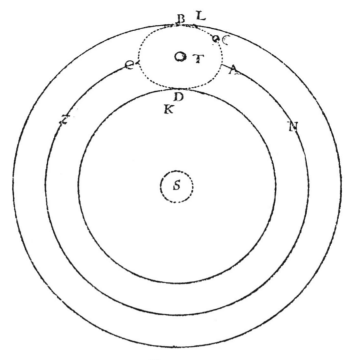

Figure 5.7

strengthened by the rapid revolution (on this interpretation more rapid than the initial speed of the vortex at the periphery) of the Moon at its periphery.

There are undeniably loose ends in Descartes' cosmology, but his vortex theory dominated cosmology before the publication of Newton's *Principia*, and, on the continent, for many years afterwards. Descartes provided the first comprehensive mechanist cosmology, and Newton was well aware that if he was to establish his own system it was Cartesian cosmology that he had to destroy. The General Scholium to the *Principia* begins with the sentence: 'The hypothesis of vortices is beset with many difficulties',[22] and Book II has as one of its principal aims the demolition of Descartes' account of motion in fluids. Unlike that of Descartes, Newton's cosmology, building above all on the work of Galileo and Huygens, starts from the behaviour of an idealised body – a mass-point – in a vacuum, and he treats the planets as moving through a resisting

---

[22] *The Principia*, 939.

medium rather than being carried by the medium. On this basis, he is able to show that in a medium as dense as the body in motion, the body would lose half its motion before it travelled a distance equal to twice its diameter, and that Jupiter would lose a tenth of its motion in thirty days.[23] But Newton's system had one outstanding disadvantage: it postulated the existence of an 'occult force', gravitation, which was postulated to act at a distance. Of course, Newtonians were loath to see this as an 'occult quality',[24] but Descartes had his own explanation of gravitation, as we shall see in the next chapter, which worked in terms of his vortex theory and did not require action at a distance. More than anything else, it is as a consequence of this that the vortex theory received such staunch support well into the eighteenth century. As Bulffinger, winner of the Paris Académie prize of 1728 for his attempts to save the vortex theory, put it: 'Nothing is simpler than the Cartesian vortices; hence I think everything should be tried before they are given up; and if they do not work properly, I should wish them to be changed as little as possible.'[25] Seventeenth-century Cartesians such as Régis could not understand why Newton's advances could not be accommodated to vortex theory, and set out to show (as Descartes himself had suggested) that vortices can be adapted to elliptical shapes if they are squeezed by neighbouring vortices, that the precessions of Mercury and Venus can be explained, that an improved account of the tides can be developed by correlating them with the position of the moon by means of vortices, and so on.[26] Although Descartes' presentation of vortex theory was qualitative and suggestive, later accounts were often very precise and developed with a high degree of mathematical sophistication, the high point probably being Jean Bernoulli's 1730 prize-winning essay on elliptical orbits, in which he derived Kepler's third law from vortex theory, and called into question the mathematics behind Newton's claim that the two were

---

[23] See Westfall, *Force in Newton's Physics*, 510–12; Mouy, *Le Développement de la physique cartésienne*, 239–41; and my 'The Foundational Role of Statics and Hydrostatics in Descartes' Natural Philosophy'.

[24] See Cotes' preface to the second edition of Newton's *Principia*: 'I can hear some people disagreeing with this conclusion and muttering something or other about occult qualities. They are always prattling on and on to the effect that gravity is something occult, and that occult causes are to be banished completely from philosophy. But it is easy to answer them: occult causes are not those causes whose existence is very clearly demonstrated by observations, but only those whose existence is occult, imagined, and not yet proved. Therefore gravity is not an occult cause of celestial motions, since it has been shown from phenomena that this force really exists. Rather, occult causes are the refuge of those who assign the governing of these motions to some sort of vortices of a certain matter utterly fictitious and completely imperceptible to the senses', Newton, *The Principia*, 392.

[25] Cited in J. L. Heilbron, *Electricity in the Seventeenth and Eighteenth Centuries* (New York, 1999), 121.

[26] See Aiton, *The Vortex Theory*, chs. 7–10.

inconsistent.[27] The vast literature defending vortex theory from the publication of Descartes' *Principia* in 1644 to Fontenelle's *Théorie des tourbillons* of 1752, a literature to which some of the greatest mathematicians and natural philosophers of the age contributed, indicates the lasting power of the model that Descartes advocated.

---

[27] See ibid., 214–19.

CHAPTER 6

Principia, *Part IV: The Earth*

In Part IV of the *Principia*, Descartes made the Earth an object of natural–philosophical/scientific investigation for the first time. There had, of course, been theories about such phenomena as earthquakes and volcanic activity, but these were considered – most notably by Aristotle – to be something that affected only the superficial layers of the Earth: the Earth's great mass was inert.[1] As Jacques Roger has put it, Descartes' was 'the first attempt to understand systematically the Earth's structure and its actual topography'.[2] Having not only moved the Earth from the centre of the cosmos, but also made it little more than a piece of refuse from another solar system, Descartes puts himself in a position where he can consider it in the same way as any other concentration of solid matter, and indeed can consider any other planet as being like the Earth. Descartes is not unaware of the radical consequences of what he is advocating. As he points out to Burman:

It is a common habit of men to suppose that they themselves are the dearest of God's creatures, and that all things are therefore made for their benefit. They think their own dwelling place, the Earth, is of supreme importance, that it contains everything that exists, that everything else was created for its sake. But what do we know of what God may have created outside the Earth, on the stars, and so on? How do we know that he has not placed on the stars other species of creature, other lives and other 'men' – or at least beings analogous to men?[3]

Descartes' attempt to account for the formation of the Earth lay at the foundation of a complete transformation of our understanding of the nature of our planet and its age, a transformation that was to have far

---

[1] On theories of the Earth in antiquity and in the Middle Ages, see Clarence J. Glacken, *Traces on the Rhodian Shore* (Berkeley, 1967), chs. 1–7.

[2] Jacques Roger, *Buffon: A Life in Natural History* (Ithaca, 1997), 94. See also his 'The Cartesian Model and its Role in Eighteenth-Century "Theory of the Earth" ', in T. Lennon et al. eds., *Problems of Cartesianism* (Kingston, 1982), 95–112.

[3] AT v. 168.

greater consequences than the removal of the Earth from the centre
of the cosmos. Descartes and his contemporaries took the Earth to be
about six thousand years old, on the grounds of biblical chronology. By
the second half of the eighteenth century, the calculations of Buffon –
whose great *Histoire Naturelle* was prefaced, with obvious Cartesian prece-
dents, by a 'Discourse on Method' followed by 'examples of this method
in the following discourses, the Theory of the Earth, the Formation of
the Planets, and the Generation of Animals'[4] – were putting the figure
at up to ten million years.[5] Although biblical chronology, with its natural disasters such as the Flood, was far more conducive to the idea
of a natural history of the Earth than the cyclical model of history of
the ancients, in which there were no irreversible events in the history
of the Earth,[6] its narrative was a mythological one, and when natural
philosophy replaced biblical chronology it was not only one of the most
important developments in our understanding of the sequence of natural
events at a cosmological level, but a watershed in the establishment of
the autonomy of natural philosophy.[7]

THE NATURE OF THE EARTH

In Part III of the *Principia*, Descartes had explained how the occlusion of
stars by spots – which gradually build up as the star becomes less and less
able to expel the hardened material that forms on it surface – causes the
vortex in which the star is located to collapse, and the occluded star is
forced into a neighbouring vortex, where, moving inwards until it finds
a layer in which it is in equilibrium with the surrounding celestial fluid,
it becomes a planet and is carried around the centre by that fluid. This
account is now used in Part IV as a basis for a hypothetical theory of
the formation of the Earth, in which events are reconstructed so that
the outcome of this process would result in the Earth having exactly the
same features as those it actually has (art. 1). Descartes is interested only
in what kind of physical processes could have resulted in the formation

---

[4] Roger, *Buffon*, 91.
[5] See Paolo Rossi, *The Dark Abyss of Time: The History of the Earth and the History of Nations from Hooke
to Vico* (Chicago, 1984), 107–12, and Roger, *Buffon*, 409–13.
[6] On this contrast see G. W. Trompf, *The Idea of Historical Recurrence in Western Thought: From Antiquity
to the Reformation* (Berkeley, 1979).
[7] The context in which these events occurs is, of course, extremely complex, and there was continuous dispute over the kind of guidance offered by the Bible in the early modern era; see, for
example, Peter Harrison, *The Bible, Protestantism, and the Rise of Natural Science* (Cambridge, 1998),
and Henning Graf Reventlow, *The Authority of the Bible and the Rise of the Modern World* (Philadelphia,
1985).

of the Earth, not in whether it was physical processes or a supernatural act of creation that resulted in its formation:

it will rightly be concluded that the nature of [natural things] is the same as if they had indeed been formed in such a way, although the world was not formed in that way in the beginning, but was created directly by God. (art. 1, French version)

In other words, God having decided to give the Earth the characteristics it has, he could have chosen the physical process that Descartes describes and have got the same result as that he achieved by supernatural means.

The reconstruction of the Earth's formation from a star and its journey into this solar system provide an indication of what its internal constitution must be like. The innermost region of the planet, marked I (see Fig. 6.1), is composed of subtle matter and is of the same consistency

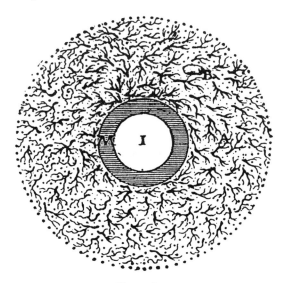

Figure 6.1

as the Sun, except that it is not so pure. The middle region consists of dense material, of a similar consistency to sunspots, which is impervious to the globules of the second element but able to admit grooved particles and other subtle matter. Finally, the outermost region, which is what Part IV is primarily concerned with, consists of particles of the third and, to a lesser extent, second element. Descartes tells us that 'the innermost nature of these particles can be known from the way in which they were generated' (art. 5), leaving us in no doubt that the physical reconstruction he is offering is really the only way to understand how the Earth is composed.

Descartes derives the properties of the particles of third-element matter that predominates on the surface of the Earth from the way in which they are formed. The particles that can be formed from the joining together of subtle matter are much larger than globules, although they are much less active, and unlike globules, which are spherical, they take their shape from the irregular scrapings from which they are formed, and so can form a large range of different shapes (art. 8). Moreover, in the planet's sunny past it was formed from the subtle matter pushed to the centre of the vortex by heavier rapidly moving globules. There was great pressure towards the centre, and this remains the case as the Earth moves out of its own vortex and into that of the Sun, but its internal material constitution is changed by this move, for many globules at the periphery of the Earth which, because of their mass/bulk, were in equilibrium with surrounding layers when they revolved close to the centre, while it was still a star, will no longer be in equilibrium once the Earth has settled into a stable orbit as a planet in our solar system, and they will move towards the centre of the solar system, being replaced by heavier globules. It is this outer region that Descartes is interested in, as the two inner regions of the Earth are covered by a shell of occluded material (art. 13).

The body that emerges from a collapsed vortex, and establishes itself in an orbiting layer of celestial fluid around the Sun, is still unlike the Earth as we know it in many respects, and in articles 14–31 Descartes sets out the four basic kinds of 'action' by which the different kinds of typically terrestrial phenomena are produced: these are the production of transparency by the motion of globular matter, the production of weight or gravity, the production of light, and the production of heat. The 'action' involved here is, of course, purely mechanical, and Descartes employs the mix of kinematic and dynamic terminology that has effectively been in use since matter theory was introduced early in Part III.

Transparency is an effect of the action of celestial globular matter on the particles of terrestrial matter. Globular matter has a high degree of activity, evident in the fact that it is able to revolve around the Sun annually, and around the Earth daily, and in mixing with particles of terrestrial matter its comparatively great activity is able to modify them in various ways. The first of these modifications consists in the opening up of straight passages through terrestrial bodies. The great activity of globular matter means that it is able to realise the tendency of all matter to move in a straight line to a significant degree, so it tends to move through the regions of subtle matter between particles with sufficient force to be able to open up a rectilinear path in some bodies, altering the arrangement of the particles, and thereby making the gap (which is actually a region of subtle matter) suitable for 'the transference of the action of light'. Descartes maintains that all pure liquids (except mercury, the parts of which are too bulky to allow globules through) are transparent, and although the point seems little more than definitional, for any non-transparent liquids – milk, ink, blood – are immediately dubbed impure on the grounds that they have small grains of hard bodies in them, there is support to be had for this view from distillation, which does routinely clarify liquids, and Descartes mentions the related process of the purification of wine in article 18. Transparent solids are accounted for similarly, on the grounds that all transparent solids are always formed from the cooling of transparent liquids, so that the parts have retained the same relative locations, leaving open the passages that formed when they were liquids.[8]

The second action is weight or gravity, and given the intense interest in gravity in the wake of the publication of Newton's *Principia*, Descartes' treatment of the phenomenon took on a great significance. Indeed, it became one of the key issues in disputes over the vortex theory, for, unlike the approach of Kepler and Newton whereby weight or gravity is to be explained in terms of a mutual attraction between heavy bodies and the Earth, Descartes' account of weight is formulated in terms of his vortex theory. He begins with an account of the formation of spherical drops of water, whereby the celestial globules circulate in all directions around the water, exerting equal forces towards the centre at all points. In the same way, the globular matter circulating around the Earth acts inwards towards the centre, giving it a spherical shape and pushing it towards those bodies we call heavy. In other words, the parts of matter do not just naturally cohere: they are pushed together by the action of the surrounding globular matter, which is squeezed to the centre as heavier matter is pushed outwards through centrifugal force, and it is this pressure that is the cause of, indeed is constitutive of, weight or gravity.

---

[8] We shall look at Descartes' account of the manufacture and properties of glass, in articles 124–32, below.

What this means is that weight is not an intrinsic property of bodies: nothing is intrinsically heavy. If the region around the Earth were a void, then bodies would fly off its surface unless they were firmly attached, 'but since there is no such void, and since the Earth is not carried along by its own motion, but is moved by the celestial matter which surrounds it and penetrates all its pores, the Earth has the mode of a body that is at rest' (art. 22).[9] The weight of a terrestrial body is not a function of all the matter flowing around it, however, but only of that matter which moves into the region vacated by the matter moving towards the centre, and which is therefore equal in size to it:

For example, if B is a terrestrial body [Fig. 6.1] suspended in mid-air and united with more particles of the third element than a quantity of air equal to it, and which therefore has fewer or narrower pores in which heavenly matter is contained, then it is evident that if this body B descends towards I, a quantity of air equal to it must ascend into its place. And because this quantity of air contains more celestial matter than there is in B, it is also evident that there must be, in this quantity of air, the force to drive B down. (art. 23)

As regards the third and fourth kinds of action, light and heat, Descartes notes that light, 'being nothing other than a certain pressure that occurs along straight lines drawn from the Sun to the Earth', can exert a pressure through layers of matter and that matter can be agitated by the Sun's rays, although this does not happen in a regular way. This agitation is called heat – or rather, it is what causes the sensation of heat in us – and the heat may remain after the light has ceased. Moreover, because it is an irregular form of agitation, it breaks up practically all terrestrial bodies and causes them to expand.

THE FORMATION OF THE EARTH

As the Earth enters the solar system and moves into the appropriate layer of celestial matter, there will be an exchange of matter between the Earth and the fluid in which it is embedded, the smaller globules on its surface changing places with the heavier globules of the surrounding fluid, a process that forces the third element matter to join together to form large clumps which inhibit the activity of celestial globules. The process is illustrated in Figure 6.2, which represents various stages in the

[9] Unfortunately, as Régis was later to point out, if weight results from circulation of surrounding matter, it should be directed not towards the centre but towards the axis of rotation; Régis, *Système de philosophie*, I. 443.

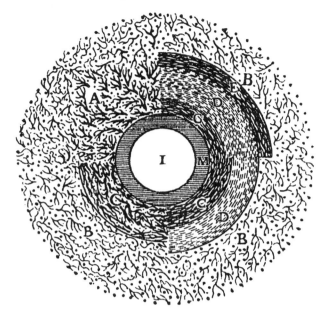

Figure 6.2

Earth's formation, beginning on the left and moving counterclockwise. At first, the highest region of the Earth, A, is divided into two kinds of body, B, which is rare, fluid, and transparent, and C, which is hard, dense, and opaque. The reason for this is that the parts of C have been pressed downwards by celestial globules and have adhered to one another. But C is not completely homogeneous, and under pressure parts of C which are less inclined to bind with one another because of their shape (long as opposed to branching) are forced up and form a separate layer between A and C, namely D, which is neither completely solid like rock nor completely fluid like water. Particles of D, some of which are hard and some flexible, can separate and unite with C, on the one hand, and C itself could separate into several regions as a result of a mixture of different particles. On the other hand, this separation is responsible for the formation of a rind or shell, E, at the interface between D and B. In this way, the make-up of the planets comes to be relatively stable, but, because of the action of the Sun in lighting and heating the Earth, a layer of agitated matter, F (see Fig. 6.3 upper half) is formed beneath E, trapped between two hard layers, and causing fissures in E to occur. As

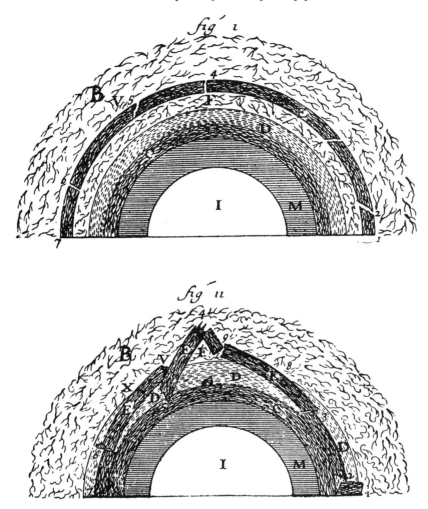

Figure 6.3

depicted in the lower illustration of Figure 6.3, fissures can occasionally erupt violently, emitting the liquid (D) and vapours (F) trapped between the two concentric crusts, causing the thick outer crust to crack and tilt, which is how continents (4 in Fig. 6.3), mountain ranges (8), and oceans (3, 6) are formed. Here, B is air, C is a thick crust from which metals originate, D is water, E is the surface of the Earth, comprising stones, clay, sand, and mud, and F is air (art. 44).

AIR, WATER, EARTH, AND FIRE

The bulk of Part IV of the *Principia* is devoted to what is in many ways a reformulation of the traditional theory of the elements: air (arts. 45–7), water (48–56), earth (arts. 57–79), and fire (80–132). Air is treated very briefly (it would be another ten years before Guericke would demonstrate the elasticity of air in his famous Magdeburg hemispheres, and begin a period of intense interest in decompression). Air comprises particles so separated from one another that their behaviour is completely regulated by the globules of secondary matter. It is more active than the globules, however, and as a consequence requires larger regions for its activity than the globules. This is manifest in the phenomenon of compression, whereby air particles and globules compete for space when their agitation is checked, as it is under compression, attempting 'to drive one another out of their place, and thus together producing the force to occupy a greater space' (art. 47).

Descartes' main interest in water in Part IV lies in the tides. This is a topic which he had investigated in detail in *Le Monde*, writing to Mersenne at the time that accounting for the tides had given him a great deal of trouble, and that while he was not happy with all the details, he did not doubt the success of his account.[10] The tides were one of the keys to the defence of the heliocentric theory for Galileo, as they were one of the best forms of observational evidence for the motion of the Earth, but they were extremely difficult to deal with.[11] A theory of the tides has to account for four cycles[12]: (1) the *daily cycle* with high and low tides recurring at intervals of twelve hours; (2) the *monthly cycle* whereby the tides lag behind 50 minutes each day until they have gone round the clock and are back to their original position; (3) the *half-monthly* cycle with high tides at new and full Moon and low tides at quadratures; and finally, (4) the *half-yearly cycle* with greater tides at the equinoxes than at the solstices.

All of these are explained by Descartes in terms of the vortical motion of celestial matter around the Earth. In Figure 6.4 the Earth is represented as being surrounded by a circulating layer of celestial matter ABCD, its surface being covered by water 1, 2, 3, 4, and this in turn is enveloped by air 5, 6, 7, 8. Because the distance between the Moon, in the position marked, and 6 is greater than between B and 6, the celestial

[10] Descartes to Mersenne [November or December] 1632; AT I. 261.
[11] See William Shea, *Galileo's Intellectual Revolution* (New York, 1972), 172–89.
[12] I follow the useful summary of Shea, *The Magic of Numbers and Motion* (Canton, Mass., 1991), 289.

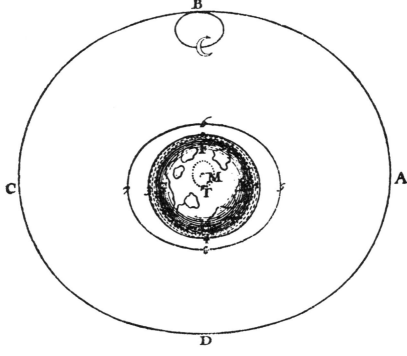

Figure 6.4

matter has to pass a little more quickly between the Moon and 6, and as a result the Earth is pushed a little towards D, so that its centre T moves away slightly from M. Because the air and water surrounding the Earth are fluid bodies, the force that moves the Earth slightly away from M will also move them towards T, acting on them from sides 6, 2 and 8, 4. This causes a compensatory rise at 5, 1 and 7, 3, and hence 'that part which is not at F (below the region B and where the ocean is as shallow as possible) will be at G after six hours (below the region of point C where the ocean is deepest); and after six more hours at H, below the region of point D, and so on' (art. 50). Since the Earth rotates counterclockwise once every twenty-four hours, points 5, 1 and 7, 3 will move giving rise to two high and two low tides daily.

This theory also accounts for the monthly, half-monthly, and half-yearly cycles. Monthly cycles are put down to the fact that the moon makes a full rotation around its axis once every lunar month, so that every six hours it makes 1/120 of its circuit, with the result that the tides do not change precisely every six hours but lag behind approximately twelve minutes. As regards half-yearly cycles, because the axis BD is slightly shorter than the axis AC, the Moon moves more rapidly at B, where it is full, and at D, where it is new, than at A and C, when it is at quadrature (art. 51). Finally, there is also a half-yearly cycle (not mentioned in *Le Monde*) whereby the tides are higher at the equinoxes because 'the moon's plane is near to ecliptic, whereas the Earth's diurnal motion is along the plane of the equator', and the two planes intersect at the equinoxes and are at their greatest distance at solstices (art. 52).

The third of the traditional elements, earth, is dealt with in the context of a discussion of the interior and exterior of the Earth, and here we encounter a form of matter theory of a very traditional Epicurean sort, in which mechanical considerations play no effective role, as it is shape, rather than size, speed, and direction, that drives the discussion. In such cases, explanation just takes the form of an extrapolation from macroscopic structural features of bodies to the microscopic level. The structure of the outer part of the interior shell – C, in Figure 6.3 – for example, is described in terms of branching particles, presumably because the macroscopic analogues (such as chainmail) constitute the most strongly bound material that nevertheless remains porous, and its interior is described in terms of 'smooth, rod-like, polished particles'. There is, of course, no argument for such a structure, and the best Descartes can offer is the statement that 'it is credible' (art. 57). The chemistry of changes near the Earth's core is given a similarly speculative treatment, with acids being formed from the heating of rod-like particles and their transformation into sharp, pointed particles (art. 61). The treatment of the exterior of the Earth – E in Figure 6.3 – is likewise speculative, qualitative, and again consists in an extrapolation from such physical features of macroscopic bodies as their shape and flexibility to the supposed qualities that microscopic particles must have if they are to have the effects that we experience. So, for example, just as the properties of acids are explained in terms of sharp, pointed particles, the properties of sulphur are described in terms of branching particles mingled with acrid juices and metallic particles (art. 76).

The fourth traditional element, fire, is something that Descartes had devoted some considerable attention to in *Le Monde*, and it was a test case of how a mechanical explanation could replace an elemental one. In Part IV, this mechanical construal is, of course, still what lies behind his account, but he chooses to deal here with a range of phenomena where a somewhat contingent mix of matter–theoretical details are called upon to do the main explanatory work: the lava emitted in earthquakes, kindling, the need for fuel, the production of fire through friction, its production by focusing the Sun's rays, its production from violent motion, lightning, phosphorescent illumination, the heat generated in stored hay, the nature of smoke, why alcohol ignites so easily, flammable bodies, gunpowder, charcoal, liquefaction and desiccation by heating. The most extended discussion is of the manufacture of glass (arts. 124–32), and, given the importance of glass for optics, if we were to find a mechanically guided account anywhere in Descartes' treatment of the nature of materials, it would be here, but such an account is well beyond the resources that Descartes (or any of his contemporaries) is able to draw upon, and what he offers is a matter–theoretic account whose mechanical underpinnings play little if any role. The formation of glass from lime is basically a question of irregular angular shapes being blunted, and surfaces being smoothed, through the action of fire. The hardness of glass is put down to the fact that 'it must consist entirely of fairly large and inflexible particles' (art. 127), the French text adding that these particles must themselves be hard, so that we end up with the claim that the reason why glass is hard is that its constituent parts are hard! It transparency is due to the amount of globules present in its structure, replacing those lime particles that have been forced out in heating. Finally, its elasticity when heated is explained in terms of a combination of the resistance to distortion of its pores and from the smooth joining of its particles.

This kind of approach is, of course, wholly qualitative and speculative, but it does have a definite content: it shows a clear commitment to a micro-corpuscularian form of explanation, in stark contrast with Aristotelian natural philosophy. Indeed, the matter theory it offers is very reminiscent of classical atomism, and many of Descartes' contemporaries clearly saw him as developing his basic principles from Democritus and Epicurus.[13] As regards the general thrust of Cartesian natural philosophy, this is an unsustainable claim, and at the end of Part IV he justifies his micro-corpuscularianism by distinguishing it from what he sees to be the objectionable features of classical atomism:

Democritus also imagined certain small bodies, having various shapes, sizes, and movements, from the accumulation and collision of which all perceptible bodies arose, but his method of philosophizing is commonly rejected by all. However, no one ever rejected it on account of the fact that it considers certain bodies that

---

[13] See Garber, *Descartes' Metaphysical Physics*, 119.

are so miniscule that they escape the senses, and which are said to have various sizes, shapes, and movements, because no one can doubt that there are indeed many such bodies, as has just been shown. It has been rejected, first, because it supposed these bodies to be indivisible, for which reason I also reject it. Second, because it imagined that there was a void around these bodies, which I show cannot be the case. Third, because it attributed weight to these bodies, whereas I understand that there is no weight in any body considered in isolation, but only in so far as that body depends on the situation and movement of other bodies, and relates to them. And finally, because it did not show how individual things resulted solely from the encounters of small bodies, or if it showed this about some things, not all of the reasons were consistent with one another. (art. 202)

These objections show the mechanical underpinnings of Descartes' approach to micro-corpuscularianism, and, even though those underpinnings might not be so evident in the kind of matter–theoretic approach he adopts in the cases we have just looked at, it is there in reserve, so to speak, and these reserves are now drawn upon in his treatment of magnetism.

MAGNETISM AND RELATED PHENOMENA

The remainder of Part IV (arts. 133–87) – except for some very brief concluding remarks – offers an extended discussion of magnetism and related phenomena. Descartes' account of magnetism is, along with his cosmology and his account of weight or gravity, part of the centrepiece of his vortex theory. It was, in fact, one of the most successful parts of vortex theory, with Euler, Daniel Bernoulli, and Jean Bernoulli winning Académie prizes in the 1740s for explanations of magnetism that are variations on the Cartesian account.[14] Magnetism was one of the most intractable yet pressing problems for advocates of a mechanist natural philosophy. Renaissance naturalists, whether of Neoplatonic or Aristotelian leanings, had often used magnetism as a paradigm case of an occult force acting at a distance, something wholly resistant to an atomist construal, and they had hoped to model all natural phenomena on it, rejecting any attempt to account for such attraction in terms of contact forces. Gilbert, whose *De magnete* (1600) lay at the fountainhead of seventeenth-century studies of magnetism, Descartes' included, held such a view, for example. Noting the facts that magnetic effluxions were able to penetrate dense bodies, and that when a needle was magnetised nothing physical seemed to have been added to it (its weight, shape, speed were unaffected), he

---

[14] See Heilbron, *Electricity in the Seventeenth and Eighteenth Centuries*, 31 n. 4.

concluded that the magnet is animate and acts in a similar way to the human soul.[15]

Clearly Descartes is having nothing of this, and he had raised a problem with using magnetism to explain other phenomena as early as Rule 9 of the *Regulae*, arguing that we cannot take phenomena such as astral influences and magnetic attraction to be something primitive, and explain other phenomena in terms of them, for they are more poorly understood than what they are invoked to explain.[16] Nevertheless, recourse to magnetic explanations seemed forced upon natural philosophers in a number of areas, not least cosmology. With the removal of the celestial spheres and the rejection of the Aristotelian physics underlying the traditional geocentric cosmology, magnetism provided what many – geocentrists and heliocentrists alike – saw as the key to the understanding of what keeps the planets in a stable harmonious relation to one another and to the Sun: magnetic attraction was what bound them together into a system.[17] Gilbert had provided the model in *De Magnete*, arguing that elemental earth is magnetic and that the Earth itself is, as a consequence, a giant lodestone, which he assumed rotates around its magnetic poles (since he assumed these to be identical with its geographical poles). Magnetic motion was circular, argued Gilbert, and, since the parts of the Earth are magnetic, it is hardly surprising that the Earth has a circular diurnal motion. He was followed by various Jesuit defenders of geocentrism up to the 1660s, and by defenders of heliocentrism such as Stevin, who construed stability in terms of a magnetic attraction between planets, and by Kepler, who argued that the planetary orbits were stable in virtue of a combination of several factors, including the tangential forces generated by their rotation and the Sun's central attraction, which was magnetic. Moreover Galileo, before he developed his account of circular inertia, defended a heliocentric account in terms of magnetic forces.[18]

But, whatever its apparent use, the explanatory force of something as poorly understood as magnetism prevented it from providing anything other than a stopgap measure. Descartes does not use magnetism to explain other phenomena; he sets out to explain it, using the same theory he has used to explain the stability of planetary orbits, the nature of weight,

---

[15] William Gilbert, *De magnete* (London, 1600), Book II, ch. 4.
[16] AT x. 402. See my *Descartes, An Intellectual Biography*, 146–58.
[17] See Stephen Pumfrey, 'Magnetical Philosophy and Astronomy, 1600–1650', in René Taton and Curtis Wilson, eds., *Planetary Astronomy from the Renaissance to the Rise of Astrophysics, Part A: Tycho Brahe to Newton* (Cambridge, 1989), 45–53.
[18] See ibid., 49.

and the formation of solar systems. For Descartes, the only way to deal with magnetism is to mechanise it, because that is the only way we can understand any material process. At the end of his discussion in Part IV, he tells us that he has shown that magnets have 'no qualities so occult, nor effects of sympathy and antipathy so marvellous as to render them inexplicable by the principles of magnitude, size, position, and motion' (art. 187). Descartes was not alone in pressing this view, and Mersenne for one had struggled with the question,[19] as had Gassendi, who proposed the old hooked particles of the Epicureans,[20] but Descartes' was the first mechanistic account of magnetism: and not just the first but the only detailed and remotely plausible mechanistic account.[21]

The core of his account of magnetism – which he develops in the context of the lodestone but then applies to the Earth's magnetism – is the existence of long threaded pores or channels in lodestone which admit grooved particles, depending on whether the particle has a right-hand screw or a left-hand one. These pores are aligned along the polar axes of the lodestone and one set admits grooved particles in one polar direction, the other grooved particles in opposite polar direction. The generation of these grooved particles had been set out in Part III (arts. 87–93). Their grooves derive from the fact that they are squeezed through the interstices of contiguous spherical globules (see Fig. 6.5). As a result

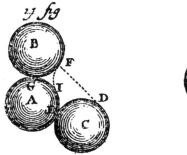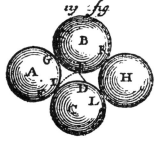

Figure 6.5

[19] See the discussions of magnetism in Marin Mersenne, *Quaestiones in Genesim* (Paris, 1623), cols. 552 and 548, and *La Verité des Sciences* (Paris, 1625), 910–21.
[20] Gassendi, *Opera Omnia*, I. 345 col. 2–346 col. 1; II. 122 col. 1–135 col. 2.
[21] I am treating Huygen's various works on magnetism (in vol. XIX of Christiaan Huygens, *Oeuvres complètes de Christiaan Huygens*, 22 vols. (The Hague, 1888–1950)) as a development of Descartes' account, even though Huygens revises this account significantly. It is worth noting that Newton had almost nothing to say on magnetism, and he did not believe that the inverse square law applied to magnetism; see *Principia*, 810 (Part II, prop. 8, coroll. 5).

of this squeezing they end up as cylinders having three or four concave sides joined by rims, depending on whether they are squeezed through three or four contiguous globules. Moreover, because they rotate on being squeezed through these interstices, the channels or grooves are rotated, forming a stream of diagonally grooved, cylindrical fragments, some of which will have a left-hand screw, some a right-hand screw, according to the direction of the twist.

This account holds for the magnetism of Earth as well as that of the lodestone. Grooved particles are initially expelled from the Sun along the plane of the equator, where the centrifugal force is greatest, and, since the axis that makes up our whole solar system undergoes a rotation in one direction, the direction of the screw of those coming from the North Pole will be different from those coming from the South Pole. In Figure 6.6, ABCD represents the Earth and A and B the Poles. The grooved particles

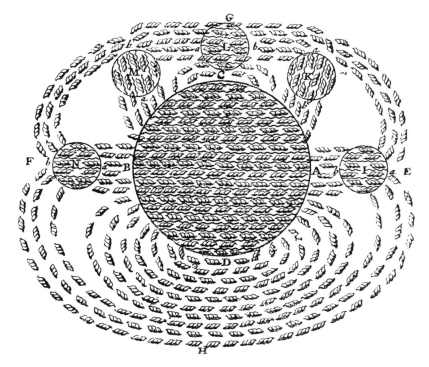

Figure 6.6

enter from one Pole and travel to the other along passages through the Earth, some allowing particles with a right-hand thread, others allowing particles with a left-hand thread. When they emerge, they are deflected by the air, whose pores are unable to accommodate them, so they return to their point of origin 'forming a kind of vortex' (art. 133). Their course during this return explains the dip and declination of the magnetic compass needle, and their right-handed and left-handed orientations explain polarity.

Grooved particles will naturally be found in significant concentrations where there are bodies with pores that can accommodate them, and this is why they accumulate in and around the lodestone. When two magnets, aligned so that their contrary poles are facing one another, come sufficiently close that the grooved particles issuing from one can reach the other before being deflected by the air, they will continue along the path of least resistance, producing a magnetic vortex on a small scale (Fig. 6.7). The resulting vortical flow drives the air from between the

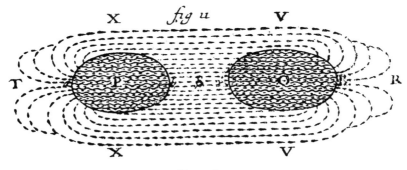

Figure 6.7

magnets, and the displaced air circling to their rears, T and R, pushes them together. The same process is at work in the magnetisation of iron by the lodestone, whose pores are of a size and situation necessary to accommodate the grooved particles, once they have been threaded by the vortex of the lodestone. Indeed, what is particularly remarkable about the magnetisation of iron is the vortical pattern formed, as when one sprinkles iron filings around a magnet (art. 179), which provides striking observational confirmation of the vortex theory.

The last topic of Part IV, electricity, follows on naturally from magnetism in that, as Descartes points out, just as magnetism exhibits a force of attraction, so, too, do 'amber, wax, resin, and other similar things' (art. 184). Moreover, the aim in both cases is to provide an account of the phenomena in terms of mechanics and matter theory, perhaps on the model of what he has just offered in the case of magnetism. But electricity was much more poorly understood than magnetism, and there was no equivalent of Gilbert's *De Magnete*, from which Descartes had culled almost all his observational information in his treatment of magnetism. He confines his treatment to the behaviour of glass, which, as we have seen, was dealt with earlier in Part IV in his examination of the properties of fire. The account of the structure of glass presented there conflicted with a theory of static electricity which had been advocated by the English natural philosophers Kenelm Digby, Thomas White, and Thomas Browne, and it was a theory that was to have wide currency in England in the mid seventeenth century.[22] Descartes writes:

> Although I cannot examine this force in jet or amber without first deducing from various observations many of their other properties, and thus investigating their innermost nature, nevertheless because the same force is also in glass (which I was obliged to discuss a little earlier in order to demonstrate the effects of fire), if I did not explain this force then perhaps the other things that I have written about glass could be questioned. Especially since some men, seeing that this force occurs in amber, in wax, in resin, and in practically all oily substances, will perhaps think it consists in the fact that certain slender and branching particles of these bodies have been moved by friction (for friction is usually required to arouse this force), scatter themselves through the nearby air, and, adhering to one another, immediately return and bring with them the tiny bodies that they strike on their way. Just as we see that a drop of liquefied fats of this kind, suspended from a rod, can be shaken by slight movements in such a way that one part of the drop still adheres to the rod, while another part descends for some distance and immediately returns and also brings with it the tiny straws or other minute bodies which it has encountered. For no such thing can be imagined in glass, at least if its nature is as we described it above; and therefore another cause of this attraction in it must be indicated. (art. 184)

The structural difference between glass and oily substances is that the latter have interlinking branching parts (see art. 76), whereas glass has large smoothly joined constituents. The explanation for the behaviour of glass is to be found in the mechanical arrangement of its constituent matter rather than in some chemical property of this matter. As with magnetism, Descartes sees the solution in the distinctive pores of glass. The heating process through which glass is formed has produced long thin channels which run from one end of the glass to the other and which are filled with subtle matter, which forms itself into long thin ribbons (Fig. 6.8). These ribbons, being formed of subtle matter, are

---

[22] See Heilbron, *Electricity in the Seventeenth and Eighteenth Centuries*, 193–5. The theory is set out in Kenelme Digby, *Two Treatises* (Paris, 1644), 172–5.

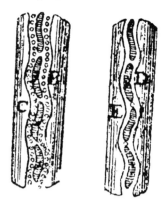

Figure 6.8

highly agitated, but are confined within the pores of the glass because their shapes have been fixed in the cooling of the glass and they cannot accommodate themselves to the pores of the surrounding air. Rubbing of the glass agitates these ribbons to such an extent that they escape into the nearby air and the pores of nearby bodies, picking up material from these as it adheres to them, but returning in the end to the glass for this is the only thing that can accommodate their shape. This account is not specific to glass, however, but should hold for at least most electrical bodies.

What Descartes believes he has achieved in Parts III and IV of the *Principia* is set out in article 187, which is the end of the proper subject matter of Part IV, namely the theory of the Earth. Taking us through some of the more recalcitrant phenomena he has attempted to explain in terms of the basic principles set out in the *Principia* – electricity, magnetism, fire, and the transmission of light over great distances – he concludes that everyone

will be easily persuaded that there are, in rocks and plants, no forces so secret, no marvels of sympathy or antipathy so astounding, and finally no effects in all of nature which are properly attributed to purely physical causes or causes lacking in mind or thought, the reasons for which cannot be deduced from these principles. Consequently, it is unnecessary to add anything else to them.

The test of this claim will now come in Part V, where Descartes' principles will be extrapolated into the realm of the organic, the most ambitious extension of his system of natural philosophy imaginable. It is here that the real test – and one of the real strengths – of his system lies.

CHAPTER 7

Principia, *Part V: Living things*

Article 188 of Part IV of the *Principia* reads:

I would not add to this fourth Part of the *Principia Philosophiæ* if, as I had previously intended, I were still going to write two other Parts; that is, a fifth Part concerning living things, or animals and plants, and a sixth concerning man . . . Up till now I have described the Earth and the whole of the visible universe as if it were a machine, and I have considered only the various shapes and motions of its parts. But our senses show us much else besides, namely colours, smells, sounds and similar things. And if I remained completely silent about these, I should seem to have omitted the principal part of the explanation of natural things.

In Parts III and IV, Descartes tells us, he has considered the inorganic world as a machine: the topic of Part V is 'living things', which Descartes also considers as machines. As he puts it at the close of *L'Homme*:

I desire that you consider that all the functions that I have attributed to this machine, such as the digestion of food, the beating of the heart and the arteries, the nourishment and growth of the bodily parts, respiration, waking and sleeping; the reception of light, sounds, odours, smells, heat and other such qualities by the external sense organs; the impression of the ideas of them in the organ of common sense and the imagination, the retention or imprint of these ideas in the memory; the internal movements of the appetites and the passions; and finally the external movements of all the bodily parts that so aptly follow both the actions of objects presented to the senses, and the passions and impressions that are encountered in memory: and in this they imitate as perfectly as is possible the movements of real men. I desire, I say, that you should consider that these functions follow in this machine simply from the disposition of the organs as wholly naturally as the movements of a clock or other automaton follow from the disposition of its counterweights and wheels. To explain these functions, then, it is not necessary to conceive of any vegetative or sensitive soul, or any other principle of movement or life, other than its blood and its spirits which are agitated by the heat of the fire that burns continuously in its heart, and which is of the same nature as those fires that occur in inanimate bodies.[1]

[1] AT x. 201–2.

The doctrine of the 'animal machine' was without doubt the most no-torious Cartesian doctrine in the eighteenth and nineteenth centuries, and brought upon him more opprobrium than all his other doctrines put together.[2] Yet, as we shall see, the doctrine has been widely misunder-stood, above all because it has been construed as eliminating any sentient and cognitive states in animals, whereas, in fact, not only does Descartes not deny such states to animals, his mechanist account is designed to offer an explanation of such states.

In the light of such misunderstandings, it is important in looking at Descartes' account of physiology to begin by asking about the aim of a mechanised physiology, that is, what Descartes hoped to achieve by such a programme. The first thing to note is that it is a direct contin-uation of his account of celestial and terrestrial phenomena. It works within the same theory of matter and the same mechanist constraints as his account of these, allowing no qualitative distinction between types of matter, allowing no internal forces or activities, and explaining vari-ous differences between the properties of things in terms of three sizes of matter. There are three kinds of approach to which his mechanist physiology can be seen as an alternative, and by contrasting Descartes' account with these we will get a better idea of the novelty and value of his approach. These approaches attempt to provide an account of physiol-ogy that aims to explain various functional differences between organs either, first, in terms of qualitatively different kinds of matter, or, second, in terms of some non-material principle guiding those functions, or, third, in goal-directed terms which cannot be captured mechanistically.

In the first case, what was usually invoked was the traditional doctrine of the four elements – earth, air, fire, and water – but, as we have seen, Descartes had questioned both the basis for this doctrine and whether the accounts it produced could have informative content or explanatory value, and he had offered his own accounts of phenomena such as burn-ing, and the different physical properties of solids and fluids, in terms of his much more economical single-matter theory. At a general level, the argument is that invoking the traditional theory of the elements explains nothing, and the cases they are invoked to explain in physical theory can actually be accounted for fully in terms of a single type of matter, material extension. When we turn to physiology, the same considerations apply. Why try to account for differences in physiological function in terms of

---

[2] On the development of the doctrine see Leonora Cohen Rosenfield, *From Beast–Machine to Man–Machine*, rev. edn. (New York, 1968), and Jean-Claude Beaune, *L'automate et ses mobiles* (Paris, 1980).

a theory of matter which would not explain anything anyway, and which can be replaced by something much more economical?

In the second case, a parallel set of considerations holds. Instead of a theory of elements, what are invoked are various classes of 'soul' – vegetative souls, sensitive souls, and rational souls – and Eustachius and Dupleix for example each set out this doctrine routinely and in detail.[3] These are supposed to capture various qualitative differences that emerge as we ascend the chain of being from inanimate matter, to vegetable life, to animal life, to human beings; or alternatively, as we ascend from those functions we share with plants, to those we share with animals, to those that are distinctively human.[4] Descartes certainly thinks that distinctively human capacities require the postulation of a separate soul, but the postulation of a hierarchy of souls – and, more specifically, the postulation of a 'sensitive soul' to account for animal sentience – is a different matter. First, it is unnecessary, since one can, Descartes believes, explain vegetable and animal capacities simply in terms of matter. Second, the postulation of a hierarchy of souls does not actually explain anything: it does nothing more than label the stages at which various differences are considered to emerge, while giving the impression that the cause of the difference has been identified. Third, a hierarchy of souls obscures the all-important distinction between the soul and the body, suggesting that the differences may be ones of degree, something that Descartes singles out for criticism in his theory of the passions, as we shall see in the next chapter.

The third case, that of the apparent goal-directedness of certain physiological processes, is the most serious challenge to a mechanist physiology, and the cases of the development of the foetus and perceptual cognition are the most problematic kinds of case for a mechanist account.[5] Descartes deals with both in some detail, and, as we shall see, his treatment of them differs considerably, highlighting two very different kinds of strategy available within a mechanist physiology. His account of embryology is radically revisionary and effectively eliminates any element of goal-directedness in foetal development. His account of perceptual cognition, on the other hand, aims to 'save the appearances' to a large extent, and is reductionist, in that nothing other than mechanical processes

---

[3] Eustachius in Part III of the *Physicus*, Dupleix in Book 8 of the *Physique*.

[4] On the late Scholastic doctrine of plants and animals, see Denis Des Chene, *Life's Form: Late Aristotelian Conceptions of the Soul* (Ithaca, 2000).

[5] Note also, however, the problem of how we conceive of a normal, well-functioning body in the case of automata, that is, how we fill out the notion of health in automata if not in terms of some goal. On this question see Dennis Des Chene, *Spirits and Clocks: Machine and Organism in Descartes* (Ithaca, 2001), ch. 3.

are involved, but these mechanical processes have a level of structuring imposed upon them that allows for recognitional capacities, something which Descartes shows, at least at an elementary level, not to be beyond the capabilities of a mechanist theory: the aim is to show how function can be generated purely within the resources of mechanism.

The account that can be reconstructed, principally from *L'Homme* and *La Description du Corps Humain*, is comprehensive, embracing basic physiology, developmental physiology, and psycho-physiology. At each of the three levels of physiology, distinctive problems arise for Descartes' mechanistic account. In terms of basic physiology, the Scholastic account had postulated something different from matter, a 'vegetative soul', to account for organic processes such as digestion, movement of the blood, nutrition, growth, reproduction, and respiration, since these processes seem to involve a kind or level of activity that was qualitatively distinct from anything found in the inorganic realm. In the case of what they considered to be distinctively animal capacities – perception, appetites, and animal motion – they postulated a different kind of soul, the 'sensitive' soul. Descartes rejects the idea that there are different kinds of soul, and, since it was common ground that a 'rational soul' was a distinctive feature of human beings, and wholly absent in plants and animals, this left him with only the resources of a mechanistic physiology on which to draw. The problems for this approach are exacerbated once we move on to developmental physiology. The development of the foetus is as good an example of a goal-directed process as one is likely to find, yet how could a foetus, which begins simply as an undifferentiated region of matter on Descartes' account, possibly harbour and realise goals? Somehow, Descartes must seemingly attempt the impossible and construe the development of the foetus in non-teleological terms. Finally, animals are sentient, and this had traditionally been accounted for by ascribing a 'sensitive soul' to them. Descartes does not deny animal sentience, indeed he gives an elaborate account of it, but it is an account that construes animal faculties purely in mechanistic terms. Descartes' ability to solve the problems at this level is of particular importance because the functioning of animal faculties is crucial to his account of human psycho-physiology (which will be our concern in the next chapter) since much of his mechanistic account of cognitive functioning is as applicable to humans as it is to animals: the treatise in which it is set out is, after all, entitled *L'Homme*.

What drives Descartes' account of basic physiology, developmental physiology, and psycho-physiology is his refusal to countenance a multiplicity of souls. The point behind his advocacy of dualism is not to give us two things – mind and body – where we might have been satisfied with one, but to show that there are only two things, not the four postulated by his Aristotelian contemporaries, namely body, vegetative soul, sensitive soul, and rational soul. Indeed, mind comes neither in different types, nor in the form of higher and lower faculties, for Descartes insists there is only one kind of mind, just as there is only one kind of matter. Many of the functions that his contemporaries ascribed to lower faculties of the mind, especially those associated with non-rational sentience, must, on Descartes' account, be assigned purely to corporeal faculties and their mechanistic underpinnings.

BASIC PHYSIOLOGY

Under the category of basic physiology, I include all those non-developmental forms of physiology that do not have a direct bearing on cognition. It is important that we restrict the term 'cognition' to those cognitive processes working by means of a cognitive representation of the stimulus, however, for Descartes also conceives of a very different kind of sensory process, which does not involve cognitive representation, namely reflex action in animals and in some plants, something that he associates with the possession of a circulatory system.

Of the functions traditionally ascribed to the vegetative soul, Descartes has little to say on digestion, respiration, and reproduction. He has a deep interest in the movement of the blood and growth, however, and he does discuss nutrition, which is closely tied to growth and will be used as a model for the mechanism of foetal development. The basic aim of the project is set out in *La Description du Corps Humain* in these terms:

It is true that it may be hard to believe that the disposition of organs alone is sufficient for the production in us of all the movements that are not determined by our thought. This is why I shall try to demonstrate this here, and to explain the entire machine of our body in such a way that we will have no more reason to think that it is our soul that excites in us those movements that we do not experience as being directed by our will, than we have to judge that there is a soul in a clock that makes it tell the time.[6]

The circulation of the blood is the basic feature of animal physiology on Descartes' account and, as we shall see, it is mirrored in plants in what Descartes and his contemporaries considered to be the analogous circulation of sap, so that, more generally, circulatory systems would seem to be distinctive of living things, for they are tied in with respiration which is crucial in the circulation of the blood,[7] nutrition, in the circulation

---

[6] AT XI. 226.   [7] *L'Homme*, AT XI. 124; *La Description*, AT XI. 236–7.

of nutrients through the blood to the various parts of the body,[8] and sensation, through the circulation of various spirits through the blood, nerve fluids, or some other medium from sense organs or sensitive parts of the body to other parts such as the brain.[9]

Descartes' account of the circulation of the blood is his most novel contribution to basic physiology.[10] Galenic physiology had distinguished diastole, in which the cavities of the heart dilate and shorten, and systole, in which the heart lengthens and the ventricles contract, but the venous and arterial systems are autonomous on the Galenic account, and blood moves away from and towards the heart in both. Harvey established that the blood circulates around the body, and supplied a mechanism for this circulation: the 'pulsific faculty' or pumping action of the heart, which is wholly muscular. Descartes rejected the details of Harvey's account of the muscular action of the heart on a number of grounds,[11] but above all he could not accept a primitive pumping action, as if it were simply a natural function of the body, for how could such a natural function be accommodated to a mechanist framework? Some cause of the pumping had to be found, and more specifically some mechanically construable process had to be invoked to explain it. What Descartes offers in its place is an ebullition theory, whereby the cause of the expansion and contraction of the heart is traced to the production of heat in the heart. Descartes tells Plempius[12] that heat of the heart instantaneously rarefies the blood by breaking up its parts, making them take up a greater volume and causing the heart to swell as a result. This forces the closing of the atrioventricular valves, which prevents more blood coming into the ventricles, and the opening of the semilunar valves, which releases the pressure by forcing the rarefied blood into the arteries, causing them to swell. As the blood cools, the arteries and ventricles that contain it contract, the semilunar valves close, and the process is repeated. Because Descartes construes heat in terms of the violent motion of the parts of matter, as we have seen, the thermogenetic processes responsible for the creation of pressure in the arteries are amenable to a purely mechanical explanation.

How seriously Descartes took his account of the cause of circulation is clear from his remark to Mersenne that he was prepared to admit that 'if what I have written on this topic ... turns out to be false, then the

<hr />

[8] *La Description*, AT XI. 246–52.   [9] *L'Homme*, AT XI. 132ff.

[10] The fullest account is in Part II of *La Description*, AT XI. 228–45, although some details are missing there, for example, on the details of his ebullition theory. On Descartes' account of the heart and circulation see Annie Bitbol-Hespériès, *Le Principe de vie chez Descartes* (Paris, 1990).

[11] AT XI. 241–5.   [12] Descartes to Plempius, 15 February 1638; AT I. 529–34.

rest of my philosophy is entirely worthless'.[13] Circulation is so important because without it we would not be able to explain how living things are able to nourish themselves, or how they are able to exhibit various degrees of sensory receptiveness.

The first stage of nutrition, digestion, is described by Descartes in terms of mechanical processes,[14] and it should be noted that, in principle, it is common to animals and plants.[15] In animals, digestive fluids derive from the heart, and so are very hot, and they break down food by gliding between its parts, separating and agitating them. The coarse parts are excreted, but the finer ones flow through pores in various veins, particularly that leading to the liver, and the separation here is purely mechanical, Descartes comparing it to the separation of the finer parts of meal from the coarser ones in a sieve. These finer parts are then mixed in with the blood, and indeed become part of it. It is arterial blood that is the primary source of nourishment for the body,[16] partly because the pressure in the arteries, being greater than that in the veins, is such that their pores are widened to a greater extent, allowing the blood, with its nutrients, to enter the pores of the membranes surrounding the solid parts of the body. I shall return to nutrition below, when we look at developmental physiology, for which it forms a model. For the present it is sufficient to note that mechanical pressure and size of particles relative to the aperture of pores which they encounter are all that Descartes invokes in accounting for nutrition.

This account is also designed to explain the production of 'animal spirits', the finest constituents of the blood, made of the first and finest kind of matter which Descartes identified with light and heat in Part III, and which here are responsible for transmission of stimuli from one part of the body to another. The most active parts of the blood that are pushed through the aorta and the carotid travel to the brain, passing through exceptionally narrow pores, and these are the 'animal spirits', some remaining in the brain and some returning to the heart and being caught up in the general circulatory process.[17]

Despite his use of their traditional name, which derives from the fact that they were considered peculiar to animals, 'animal spirits' do not seem to be peculiar to animals for Descartes. On 23 August 1638, he wrote to Mersenne:

As for the plant that you report having come from Mr de la Brosse [Head of the Jardin Royal des Plantes Médecines, Paris], the only thing I find strange is its

---

[13] Descartes to Mersenne, 9 February 1639; AT II. 501.
[14] AT XI. 121–3.   [15] AT XI. 247.   [16] AT XI. 246.   [17] AT XI. 251–2.

rarity. For after having described the movement of the heart in a way that can apply as easily to plants as to animals, if the organs found there are the same, I have no difficulty in conceiving how the movement of the plant can come about; but I would not undertake to say definitively how it happens, if I have not seen and examined it first.[18]

The plant in question here is what he refers to subsequently as '*l'herbe sensitive*' (*mimosa pudica*) which is extremely sensitive to touch, the leaflets of the bipinnate leaves folding together at the slightest contact with the fingers.[19] A plant apparently capable of sensation was very difficult to explain on the traditional view of sensation, because plants were thought of as being regulated by a vegetative soul, responsible for lower functions such as nutrition, while animals, as well as a vegetative soul, also had a sensitive soul, which conferred on them the power of sensation.

Because Descartes rejects this theory, treating plants and animals along the same mechanistic lines as being composed solely of inert matter, there is no problem in principle with plant sensation for him. There was a widely accepted analogy between the circulation of blood in animals and the circulation of sap in plants in the seventeenth century, which is presumably what Descartes has in mind in speaking of the movement of the heart: in talking of the 'organs found there' being the same he is undoubtedly referring to a functional similarity between plants and animals, that is, to a functionally, not a structurally, heart-like organ. Indeed, the circulation of the blood and the movement of sap are both caused by heat: just as we find heat in the heart, so we find the same kind of heat ('fire without light' as he calls it in *Le Monde*), in the stems and leaves of new mown hay.[20] The claim, then, is that a circulatory system is sufficient for sensation. Circulation is needed if a stimulus affecting one part of the body is to have an effect – a systematic effect, which the behaviour of the *mimosa* certainly demonstrates – on something other than the immediate area of contact, for it is by means of circulation that

---

[18] AT II. 329. Descartes did try to obtain specimens for dissection and experiment, but there is no evidence that these attempts came to anything. On 16 October, he wrote to Mersenne thanking him for an offer of seeds, telling him that he is now working 'on a part of his speculations concerning plants' (AT II. 595). On 13 November, he wrote to Mersenne again thanking him for the offer of seeds, but saying he knew they would be available at the Leiden botanical gardens, only they had not ripened and the time to sow them had already come, and asking for a plant catalogue from the Jardin Royal in Paris (AT II. 619). This is the last trace I can find of the issue in either Descartes' or Mersenne's correspondence.

[19] Descartes' remarks give the impression that he has not come across the plant before, but Beeckman had described it in his *Journal*, as early as 1617 (*Journal*, I. 124), and Descartes may well have had access to this material. There is also a later reference in the *Journal* (II. 319) dating from 1625.

[20] *Principes* (fuller than the Latin version) Part IV, art. 80.

the parts of the organism are connected. What we are dealing with here is in effect a reflex response, and comparison with Descartes' account of the reflex response in animals shows it to be essentially the same kind of thing.

Descartes is often credited with the discovery of the reflex response in animals, but his account of it has been widely misunderstood. In the account of reflex response in *L'Homme*, he gives an example of a 'man machine'. [Fig. 7.1] His foot, *B*, is next to a fire, *A*, and because the parts

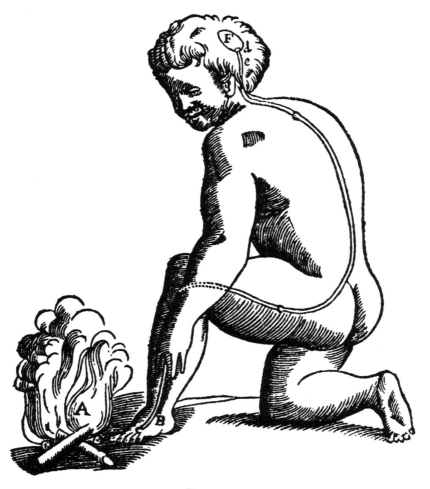

Figure 7.1

of fire move very swiftly they displace the area of skin that they touch, pulling the end of the thread *c* which is there. When this is pulled the pore *de*, which is located in the brain where the thread terminates, is opened simultaneously, just as happens when one pulls a cord and the bell at the other end rings simultaneously. The entrance to the pore *de* being opened, the animal spirits from cavity *F* enter and are carried through it, 'part into the muscles that serve to withdraw this foot from the fire, part into those that serve to turn the eyes and head to look at it, and part into those that serve to advance the hands and bend the whole body to protect it'.[21] Such automatic motion is completely mechanical and Descartes at one point compares the mechanical control of muscular motion to the operations of a church organ:

If you have ever had the curiosity to examine the organs in our churches, you know how the bellows push air into receptacles called (presumably for this reason) wind-chests. And you know how the air passes from there into one or other of the pipes, depending on how the organist moves his fingers on the keyboard. You can think of our machine's heart and arteries, which push the animal spirits into the cavities of its brain, as being like the bellows, which push air into the wind-chests; and of external objects, which stimulate certain nerves and cause spirits contained in the cavities to pass into particular pores, as being like the fingers of the organist, which press certain keys and cause the air to pass from the wind-chests to particular pipes. Now the harmony of an organ does not depend on the externally visible arrangement of pipes or on the shape of the wind-chests or other parts. It depends solely on three factors: the air that comes from the bellows, the pipes that make the sound, and the distribution of air in the pipes. In just the same way, I would point out, the functions we are concerned with here do not depend at all on the external shape of the visible parts that anatomists distinguish in the substance of the brain, or on the shape of the brain's cavities, but solely on three factors: the spirits that come from the heart, the pores of the brain through which they pass, and the way in which these spirits are distributed in these pores.[22]

The organ simply produces the music as a result of an input: it does not represent the notes to itself, in the way that the organist might. Similarly with *mimosa* and with the 'man machine'.

The crucial feature of the man machine, and the feature that has caused the greatest misunderstanding, is the organ labelled *F* in Figure 7.1. It has usually been assumed that this is the pineal gland, but the function of the pineal gland, as we shall see, is to produce cognitive representations, and no such representations are present in reflex

---

[21] AT xi. 142–3.   [22] AT xi. 165–6.

responses. Indeed, it is crucial to Descartes' understanding of reflex responses that they be immediate and automatic if they are to be effective. It is also worth noting that Descartes calls F a 'cavity', and he never refers to the pineal gland as a cavity. It is almost certainly one of the cerebral ventricles. Animals are capable of genuine perceptual cognition on Descartes' account, as we shall see, but his account of reflex, applicable as it is to plants as well as animals, is not genuine perceptual cognition. It does not require or involve the pineal gland – which means it does not involve any cognitive representation of the stimulus – only a circulatory system, and he does not consider such a system to be peculiar to animals.

DEVELOPMENTAL PHYSIOLOGY

One of the principal tasks of a mechanist natural philosophy in the seventeenth century was the elimination of teleology. In the case of mechanics, optics, and cosmology, there were, outside the question of the formation of the Earth, few reasons to question this approach once Aristotelianism had been abandoned. Physiology was a different matter, however, and among the phenomena that a mechanized physiology had to deal with were a number of processes that seemed clearly goal-directed. Here at least, it was not a question of Aristotle's misguided concern to provide teleological explanations where they weren't needed, but rather that of how one could possibly avoid reference to goals in explaining these processes.

As we saw in the previous chapter, in Part IV of the *Principia*, Descartes offered an account of the formation of the Earth that attracted wide criticism, especially in England. He was accused of 'Epicureanism', for, on his account, the processes that led to the formation of the Earth were either chance processes or were driven by necessity, and what was conspicuously absent was any providential guidance. Providential guidance introduces an element of goal-directedness into the question: the Earth is there for a specific reason and is formed so as to serve a particular function, as a home for human beings, at least until the Last Judgement. The argument was that if we ignore that function, we will fail to understand what the Earth is, just as surely as if we try to understand a watch without realising that it is designed to keep the time.

There are a number of similarities between Descartes' account of the formation of the Earth and his description of the formation of the foetus in *La Description*. Both had traditionally been construed as intrinsically goal-directed processes, and it is important to appreciate here that Descartes' concern is not with goal-directedness as such, but with intrinsic goal-directedness. He does not deny that God guides the development of the embryo any more than he denies that God guides the formation of the Earth. But such extrinsic goal-directedness simply does not fall within the domain of natural philosophy for Descartes. It would do so only if the goal-directedness were somehow internalised by the body so guided, but this would be to allow processes in the body that were incompatible with the inertness of matter. At one level, Descartes is not denying that there is a question as to why matter behaves in such a way that the foetus develops into an adult of a particular species. What he is saying is that the explanation for that is not something *internal* to the development of the foetus but *external* to it: God made it so. Nor is this necessarily an unorthodox position. Although he does not do so, Descartes could easily have cited Augustine, who writes in *De Civitate Dei* (12. 26):

We do not call farmers 'creators' of crops, since we are told, 'The planter does not matter, nor does the waterer. It is God who matters, for it is he who makes things grow' [1 Cor. 3.7]. We do not even ascribe creative power to the earth, although it is clearly the fruitful mother of growing things, promoting their growth as they burst out into shoots, and holding them safely by the roots; for as we are also told, 'God gives to the seed a body of his own choosing, its own body to each seed' [1 Cor. 15.38]. We must not attribute to a woman the creation of her child, but instead to him who said to his servant, 'I knew you, before I formed you in the womb' [Jer. 1.5].

In other words, God is the only final cause. In his natural philosophy, Descartes is concerned with internal or intrinsic causes, and these are missing, for Augustine as for Descartes, in the case of foetal development.

What Descartes denies, then, is intrinsic goal-directedness. Such intrinsic or internally generated goal-directedness is a feature of Aristotelian natural philosophy, where it was thought to be characteristic of any natural process. There, organic processes, such as a seed developing into a tree, and inorganic processes, such as the fall of a body to the earth, are put down to some intrinsic goal-directedness. Mechanism dismantles the conceptual apparatus whereby processes are construed as being goal-directed, because it removes the doctrine of forms, which is crucial to the notion of something striving to realise its natural state. It does this not just in the cases where goal-directedness seems an artificial way to construe what happens once Aristotelianism has been abandoned, however, but also in cases where this remains a natural way of construing what occurs, such as in the development of the foetus.

Most biological processes can be thought of in goal-directed terms: nutrition, respiration, excretion, sleep, etc. But then many purely physical processes can be thought of in goal-directed terms, and Aristotle had thought that the explanation of the fall of heavy bodies to the ground had to display the goal-directedness of this process: bodies fall to the ground because this is their natural place, and, when they are unconstrained, it is in the nature of heavy bodies to behave in this way. This raises the problem of where we draw the line. We may concede that a process can be described in terms of a goal without conceding that goal-directedness plays any genuine part in explaining the process. Unless we think that teleology plays a part in any natural organic process, for example, we will not be inclined to think that growth in adolescents or adults requires explanation in terms of ends or goals. On the other hand, we may be inclined to think that the development of the foetus does require an explanation in terms of ends or goals: it develops in this way because it is developing into a horse, or a person, or a bird. In the middle of these two is a grey area. We can think of Descartes' strategy as pushing foetal development into the grey area, in which case the question of the right kind of explanation will no longer be judged by a priori considerations about whether goals are relevant, but by how effective whatever concrete explanation one comes up with is in accounting for the detail.

More schematically, although Descartes does not lay out his plan for dealing with this question explicitly, it seems clear that a threefold strategy must lie behind any thoroughgoing mechanist approach to embryology. First, ordinary growth is accounted for in a way that makes no refer- ences to goals. Second, the process of formation and maturation of the foetus is treated simply as a species of growth: it involves a significantly greater increase in complexity and internal differentiation of parts than the process of growth from childhood to adulthood, of course, but this in itself does not make it qualitatively different. Third, the mechanist must show how the development from a low degree of complexity and inter- nal differentiation to a high degree of complexity and differentiation is something that can be handled in mechanistic terms.

What this strategy allows one to do is to provide a general account of growth, in terms of how raw material is introduced into the organism from outside and transformed into the kinds of highly differentiated material making up bones, blood, muscle, etc. Then, having done this, one shows how the kind of account developed in this way can be extended to the case where the organs are not being built up but are actually being formed anew.

The phenomenon of growth, in the less problematic non-foetal case, comes under the maintenance of bodily organs. In his treatment of nutrition in *La Description*, Descartes argues, as we have seen, that the organs of the body are nourished by blood from the arteries. To understand this more distinctly, he tells us,

we must bear in mind that the parts of those living bodies that are maintained through nourishment, that is, animals and plants, undergo continual change, in such a way that the only difference between those that are called *fluids*, such as the blood, humours and spirits, and those that are called *solids*, such as bone, flesh, nerves, and membranes, is that the latter move much more slowly than the others.[23]

That all the parts of the body move, those of the solid bodily members just as much as the parts of bodily fluids, is a crucial point, increasing the degree of homogeneity of the matter making up the body, and hence making it easier to account for the transformation of nutrients into the fabric of the body. This constant motion causes rubbing, which, in turn, can cause various bodily parts to become smaller, or to combine into larger parts. At this point we get the explanation of growth, change of bodily shape, and aging of the body:

When one is young, for example, because the filaments that make up the solid parts are not joined to one another very firmly, and the channels along which they flow are quite large, the motion of these filaments is not as slow as when one is old, and more matter is attached to their roots than is detached from their extremities, which results in their becoming longer and stronger, and their increase in size is the means by which the body grows. When the humours between these filaments do not flow in great quantity, they all pass quite quickly along the channels containing them, causing the body to grow taller without filling out. But when these humours are very abundant, they cannot flow so easily between the filaments of the solid parts, and in the case of those parts that have very irregular shapes, in the form of branches, and which consequently offer the most difficult passage of all between the filaments, they gradually become stuck there and form *fat*. This does not grow in the body, as flesh does, through nourishment properly speaking, but only because many of its parts join together and stick to one another, just as do the parts of dead things. And when the humours become less abundant, they flow more easily and more quickly, because the subtle matter and the spirits accompanying them have a greater force to agitate them, and this causes them little by little to pick up the parts

[23] AT XI. 247.

of the fat and carry them along with them, which is how people become *thin*. And as we get older, the filaments making up the solid parts tighten and stick together more closely, finally attaining such a degree of hardness that the body ceases entirely to grow and even loses its capacity for nourishment. This leads to such an imbalance between the solid and the fluid parts that age alone puts an end to life.[24]

Descartes then turns to the question of how the requisite form of nourishment gets to the right part of the body. This is, of course, something one might be inclined to think of in goal-directed terms, but Descartes' approach is resolutely mechanical. Can we seriously suppose, he asks, that each bodily part can choose and guide the parts of the food to the appropriate place? To do so would be 'to attribute more intelligence to these than even our soul has'.[25] Rather, he argues, there are only two factors that can be responsible for the movement of nutrients to the appropriate place: their initial position in relation to that organ, and the size and shape of the pores in the membranes through which the nutrients pass, and in this connection Descartes looks at the paths which the blood takes around the body and discusses the sieving effects of the pores.

At this point, Descartes tells us that we will have a better knowledge of how nutrition works if we consider 'how the bodily parts are formed from seed',[26] and we are thereby launched into the formation of the foetus via a consideration of nutrition: just about as mechanist a route as is possible. The reproduction of plants, which Descartes, of course, treats as asexual, is distinguished from the conception of animals, which is sexual, comprising the mixing of male and female fluids, 'which act on each other like a kind of yeast, heating one another so that some of the particles acquire the same degree of agitation as fire, expanding and pressing on the others, and in this way putting them gradually into the state required for the formation of parts of the body'.[27] The shift from a liquid state to one on a par with fire is simply an increase in the degree of fluidity in Descartes' natural philosophy; the point in the present context is that the materials from which the foetus is initially formed are as fluid as possible, allowing them to take on any form.

The explanation of the differentiation of these parts now begins. The initial form of differentiation occurs due to the heat generated in this mixture, 'which acts in the same way as does new wine when it ferments, or as hay which is stored before it is dry, causing some of the particles

[24] AT XI. 249–50.   [25] AT xi. 251.   [26] AT XI. 252.   [27] AT XI. 253.

to collect in a part of the space containing them, and then makes them expand, pressing against the others'.[28] This is how the heart begins to be formed. But, because the tiny parts of matter which have been expanded by the heat in this way tend to continue in their movement in a straight line, following Descartes' principle of rectilinear inertia, and because the heart, which is now forming, resists them,

> they slowly move away and make their way to the area where the brain stem will later be formed, in the process displacing others which move around in a circle to occupy the place vacated by them in the heart. After the brief time needed for them to collect in the heart, these in turn expand and move away, following the same path as the former. This results in some of the former group which are still in the same position – together with others that have moved in from elsewhere to take the place of those that have left in the meantime – moving into the heart. And it is in this expansion, which occurs thus in a repeated way, that the beating of the heart, or the pulse, consists.[29]

We are then taken through an explanation of the formation of the spine, pulmonary artery, pulmonary vein, the brain, the sense organs, and so on, with occasional explanations of how the mechanical processes as described account for various observed phenomena, such as the colour of the blood.[30]

The basic explanatory tools are: the fermentation-like process that produces heat and a breakdown of matter when the seeds of the two sexes are combined; the ways in which these parts subsequently recombine simply under the action of heat and the expansion and increased pressure this produces; and the rectilinear tendency of the parts projected under this pressure and the barriers to a rectilinear motion, causing various forms of branching and the collection of matter at different termini of this branching depending on degree of fluidity, degree of agitation, size of pores in the membranes formed, as well as various other mechanically

---

[28] AT XI. 254.   [29] AT XI. 254.

[30] Even sexual differentiation in the foetus is covered, although not in *La Description*, but in the Latin notes *Prima cogitationes circa generationem animalium* (AT XI. 505–38). Here Descartes offers two quite different accounts. On the first of these, when the head of the foetus is facing towards the mother's navel, its buttocks pushed towards her spine, the penis will be formed outside the body and the foetus will develop into a male; when the body of the foetus is facing in the other direction, the penis curves back into the interior of the foetus becoming a vagina, so that the foetus develops into a female. But Descartes follows this with a different explanation, whereby the foetus either excretes liquids and retains solids, causing the penis to extrude from its body, or, being 'less robust', excretes solids and retains liquids, causing the penis to form inside the body, and inside out, as it were. See the discussion in Des Chene, *Spirits and Clocks*, 47–52. Des Chene plausibly suggests that Descartes may have come up with the second account as a result of realising that foetuses are not randomly oriented in the womb (47 n. 25).

conceived variables. Using these tools, Descartes offers an account that is designed to explain the development of the veins, arteries, and epigastrics in the foetus in terms of the initial state of the combination of 'seeds', the natural tendency of matter to move in the straight line, and the branching and conglomerations of matter that result from the constraints on its motion. The final part of *La Description* then turns to the formation of organs, or, more specifically, to the heart, brain, muscles, and the various skins and membranes that enclose organs.

While the details that Descartes provides are completely hypothetical and speculative, there is little to be gained from asking how these details match up with those provided by modern developmental physiology. Rather, we must ask whether, in making no reference to intrinsic ends or goals, he has deprived himself of an essential ingredient in any satisfactory explanation of this development. Ideally, the kind of picture he wants, as I have indicated, is that where the development of the foetus can be seen as a variant on the assimilation of nutrients, like adolescent growth, getting fat, and getting thin. No one would see ordinary weight-gain as a process directed towards a state in which one is fat: this would be to get the causality the wrong way around. Similarly, it is the (mechanistically construable) chemical and mechanical processes that occur in the foetus that cause it to develop into an adult of a particular species, not the fact that it is going to develop into a member of a particular species that causes the particular chemical and mechanical processes to occur in the way they do.

ANIMAL PSYCHO-PHYSIOLOGY

Descartes' basic physiology requires nothing more than inert matter, differentiated in three sizes, and an understanding of circulatory systems. His developmental physiology can also get by with these, but his account of psycho-physiology requires an expansion in the resources of his mechanism. In his account of the development of the foetus he pursues a programme designed to show that what had traditionally been seen as a goal-directed process need not be thought of as goal-directed at all, and could be construed in terms of straightforward mechanical causation. However, in his treatment of perceptual cognition in animals – and in humans in cases where the intellect is not operative, that is, where it is simply a case of psycho-physiology – he does not attempt to show that perceptual cognition does not occur, but rather invokes a kind of receptive capacity which stretches what one might normally think of as the limits of explanations that have recourse only to mechanical causation.

Descartes' account of the physical and physiological processes involved in visual cognition, to take the case he deals with in detail, is in outline as follows. Light corpuscles/rays strike the relevant external sense organ, namely the eye, and an image of the stimulus is formed. This image is transmitted instantaneously through the nerves to the first of the internal senses, the 'common sense', whose function, as the name implies, is to unify the stimuli from the various external senses into a single representation. This representation is then passed on to memory, where the representation is matched against stored mnemonic representations, until finally it arrives at the 'imagination', which is the *locus* of cognition, and which Descartes identifies in his later writings with the pineal gland, on the grounds that the pineal gland is the only organ in the brain of any significant size that is not duplicated in each hemisphere, and it is very centrally located (as well as being of otherwise unknown function). Note how different this account is from what happens in reflex action. Here, in the case of genuine visual cognition, a representation is formed which is unified with other representations, then compared with other representations, and finally formed into an image on the surface of the pineal gland. In the reflex case, no cognitive representation is involved, and the internal senses are not needed.[31]

In spite of the fact that his treatment of the optics of vision is completely different from the traditional account, and the fact that he uses this optics to reinforce an account whereby the visual representation represents but need not resemble the stimulus, what he offers is in many respects simply a mechanised version of medieval faculty psychology. And although, as we shall see, he realises that a mechanical–causal account cannot give us a full understanding of perceptual cognition, and supplements it with a different kind of model, it is important to understand what the novelty of Descartes' attempt to mechanise physiology lay in, for it lies at the heart of his project. The novelty did not consist in construing psycho-physiological functions corporeally. Many psycho-physiological functions had been construed corporeally before Descartes by writers on physiology, and indeed there had been an extensive concern from Galen

---

[31] There is a grey, 'quasi-reflex' area here: for example, when an animal spots a predator, and responds immediately by fleeing. We shall see below that, in his account of memory, Descartes talks of associative cases where we construct a cognitive representation from very partial information. I believe such an account could be used to explain the case I have mentioned, but there are all kinds of instinctual and habitual forms of behaviour which Descartes does not clearly distinguish from reflex, which would have to be distinguished in any full account of these matters.

onwards with the localisation of particular faculties in the brain. There was even an orthodox tradition, dating back to the Church Fathers, of construing thought in corporeal terms, a tradition which the 'theologians and philosophers' who compiled the sixth set of objections to Descartes' *Meditationes* describe explicitly and approvingly as the 'soul thinking . . . by means of corporeal motions'.[32] Descartes' aim was to show that a number of psycho-physiological functions that had traditionally been recognised as being corporeal could be accounted for in a way that did not render matter sentient. That is the novel part of the programme. What is original about Descartes' project is not that it construes the faculties in corporeal terms, but his attempt to show that construing them in corporeal terms did not contradict the central tenet of mechanism that matter was inert.

It is also worth asking just what picture of biological entities emerges from the more revisionary aspects of Cartesian mechanist physiology. Descartes speaks of animals as 'automata', a term that also covers human bodies when not considered as animated by a soul. The terminology is misleading, however, for in the seventeenth century it meant little more than a 'self-moving thing' and John Cottingham has reminded us in this context that Leibniz, 'defending his claim that we possess "freedom of spontaneity" speaks of the human soul as a "kind of spiritual automaton", meaning no more than that its action-generating impulses arise solely *ad interno*, and produce effects without the intervention of any external cause'.[33] Indeed, the terminology of machines, which carries with it the strongest connotations for our understanding of what a mechanistically construed animal might be like, is also somewhat misleading here. We tend to think of seventeenth-century machines as rigid wooden and metal clockwork constructions, like the famous Strasbourg clock. On this conception, 'animal machines' come out looking like the metal robots of twentieth-century imagination. But the machines that Descartes takes as his model are hydraulically powered statues and mechanically driven fountains: the kinds of devices he describes in *L'Homme*[34] resemble, and probably derive from, the hydraulically powered devices in the underground grottoes at the Saint-Germain gardens, which Descartes was certainly familiar with from illustrations,[35] and which he may well have

---

[32] AT VII. 413–4.

[33] John Cottingham, 'A Brute to the Brutes?', *Philosophy* 53 (1978), 551–9: 553. The association of the mechanical with the inert, by contrast with the organic, seems to be a late eighteenth-century notion; see Judith Schlanger, *Les métaphores de l'organisme* (Paris, 1971), 50–1.

[34] AT XI. 120.

[35] Engravings of a number of these hydraulic devices appeared in Salomon de Caus, *Les raisons des forces mouvantes avec diverses machines tant utiles que plaisantes ausquelles sont adjoints plusioeurs desseigns de grotes et fontaines* (Frankfurt, 1615), with which Descartes was familiar.

known at first hand. He mentions the analogy with clocks in *La Discours de la méthode*,[36] but there is no evidence that clocks ever formed a model for a mechanistic physiology. Just as in his cosmology, where bodies are carried along in fluids, so in *L'Homme* and *La Description* the kind of image Descartes' model conveys is that of fluids being pushed through tubes, not wheels working cogs, and this has a much more intuitively 'organic' feel to it. The difference between an animal as traditionally conceived and a Cartesian automaton is not a difference between soft, fleshy organic entities and clockwork robots, but a conceptual difference between how physiological processes are to be modelled. Descartes' conception of animal capacities and behaviour is, in essence, no different from that of most of his contemporaries, and he attributes not just cognitive but also affective states to them.[37] What is novel about his treatment is the way he accounts for these states.

Descartes has a particular quarrel with the attempt to treat perception as a goal-directed process: it is not just that thinking of goals gets us nowhere. Rather, trying to think through perception in terms of its goals points us in a direction that is demonstrably wrong. Aristotle had maintained that we have the sense organs we do because they naturally display to us the nature of the world, and his account of the optics and physiology of perception turned around what he took its function to be. Among other things, the optics and physiology had to be construed in such a way as to yield perceptual images that resembled what was perceived.[38] The optics and physiology that Aristotle's account yielded turned out to be completely wrong, however, as Descartes knew, and his own account of perception, in the *Regulae* for example, starts from a new understanding of the optics and physiology of vision and uses this understanding to explore what form visual cognition might take.

Visual cognition involves cognitive response. This is not a problem for an account that construes the sense organs primarily in terms of their function, that subordinates structure to function, as Aristotle's account did. Descartes wants to subordinate function to structure, he wants there to be nothing more to function than what an examination of structure reveals. The problem in perceptual cognition is to

---

[36] AT VI. 50 and 59. The analogy is repeated at the end of article 16 of *Les Passions de l'Ame*. It also appears at the beginning and end of *Le Monde*.

[37] See, for example, Descartes to the Marquess of Newcastle; AT IV. 574. We shall return to this question at the end of this chapter.

[38] See my 'Aristotle on the Function of Sense Perception', *Studies in History and Philosophy of Science* 12 (1981), 75–89.

recognise the goal-directedness of perceptual cognition – the goal is cognition, the means perception – without rendering this a teleological process. It is basically the problem of capturing the idea of realising a function without the Aristotelian/Scholastic notion of intrinsic final ends.

The faculties involved in perceptual cognition – the 'external' sense organs, the common sense, the memory, and the imagination – had traditionally been construed in corporeal terms, with a good deal of attention having been given to localisation of faculties in the brain by physiologists. But the construal of some level of cognitive functioning in corporeal terms had been associated with various attempts to render matter itself sentient, by invoking the idea of a 'sensitive soul' regulating the corporeal processes from inside. To the extent that he is concerned to show that organic processes, including some cognitive operations, can be construed wholly mechanistically, Descartes has to make sure that his account is compatible with the inertness of matter. His aim is to show that the structure and behaviour of bodies are to be explained in the same way that we explain the structure and behaviour of machines, and in doing this he wants to show how a form of genuine cognition occurs in animals and that this can be captured in mechanistic terms. He does not want to show that cognition does not occur at all, that *instead of* a cognitive process we have a merely mechanical one. The aim is to explain animal cognition, not explain it away.

The case of visual cognition is the key one. We can distinguish between mere response to a visual stimulus, in which the parts of the automaton simply react in a fixed way; visual awareness, in which the perceiver has a mental representation of the object or state of affairs that caused the visual stimulus in the first place; and perceptual judgement, the power to reflect on and make a judgement about (such as a judgement as to the veridicality of) this representation. Descartes clearly restricts the last to human beings – it requires the possession of a mind/rational soul. Which of the first two are we to attribute to animals on Descartes' account? The automaton could react directly to the corpuscular action that makes up light without actually *seeing* anything, as a genuine machine might, but this is not how Descartes describes the visual process in automata in *L'Homme*. He tells us, for example, that the 'figures traced in the spirits on the [pineal] gland, where the seat of imagination and common sense is, should be taken to be ideas, that is, to be the forms or images that the rational soul will consider directly when, being united to this machine, it will imagine or will sense any object'.[39] This indicates that there are representations on the pineal gland of the automaton. It is, in fact, difficult to see how they could not have representations of the world if we are to talk about visual cognition. And it makes no sense to talk about them having representations but not being aware of the content of these representations. Moreover, Descartes certainly does not deny states such as memory to animals, and remembering something is just about the paradigm case of grasping the content of a representation.

By contrast, in the Replies to the sixth set of Objections to the *Meditationes*, Descartes seems to move in exactly the opposite direction, effectively denying that automata have sensations at all. Distinguishing three 'grades of sensory response', he remarks:

> The first is limited to the immediate stimulation of the bodily organs by external objects; this can consist in nothing but the motion of the particles of the organs, and any change of shape and position resulting from this motion. The second grade comprises all the immediate effects produced in the mind as a result of its being united with a bodily organ that is affected in this way. Such effects include the perceptions of pain, pleasure, thirst, hunger, colours, sound, taste, smell, heat, cold and the like, which arise from the union and as it were the intermingling of mind and body, as explained in the Sixth Meditation. The third grade includes all the judgements about things outside us which we have been accustomed to make from our earliest years – judgements that are occasioned by the movements of these bodily organs.[40]

Descartes describes the first grade of sensation as being common to us and brutes, suggesting that the perceptions of sound and smell, for example, are unique to us. This is very peculiar, since *L'Homme*, which is explicitly devoted to the description of an automaton, sets out in detail the psycho-physiology of automata, describing distance perception, the operation of memory, and other essentially cognitive operations, whereas here it would seem that a mind–body union is a prerequisite for such operations. I do not think there is any wholly satisfactory solution to this question, but it is worth noting that, if we follow the implications of the account in *L'Homme*, this does not commit us to the view that the phenomenology of cognitive experience is the same in us and in automata. That is to say, the automaton can have a representational response to a visual stimulus without that response taking exactly the same form as a human sensation: what an animal experiences when it perceives colour as a result of a visual stimulus is not necessarily the same as what we experience when we perceive colour under these circumstances. Usually, Descartes is careful to make this point in his discussion of animal sensation and thought. In a letter to Mersenne of 30 July 1640, he writes 'as for brute animals, we are so used to believing that they have feelings just like us/just like ours (*ainsi que nous*) that it is hard to rid ourselves of this opinion'.[41] In a letter to the Marquess of Newcastle, 23 November 1646, he responds to the idea that animals may have some thoughts such as we experience in ourselves with the remark that if they were 'to think as we do' then they would need an immaterial soul.[42] And in a letter to More of 5 February 1649, he makes it clear that his concern is specifically with whether animals 'have sensations like ours'.[43]

If we take the unqualified statement of the Replies to the sixth set of Objections as our guide to Descartes' thinking, as commentators (in ignorance of *L'Homme*) have traditionally done, denying any genuine cognition in automata, then Descartes' detailed account of the psychophysiology of automata, in chapter 3 of *L'Homme*, for example, would either be completely mysterious, or we would have to say that, by the time of the *Meditationes*, Descartes had abandoned this potentially fruitful approach, which he worked out in detail, in favour of the view that only human beings are capable of genuine cognition, without giving us any reason why he has moved to this sterile doctrine, a doctrine clearly not required by his mechanistic construal of physiology. I do not deny that Descartes is treading a fine line here, or that there is a significant degree of unclarity. The distinction between the claim that animals have no thoughts or sensations, and the claim that they have no thoughts or sensations like the ones we have, seems a central one to us,[44] and Descartes can be criticised for carelessness in not always making clear which he means; but the point remains that he does often explicitly make the second claim, and the second claim is the only one that enables us to make sense of the ambitious programme of *L'Homme*.

In sum, we have three kinds of account in Descartes. First we have the statement in the Replies to the sixth set of Objections that animals do not

---

41 AT III. 121.   42 AT I. 576.   43 AT V. 276–7.

44 This distinction might be questioned on the grounds that anything – tables, chairs, hydrogen atoms – might be said to have sensations 'but not like ours', if this latter qualification is construed broadly. On the other hand, if we insist that something has sensations only if they have sensations just like mine, then we may find ourselves with the problem of other minds, for other human beings may not have sensations exactly like mine. The fact that we have no difficulty recognising cognitive advance up the evolutionary scale – there is an increase in the complexity and quality of the sensation we are prepared to ascribe to earthworms, dogs, apes, and humans – suggests that we have no practical difficulty in distinguishing forms of sensation different from ours, even if we are wholly unable to describe the phenomenology of such sensations.

have sensations; second, we have several statements that animals do not have sensations like ours; and, third, we have a detailed account of vision and memory in animals which clearly construes them as cognitive states, that is, genuine sensations. The second and third are unproblematically reconcilable and suggest an interesting programme of research which is quite compatible with his post-*Meditationes* accounts of these matters, such as *La Description* and *Les Passions de l'Ame*, whereas the statement in the Replies to the sixth set of Objections is anomalous and provides an account wholly lacking in natural–philosophical interest. Let us, therefore, pursue the former approach and see how far Descartes can get with it.

The problem is that, while Descartes can allow that automata have representations, it is not immediately clear how he can allow that they grasp the content of these representations if they are not aware of them as representations: if, unlike human beings, they cannot make judgements about them as representations, for example about their veridicality.

In what sense can automata be aware of the content of representations without being able to respond to them as representations? Descartes' problem might be put in these terms. The behaviour of automata is such that they must be construed as responding to perceptual and other cognitive stimuli in a genuinely cognitive way, that is, in a way that goes beyond a stimulus–response arc. In other words, their behaviour indicates that they are sentient. But they are not conscious: that is, they have no awareness of their own cognitive states as such and so cannot make judgements as to their content. Consequently, Descartes has to account for the behaviour of sentient but non-conscious automata. Because automata lack a rational soul and so are literally 'mindless', this can only be done in terms of a mechanistic physiology.

In general terms, what we need to do is to capture the difference between sentient and non-sentient behaviour, and set out how this is reflected in differences at the level of a mechanistic physiology. On the first question, the difference between sentience and non-sentience, this is, of course, a grey area, but one crucial difference that we might point to is that there is a sense in which sentient beings are able to process information: they are able to interpret stimuli, and this interpretation determines their response. Descartes gives us some hints as to how this difference might be manifested in chapter 1 of *Le Monde*, for not only is it established there that there is a certain level of processing of visual information that requires nothing over and above corporeal organs, but we are also given some account of what such processing would consist in.

In chapter 1 of *Le Monde*, Descartes looks at the relation between the physical agitation of matter that results in a stimulation of the eye, and the visual cognition that we have as a result of this. Previously, his account had focused on getting the 'perceptual' part of perceptual cognition right, whereas here he concentrates on the 'cognition' side of the question. By contrast with the *Regulae*, for example, in *Le Monde* perceptual cognition is not thought of in causal terms, and it is not thought of as a multi-stage process. Rather, the treatment focuses on two questions: the form of the representation, and the question of how we are able to respond to certain properties or events as information.

On the first question, Descartes rejects a resemblance theory of perception of the kind that Aristotle and his followers had assumed must hold if perception is to be veridical. He argues that in order to represent the world, the perceptual image need not resemble it.[45] Indeed, many features of our perceptual image of the world – colours, sounds, odours etc. – are not features of the world at all. In *L'Homme* he goes on to apply the representation account to another cognitive operation, namely memory, with very significant consequences. Because his contemporaries had assumed that mnemonic representations, or memory traces, must resemble the original perceptual source, since that is what we recall, their attention was devoted to how such a huge amount of detail could possibly be stored, and they proposed various accounts of storage, many of which focused on the large surface area provided by the crinkled surface of the brain. Descartes' approach is completely different to this.

What memory does, on Descartes' account, is to enable previous representations on the pineal gland to be formed again, without the existence of the objects to which they correspond.[46] His account of both storage and retrieval of memory is organised around ease of accommodation to a mechanistic model, and this dictates what questions he is and is not concerned with. He shows no interest at all in the traditional practical questions of memory which had dominated sixteenth-century discussions, which centred around mnemonics, for example, but nor does he show much interest in the details of localisation of memory, which had played such a crucial role not just in the anatomical tradition but in the late Scholastic treatment of memory also. Rather, he is concerned with *how* memory is stored, and the account he offers has two distinctive features. First, just as in his account of visual cognition, no resemblance between experience and memory is required, and this gives the account a significant degree of flexibility. Contrary to what was a universal assumption at the time, on Descartes' account pineal patterns do not have to be stored

[45] AT xi. 3–6.   [46] AT xi. 178.

separately and faithfully – they do not have to be kept in the same form between experiencing and remembering – but just in a way that enables the idea to be presented again on the pineal gland. His account suggests a dispositional model in which storage may be implicit rather than explicit: a memory may be generated from stored items without itself being a stored item.[47] Secondly, storage and retrieval are accounted for in exclusively physical terms. Storage is effected through bending and rearranging of brain filaments, and retrieval is helped by repetition of recall. An analogy is drawn with a linen cloth which has several needles repeatedly passed through it (see Fig. 7.2). The holes in the cloth will

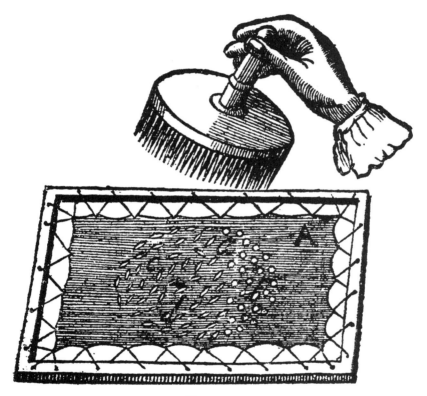

Figure 7.2

mostly remain open after the needles have been withdrawn, but those that do not will still leave physical traces which can easily be reopened.

[47] See John Sutton, *Philosophy and Memory Traces* (Cambridge, 1998).

The importance of this is that the associative basis of Descartes' account of recall can be captured, as total recall as a result of partial input can be accounted for: 'if I see two eyes with a nose, I at once imagine a forehead and a mouth and all the other parts of a face, because I am unaccustomed to seeing the former without the latter'.[48]

On the second question, what Descartes effectively proposes is that we conceive of visual cognition, not in terms of the mechanical–causal process involved in perception, but in terms of a single unified act of comprehension. He spells this out in terms of a new linguistic model of perception:

As you know, the fact that words bear no resemblance to the things they signify does not prevent them from causing us to conceive of those things, often without our paying attention to the sounds of the words or to their syllables. Thus it can turn out that, having heard something and understood its meaning perfectly well, we might not be able to say in what language it was uttered. Now if words, which signify something only through human convention, are sufficient to make us think of things to which they bear no resemblance, why should not nature also have established some sign which would make us have a sensation of light, even if that sign had in it nothing that resembled this sensation? And is it not thus that nature has established laughter and tears, to make us read joy and sorrow on the face of men?[49]

If we distinguish between the question of how perceptual information is conveyed, and the question of how perceptual information is represented, then we can see that Descartes is retaining a causal–mechanical model for the first, and advocating a linguistic model for the second. On the linguistic model, we grasp an idea in virtue of a sign which represents that idea to us. So, in the case of a conventional linguistic sign, when we know English, the word 'dog' conveys to us the idea of a dog. And just as conventional signs do not resemble what they signify, so, too, natural signs do not resemble what they signify either. Descartes tells us that there is in nature a sign which is responsible for our sensation of light, but which is not itself light, and which does not resemble light. All there is in nature is motion. In the case of a natural sign like motion, provided we have the ability to recognise and interpret it, when we grasp motion what it will convey to us is light. Light is what we will experience when we respond in the appropriate way to the sign. As examples of natural signs, Descartes tells us that tears are a natural sign of sadness and laughter a

[48] AT XI. 179.   [49] AT XI. 4.

natural sign of joy. One of the things that distinguishes signs from causes is that whether a sign signifies something to us – that is, whether we can call it a sign in the first place – depends on our ability to recognise and interpret the sign, and it is this ability on our part that makes the signs what they are. Causation is clearly different from this, for causes do not depend in any way upon our ability to recognise them. The question is what makes natural signs *signs*. It cannot be, or cannot merely be, something in nature, for something cannot be a sign for us unless we can recognise it, so it must be something in us that makes tears, or laughter, or a particular kind of motion, signs. This something in us must be an acquired or an innate capacity; and Descartes' view is that it is an innate capacity which, it will turn out, God has provided us with. There would be no natural signs unless we had the capacity to recognise them as such.

Here, I suggest we have the two key pieces in the account of sentience. Sentient responses are different from non-sentient responses in that, in the latter case, we can give a full account merely by showing the causal–mechanical processes involved. In the case of sentient responses, this will not tell us everything we need to know, and we need to supplement it with a different kind of account. There is an element of reciprocity in perceptual cognition as linguistically modelled that we do not find in the causal–mechanical account. The linguistic model enables us to grasp what perceptual understanding consists in, whereas the causal–mechanical account describes what physical-cum-physiological processes must occur if this understanding is to take place. This is the core difference between sentience and non-sentience. Non-sentient responses to stimulus, such as reflex activity in animals and in 'sensitive' plants, are accounted for fully when we are able to provide the appropriate causal–mechanical account, but this will only ever be an ingredient in a complete account of sentient responses, the characteristic feature of which is that they involve a representation of the stimulus.

The next question is whether the form of interpretation modelled on language is realisable in a mechanistic physiology alone. What we need, over and above the causal–mechanical account that we provide of non-sentient responses, is some means of forming representations in response to perceptual stimuli, and we need some means of storing and recalling these representations. In one sense, many automata – those to which we are inclined to ascribe some kind of sophistication in perceptual cognition, such as higher mammals – clearly have the physiological means to do this. They have pineal glands, which is where perceptual representations are formed, and they have memories, i.e. corporeal means of storage of representations.

But Descartes needs to say more than this, and it is in his tantalisingly brief account of light in the first chapter of *Le Monde* that he gives his indication of what this 'more' might be. Remember that we are told that light is not the stimulus but the response to the stimulus. The stimulus is a particular kind of motion in the smallest kind of matter which is transmitted via the second matter. Now note also that, in order to respond to this particular kind of motion by perceiving light, we have to be able to respond in the right way (this is what makes this a significatory event as well as a causal one). To be able to respond in the right way, we need some kind of innate or built-in capacity. Here the question arises as to whether such innate capacities are part of our corporeal organs or our minds. One only has to note the fact that automata are able to see, that is, perceive light, whereas disembodied minds are not,[50] to recognise that the capacity to grasp various kinds of translational and rotary motion as light must naturally reside in corporeal organs. Descartes never suggests that automata cannot respond to natural signs; indeed, such functions as nutrition in higher animals, where the appropriate kind of food has to be sought out visually or olfactorily, clearly require such recognitional capacities. Indeed, more generally, it is difficult to explain how animal instincts are to be accounted for if not in terms of some innate capacity.

In more modern terms, what we need is 'hard wiring'. The brain needs to be fitted out so as to respond in the appropriate way. The hard wiring makes sure you get the right kind of representations: that you see light, that is, have a visual image which displays shapes and colours, when stimulated in the requisite way. It is not something in nature that causes us to have visual images, it is a combination of a stimulation produced by nature and certain features of an animal's physiology which result in a particular kind of representation, a visual perception.

It is important to realise here that, in the case of perceptual cognition in automata, Descartes' aim is not to deny that there is a functional story to be told, but rather to indicate how the functional story can be translated into the terms of a mechanistic physiology without losing the key insight that perception of x by y involves x *meaning something to* y, so that, for example, y perceives x as a lion. What is needed is the capacity to translate the visual stimulation, which might be characterised

---

[50] 'The human mind separated from the body does not have sense-perception strictly so called' (Descartes to More, August 1649; AT v. 402).

as agitation of the corpuscles making up the retina, into the requisite perceptual representation, that is, one that conveys the idea of a lion. This can be achieved by the requisite corporeal organs in the brain.

We should not underestimate the degree of sophistication possible within Descartes' version of a mechanised psycho-physiology. In particular, along with memory, there are a number of very advanced cognitive operations that we can attribute to animals on Descartes' account, and two such operations will serve to give a good indication of just how powerful his account is.

The first of these is colour perception, which involves enhancement of visual information on the Cartesian account. This a capacity which, like distance perception, involves no conscious intellectual activity on our part, and seems similarly ordained by nature, but it requires significant cognitive processing. On Descartes' account of colour, the natural world is colourless, but when the fine corpuscles making up light rays are reflected off surfaces having particular structural features they are given a spin, which results in a rotation of the rays. What we experience when our eyes are stimulated by this rotation is colour, because of an innate faculty that we have to respond in this way.[51] Now we perceive colours as if they were in the world, so it might seem that God has given us deceptive faculties in this respect. Descartes denies this, arguing that sensory perception has been given to us by God for the preservation of our bodies: as he puts it in Meditation 6, 'the proper purpose of sensory perceptions given me by nature is simply to inform the mind of what is beneficial or harmful for the mind/body composite'.[52] This is one of the few doctrines on which all Cartesians in the seventeenth century were agreed, even Malebranche and Arnauld, who agreed on little else. Arnauld gives the best statement of the doctrine:

It must not be imagined that there is nothing in [a body] which causes it to appear to me to be of one colour rather than another. This is surely due to a different arrangement of the small parts of their surface, which is responsible for the corpuscles which are reflected from the [body] towards our eyes stimulating the fibres of the optic nerve in different ways. But because our soul would find it too difficult to discern the difference in these stimulations, which is only one of degree, God has decided in this respect to give us the means to discern them more easily by those sensations of different colours, which he has willed be caused in our soul on the occasion of these various stimulations of the optic nerve, just as tapestry workers have a pattern, which they call a 'rough pattern', where the

[51] See *Notae in Programma*; AT VIIIA. 359.   [52] AT VII. 83.

various shades of the same colour are indicated by completely different colours, so that they are less liable to mistake them.[53]

Arnauld talks of the 'soul' here, because he is concerned with human visual cognition, but there is no conscious interpretation on our part, and nothing in principle to prevent the same capacity in animals: and we must remember here no one in the seventeenth century even raised the question of whether animals might not see the world as coloured. Indeed, colour enhancement in visual cognition is a paradigm psycho-physiological operation.

The second advanced cognitive operation which is a matter of pure psycho-physiology, and hence available to animals lacking a rational soul, is distance perception. What makes contact with the eye from the observed object – rays made up of streams of light corpuscles[54] – does not and cannot convey information in itself about the distance of its source. Yet a mechanist account such as Descartes', which restricts causal processes to those involving contact action, requires that the perceiver be able to gauge the distance of any source purely from information given within the visual process itself. In *L'Homme* and in *La Dioptrique*, Descartes offers a number of criteria by which we are aware of distance in visual perception. Two of these, namely distinctness of outline or of colour, and inference of size from past experience, are traditional, and another – degree of deflection in the pineal gland resulting in changes in the flow of animal spirits – is not illuminating. But the two others are interesting. The first is the degree of curvature of the lens: it is a matter of elementary optics that the lens must be flatter the more distant the object, and since the shape of the lens is controlled by the lens' muscles, which in turn are controlled by the degree to which the pores admitting spirits to the nerves which control these muscles are open, there will be a significant difference between focus on close and on distant objects. How we are aware of this difference is not specified, however, and Descartes simply tells us that 'the soul will be able to know the distance'.[55]

The other means of determining distance is by far the most ingenious, and the most important of them all from the point of view of mechanism.

[53] A. Arnauld, *On True and False Ideas*, ed. and trans. Stephen Gaukroger (Manchester and New York, 1990), 131–2.
[54] Strictly speaking, what we have here is a transverse motion of the fine matter packing the interstices between the corpuscles making up the medium, whose action is transmitted instantaneously in a straight line; see ch. 14 of *Le Monde*, AT x. 97–103.
[55] AT xi. 159–60.

The criteria just mentioned simply tell us how we judge distance, without explaining how it is possible in the first place that we might see things that we are not in contact with. Mechanism restricts all action to contact action, and this is, at least in the first instance, a problem for distance perception such as that which occurs in vision. In visual perception, we not only see distant things, we see them (within limits of precision) as being at a particular distance: how is this possible when our eyes are stimulated simply by corpuscles in contact with them? Here Descartes' theory of the eye's 'natural geometry' is crucial, because it is designed to tell us how something in contact with the eye can convey information about the distance of its source. Descartes compares our distance vision to a blind man holding out two sticks so that they converge on an object (Fig. 7.3), and calculating the distance of the object from the base angles

Figure 7.3

of the triangle so formed, where the base is simply the distance between the sticks in the man's hands. The blind man does not know the lengths of the sticks, but he can calculate this by means of a 'natural geometry'

from the length of the base and the base angles. Analogously with the
eyes (Fig. 7.4): here the base angles are given by the angles at which the

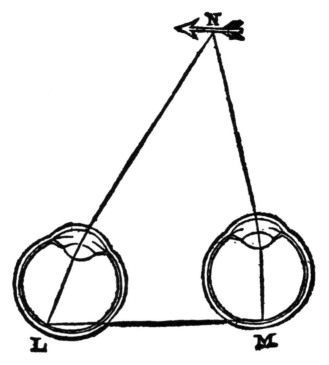

Figure 7.4

light rays strike the eye, and an apparently innate 'natural geometry'
enables us to calculate the distance of the object in the same way that the
blind man does. This doctrine, which is fully in accord with the account
of the nature of light and its action offered in *Le Monde*, secures both the
restriction of all influence to contact action, and the possibility of genuine
distance vision. We are not aware of any such calculation, of course, and
Descartes describes the process as being 'ordained by nature',[56] which
indicates it comes under psycho-physiology rather than mental activity
proper: in particular, it is not a matter of intellectual judgement.

It might be asked how an inferential process like calculation, unconscious or otherwise, could be ascribed to a mindless animal. But in
Rule 2 of the *Regulae*, Descartes tells us that 'none of the errors to which

[56] AT X. 134–5.

men – men, I say, not brute animals – are liable is ever due to faulty inference'[57] because our inference is always guided by the natural light of reason, which is infallible. In other words, brute animals make inferences, but, lacking the natural light of reason, these are at least occasionally faulty: Descartes is prepared to construe inference, at least at some level, as a psycho-physiological process. Animals are, of course, unable to reflect upon the inferential processes they engage in, and, to the extent that they calculate, in distance perception for example, they are completely unaware of what they are doing.

AFFECTIVE STATES IN ANIMALS

Sentient animals have not only cognitive states but affective ones as well. Descartes make it clear that animals can express fear, hope, and joy:

> If you teach a magpie to say good-day to its mistress when it sees her approach, this can only be because you are making the utterance of this word the expression of one of its passions. It will be an expression of the hope of eating, for example, if it has always been given a tidbit when it says it. Similarly, all the things which dogs, horses, and monkeys are taught to perform are only expressions of their fear, their hope, and their joy; and consequently they can be performed without any thought.[58]

Moreover Descartes has no doubt that these affective states in automata can be explained in the same way as cognitive states:

> I am not disturbed by the astuteness and cunning of dogs or foxes, or all the things which animals do for the sake of food, sex, and fear; I maintain that I can easily explain the origin of all these things from the constitution of their organs.[59]

In the early modern era, parallels between animals and human beings were predominantly parallels between their affective states rather than between their cognitive states. The idea that different species of animals manifested particular passions and/or virtues goes back at least to the Patristic writers, and supplied a staple diet of iconography for medieval and Renaissance writers and painters. Early modern writers continue in this tradition.[60] 'Animals are always uniform in all their actions', one anonymous seventeenth-century writer, summing up centuries of reflection

---

[57] AT x. 365.
[58] Descartes to the Marquess of Newcastle, 23 November 1646; AT IV. 574–5.
[59] Descartes to More, 5 February 1649; AT v. 278.
[60] See Peter Harrison, 'Reading the Passions: the Fall, the Passions, and Dominion over Nature', in Stephen Gaukroger, ed., *The Soft Underbelly of Reason* (London, 1998), 49–78. The references in this paragraph derive from Harrison's enlightening account.

of these matters, tells us, 'the Lyon is always generous, the Hare ever cowardly; the Tyger, cruel; the Fox, crafty'.[61] Moreover, these features generally had an explanatory role. Thomas Wright, for example, in his *Passions of the Minde* (1601) introduces eleven basic passions, and illustrates them by making reference to the behaviour of the sheep and the wolf.[62] Marin Cureau de la Chambre, one of the most influential writers on the passions in the seventeenth century, sets out his account of the various passions in terms of the characteristics of various animals, so that courage, for example, is illustrated in terms of the behaviour of lions.[63] It is instructive here that having a low view of a particular species means attributing a disreputable distinctive affective state to it: not refusing to attribute an affective state to it at all. Affective states appear to be widely attributed to animals, and Descartes is no exception. But what Descartes sees as distinctive about human beings in this respect is instructive. He notes that the signs of passions in animals are, like their cognitive behaviour,[64] natural and invariant, and that animals are unable to disguise their affective states, whereas those in humans can be modified by the soul: 'the soul is able to change facial expressions', he tells us, 'as well as expressions of the eyes . . . Thus we may use such expressions to hide our passions as well as reveal them.'[65]

What distinguishes us from automata, at the level of affective states, is not the absence of such states in automata, any more than what distinguishes us from automata at the level of cognitive states is the absence of cognitive states in automata. Moreover, although there are differences between the kinds of cognitive and affective states available to human being and those available to automata, this does not seem to be the crucial issue either. Rather, the key difference seems to lie in the ability of human beings to stand back from, make judgements about, and ultimately control their cognitive and affective states. Human beings are able to shape and reform their cognitive and affective lives in a way automata are not. It is to these questions that we now turn.

---

[61] G. Havers, *A General Collection of the Discourses of the Virtuosi of France* (London, 1664), 139.

[62] Thomas Wright, *Passions of the Minde* (London, 1601), 41.

[63] Marin Cureau de la Chambre, *Les Charactères des passions* (4 vols. in 2, Paris, 1658–1662).

[64] See Descartes to the Marquess of Newcastle, 23 November 1646: 'I know that animals do many things better than we do, but this does not surprise me. It can even be used to prove that they act naturally and mechanically, like a clock that tells the time better than our judgement does. Doubtless when swallows come in Spring, they operate like clocks. The actions of honey bees are of the same nature; so also is the discipline of cranes in flight, and of apes in fighting, if it is true that they keep discipline. Their instinct to bury their dead is no stranger than that of dogs and cats who scratch the earth for the purpose of burying their excrement; they hardly ever bury it, which shows that they act only by instinct and without thinking' (AT IV. 575–6).

[65] *Passions de l'Ame*, art. 113; AT XI. 412–13.

CHAPTER 8

Principia, *Part VI: Man*

If Descartes is prepared to attribute a range of cognitive and affective states to animals, including some kind of reasoning processes, even if unconscious ones, the problem is less that he makes animals into mere machines, but rather that animal faculties are capable of so much that the line between animals and human beings becomes blurred. Could not the account of animal faculties be extended into the explanation of human behaviour? La Mettrie's Cartesian-inspired doctrine of 'man machine' may have been the only significant positive construal along these lines,[1] but the opprobrium that Descartes' doctrine of the 'animal machine' attracted over more than two centuries was not due to the fact that his critics were animal lovers who thought him unfair to animals,[2] but to the fact that the sharp distinction between animals and humans seemed to have been compromised. In fact, in Descartes' view, the gulf was as wide as ever, and indeed it rested on the very traditional basis of human beings being unique in having the faculty of free will, although, when it came to the detail, what Descartes had to offer on the question of what made human beings different from animals was a novel and uncompromising theory about the unity of one's mental life, for it is this unity that ultimately supplies the possibility of moral responsibility, something that is lacking in animals.

There is, nevertheless, something distinctive about human cognitive states that marks them out from the cognitive states of automata. There is a kind of reflective perceptual cognition possible in human beings which is quite different from anything we find in automata, and which depends on the possession of a mind. This prompts us to reflect on the question

---

[1] See Aram Vartanian, *La Mettrie's L'Homme Machine: A Study in the Origins of An Idea* (Princeton, 1960), which includes a critical edition of the text.

[2] The treatment of animals in the seventeenth century was undeniably cruel by modern Western standards, but it was not as dire as it is sometimes made out to be; see Keith Thomas, *Man and the Natural World: Changing Attitudes in England 1500–1800* (London, 1983).

of what exactly it is, on Descartes' account, that the mind does over and above the psycho-physical operations we share with automata.

COGNITION

What is at stake in Descartes' account of representational cognition in automata is the construal of all cognitive functions in terms of corporeal processes which involve only inert matter. It might be thought that this rids cognition of goal-directedness. If it did, if animal cognition were not to be construed in terms of cognitive goals, then surely this would be tantamount to eliminativism. But, in fact, Descartes does not deny cognitive goals in animal cognition any more than he denies developmental goals in his embryology. In his account of the development of the foetus, he does not deny that there is a question as to why the constituent matter of the foetus behaves in such a way that the foetus develops into an adult of a particular species: a camel foetus develops into a camel, a horse foetus into a horse, and so on. But it develops into an animal of a particular species not because the foetal matter in camels and horses is different: there is only one kind of matter, namely material extension. Nor is it because there is some soul or spirit in the foetus which guides it in different ways. Nor, finally, is there some internally goal-directed process at work here, for to admit that would be to admit that matter could harbour goals. His argument is that the explanation for foetal development is not something *internal* to the development of the foetus, but something *external* to it. God made it so; that is, he structured the animal's womb in such a way that foetal matter contained in it developed in one way rather than another. God is the only final cause. And God is an external cause, whereas what Descartes is concerned with are internal causes. The same holds for his account of perceptual cognition. Descartes does not deny that God has given automata the sense organs they have, along with various cognitive abilities such as distance estimation and colour enhancement, so that they might protect and sustain themselves in the world. It is just that the question of *how* the sense organs operate, which is what he is concerned with, is different from *why* they operate in that way. Indeed, on Descartes' account, these are *completely* different questions.

However, when the body is considered, no longer as the body of an animal or an *homme machine*, but as part of what Descartes will refer to as 'the substantial union of mind and body' then intrinsic goals re-enter the picture. Human beings are able to reflect upon and make judgements about the content of their perceptual representations – they are to able to make judgements as to their veridicality, for example – and the nature of perception is transformed as a result. Unlike the perceptual cognition of an automaton, which has no intrinsic goals, human perception must be considered in terms of a goal, the goal of understanding the world, and it can be criticised, for example, to the extent to which it fails to achieve that goal. Intrinsic goals enter the picture because of the presence of a conscious intelligence, and that, on Descartes' account, is their proper place.

It will be helpful here to consider a case of distinctively rational or human perceptual cognition. In *La Discours*, describing the project he had pursued in *L'Homme*, Descartes separates out those cognitive operations we share with animals and those we do not:

When I looked to see what functions would occur in such a body, I found exactly those that occur in us without our reflecting upon them, and hence having no contribution from our soul: that is, from that part of us, distinct from body, whose nature, as I have said, is simply to think. These functions are just those in which animals that lack reason may be said to resemble us. But I could find none of the functions which, because they depend on thought, are the only ones that belong to us men; though I found these later, as soon as I supposed that God created a rational soul and joined it to this body in the way I have described.[3]

What is an example of the latter? What we need is a case of perceptual cognition that is not found in animals but is unique to us, and this rules out some cognitively sophisticated operations such as memory, colour perception, and distance perception, which I have argued Descartes can legitimately ascribe to automata. The only case of distinctively rational or human perceptual cognition that Descartes examines at any length is the case of our quantitative understanding of natural processes: the sort of understanding we have, in a sophisticated form, in pursuing a mathematical physics of the kind that Descartes pursues in optics, for example. This case is of interest for a number of reasons, not least because it shows just how such perceptual cognition genuinely lies between purely animal cognition, for example in the case of distance calculation in visual cognition, on the one hand, and intellectual cognition, as in the case of contemplation of universals abstracted from sense perception.

This case is dealt with in Rules 12 to 14 for the *Regulae*, where Descartes, working with a model of cognition which is still in some respects close to that of traditional Scholasticism, deals in a very ambitious fashion with the issue of how a quantitative understanding of the corporeal world is

[3] AT VI. 46.

possible. Three things are involved in this form of cognition. The first is the corporeal world, the second the pure intellect, which contains abstractions, and the third the imagination, which is a corporeal organ which Descartes will later identify with the pineal gland. The title of Rule 14 reads: 'The problem should be re-expressed in terms of the real extension of bodies and should thus be pictured in our imagination entirely by means of bare figures. Thus it will be perceived much more distinctly by our intellect.' Given the context of the questions he is concerned with in Rule 14, what this looks like is the claim that, first, we should represent the corporeal world – this is what he refers to as the 're-expression' of the problem – in the imagination in terms of geometrical lines, and that, second, when we have done this, our intellect can inspect the contents of the imagination. But, when we look at the details, the second part of the process turns out to be achieved by representing the contents of the intellect in the imagination. In the case of our quantitative cognitive grasp of the world, what such grasp consists in is a twofold mapping in which the concrete contents of the corporeal world are represented symbolically in the imagination, and in which the abstract contents of the pure intellect are represented symbolically in the imagination. As a result of this, the one can now be mapped on to the other, such mapping being constitutive of quantitative cognition of the world.

This is a radical departure from the standard Thomist account, where the role of the imagination (taken to be a corporeal faculty) is to present sensory information to the (incorporeal) intellect, the imagination then dropping out of the picture as the intellect acts on the information in a way that is constitutive of perceptual cognition. The process Descartes envisages is one where the end point, the *locus* of perceptual cognition, is the imagination rather than the intellect. This must be the case in his account because the cognition consists in a particular kind of mapping of representations, which can only take place in the imagination, not in the intellect, because the mapping is a spatial one which needs a spatially extended region in which to occur.

Descartes' argument runs along the following lines. 'Extension' and 'body' are represented by different ideas in the intellect, because we can imagine all objects in the universe being annihilated and spatial extension remaining, but they are represented by one and the same idea in the imagination:

By 'extension' we mean whatever has length, breadth and depth, leaving to one side whether it is a real body or merely a space. This notion does not, I think, need further elucidation, for there is nothing more easily perceived by our imagination . . . For even though someone may convince himself, if we suppose every object in the universe annihilated, that this would not prevent extension per se existing, his conception would not use any corporeal image, but would be merely a false judgement of the intellect working alone. He will admit this himself if he reflects attentively on this image of extension which he tries to form in his imagination. For he will notice that he does not perceive it in isolation from every subject, and that his imagination of it and his judgement of it are quite different. Consequently, whatever our intellect may believe as to the truth of the matter, these abstract entities are never formed in the imagination in isolation from subjects.[4]

Just as with extension, similarly with number. When we say that 'number is not the thing counted' or 'extension or shape is not body', the meanings of 'number' and 'extension' here are such that there are no special ideas corresponding to them in the imagination. These two statements are 'the work of the pure intellect, which alone has the ability to separate out abstract entities of this type'.[5] Descartes insists that we must distinguish statements of this kind, in which the meanings of the terms are separated from the content of the ideas in the imagination, from statements in which the terms, albeit 'employed in abstraction from their subjects, do not exclude or deny anything which is not really distinct from what they denote'.[6]

The intellect, for Descartes as for Aquinas, has the role of separating out components of ideas by abstraction. But, for Descartes, entities conceived in the intellect, because they are free of images or 'bodily representations', are indeterminate. The imagination is required to render them determinate. When we speak of numbers, for example, the imagination must be employed to represent to ourselves something which can be measured by a multitude of objects. The intellect understands 'fiveness' as something separate from five objects (or line segments, or points, or whatever), and hence the imagination is required if this 'fiveness' is to correspond to something in the world. Descartes wants to argue that, in the mathematical case, what the intellect grasps are formal algebraic quantities. It is in so far as the objects of algebra, the indeterminate content of which has been separated out by the intellect, can be represented and conceived symbolically as lines and planes that they can be identified with the real world. Algebra deals with completely abstract entities, conceived in the intellect, but these abstract entities must be represented symbolically, and thus rendered determinate, which requires the aid of the imagination. The imagination thereby represents

---

[4] AT x. 442–3.   [5] AT x. 444.   [6] AT x. 445.

general magnitudes (abstract entities) as specific magnitudes (which are not distinct from what they are the magnitudes of).

As Descartes envisages this operation, the contents of the intellect and the contents of the world must both be represented in the imagination. The purely abstract entities of the intellect are represented as lines and line lengths, and the corporeal world is represented purely in terms of spatially extended magnitudes. The former, which are effectively measures of extended magnitudes, are mapped on to the latter, which are extended magnitudes. In other words, the pure thought characteristic of algebra which the intellect engages in does not map directly onto the corporeal world: it could not do so because it is indeterminate. Rather, a representation of it in the form of proportions depicted by line lengths maps onto a representation of the corporeal world, the latter representation consisting exclusively of two-dimensional shapes.

Because of the role that the imagination plays, our carrying out of mathematical operations, and the application of mathematics to the corporeal world, take place in the imagination. The imagination represents to itself the contents of the world and it represents to itself the contents of the intellect, and perceptual cognition takes place when it maps these on to one another. On the traditional Scholastic understanding of perceptual cognition, perceptual cognition would take place in animals in the imagination, because they lack an intellect, so the imagination is the highest faculty they possess; whereas, in the case of human beings, it is in the higher faculty of the intellect that perceptual cognition (like intellectual cognition) takes place.[7] But Descartes' account of perceptual cognition is quite different from this. The upshot of his account of perceptual cognition is that it is the imagination, which draws on both the intellect and the information gleaned from the sense organs, that is the site of perceptual cognition, just as it is in mindless animals. The difference is that, whereas the imagination in the mindless animal has only one input, a sensory one, that in the human being has a sensory and an intellectual input.

This intellectual input has been widely misunderstood, and the kind of account that we find in Aquinas, for example, whereby the perceptual process culminates in the intellect, has been read into Descartes' account, where the perceptual process, even when engaging the intellect, culminates in the imagination. The misreading has the effect of making

---

[7] There is a good detailed account of Aquinas' understanding of cognition in J. Peghaire, *Intellectus et ratio selon S. Thomas d'Aquin* (Paris and Ottawa, 1936).

perceptual cognition into a form of intellectual cognition. The confusion began with occasionalist doctrines in the seventeenth century, above all with Book I of Malebranche's *De la recherche de la vérité* (1677), and came to a head again in the twentieth century in Ryle's famous doctrine of 'the ghost in the machine'.[8] These both construe cognition by an embodied mind as if it were something having the typical characteristics of a disembodied mind but which interacts with a body to which it is somehow mysteriously connected.[9] It will be clear from what has already been said that such a view cannot be ascribed to Descartes, and he himself indicates just how different knowledge of the physical world by means of intellectual cognition would be when he writes to Regius that: 'If an angel were in a human body, it would not have sensations as we do, but would simply perceive the motions which are caused by external objects, and in this way would differ from a real human being.'[10]

Intellectual cognition is quite a different kind of process from perceptual cognition. It is the characteristic activity of a disembodied mind, but there is also a form of intellectual cognition in embodied minds. Information on the cognitive states of a disembodied mind is very scant in Descartes, and puzzling when it is provided. A disembodied mind has no sensory input either from perception, because it has no external sense organs (the organs of the five senses) and no internal sense organs (such as the *sensus communis*), or from memory or imagination, both of which require corporeal organs on his account. It seems that all that the disembodied mind can do is contemplate without perceptions or memories. Descartes does invoke something which he calls 'intellectual memory' on a number of occasions. Such intellectual memory might seem to be a distinctive feature of the cognition of the disembodied mind, along with the contemplation of universals, but his brief remarks on it are not consistent with one another. In a letter of condolence to Constantijn Huygens on the death of his wife, he tells Huygens that we shall recognise our loved ones in the afterlife, 'for I believe we have an intellectual memory which is certainly independent of the body'.[11] This seems clear cut, but two other mentions of such intellectual memory indicate that it is not a form of memory at all. In the first place, Descartes tells Burman that 'intellectual

[8] See Gilbert Ryle, *The Concept of Mind* (London, 1949).
[9] Among those who have resisted this misreading are John Cottingham, 'Descartes' Trialism', *Mind* 44 (1985), 218–30, and Amélie Rorty, 'Descartes on Thinking with the Body', in John Cottingham, ed., *The Cambridge Companion to Descartes* (Cambridge, 1992), 371–92.
[10] Descartes to Regius, January 1642; AT III. 493.
[11] Descartes to Huygens, 13 October 1632; AT III. 580.

memory has universals rather than particulars as its objects'.[12] Second, these universals are not related as being in a temporal sequence in intellectual memory, for, he writes, 'where purely intellectual things are concerned, memory in the strict sense is not involved; they are thought of just as readily irrespective of whether it is the first or the second time they come to mind – unless, as often happens, they are associated with particular names, in which case, since the latter are corporeal, we do indeed remember them'.[13]

So the content of an intellectual memory is a synchronic relation between universals, not, as with corporeal memory, a diachronic relation between particulars. The former is surely just what would otherwise, and more helpfully, be described as contemplation of universals. The fact that universals are grasped, and that they are grasped non-temporally, suggests that in such thought we are not representing universals to ourselves, in the way in which we would represent sensible particulars to ourselves, for on Descartes' view – and indeed in the view of all philosophers in the seventeenth century[14] – we cannot grasp particulars directly, only by means of perceptual representations, whereas there is no reason why we should not grasp universals directly: the ultimate object of cognition is not in any way removed from the site of cognition. This holds not just for disembodied cognition, where the objects of contemplation appear to be *sui generis*, but also for that intellectual cognition where the objects of contemplation can be abstracted from sense perception. Intellectual cognition in the embodied case occurs when the intellect abstracts from perceptual representations in the imagination (i.e. the pineal gland) and contemplates them as abstracted universals or some other form of abstraction. As we have seen, although this process plays a role in perceptual cognition, it is explicitly not tantamount to perceptual cognition, which is representational.

THE FRAGMENTATION OF THE SOUL

If, on the Cartesian account, what marks out animals from human beings at the level of the range of cognitive operations is less significant than it has often been taken to be, it is nevertheless significant. But Descartes did not treat these differences as being the core difference between human beings and animals. The perceptual cognitive operations we have discussed,

---

[12] AT v. 150.   [13] Descartes to Hyperaspites, 13 October 1642; AT IV. 574–5.
[14] See John Yolton, *Perceptual Acquaintance* (Oxford, 1984).

including uniquely human quantitative perceptual grasp, are relatively
discrete operations: they are, in modern terminology, relatively modular.
One of the reasons why, in *Les Passions de l'Ame*, Descartes rejects accounts
of our psychology that break up the mind into higher and lower functions,
as the Scholastic accounts did, is because he fears the fragmentation of
the mind that results from such a conception:

All the struggles that people customarily imagine between the lower part of
the soul, which is called sensitive, and the higher or 'rational' part, or between
the natural appetites and the will, just consist in the opposition between the
movements which the body, by its spirits, and the soul, by its will, tend to excite
simultaneously in the [pineal] gland. For there is only a single soul in us, and
this soul has within itself no diversity of parts; one and the same soul is sensitive
and rational, and all its appetites are volitions. (art. 47)

The considerations that drive the rejection of a division into higher and
lower functions must also drive any attempt to account for the human
mind wholly in modular terms. For what cognitive unity – whereby I can
say that these experiences are *my* experiences, that these memories are
my memories – is possible on this account? How can we hold ourselves
morally responsible if there is not something that lies behind our various
cognitive and affective states? How are acts of will possible if the mind
is fragmented?

The difference between human beings and animals, on Descartes' account, lies not so much in the nature of the cognitive states available to
human beings and animals (although there are some differences, as we
have seen), but in the fact that cognitive and affective states in animals
are fragmented and dispersed, or modularised, whereas human beings
have a 'self', something that holds together these cognitive and affective
states, this being a necessary condition of our ability to question whether
these cognitive states are veridical (e.g. to ask whether the world is really
coloured, as it appears to be), or whether particular affective states which
we experience are the appropriate ones. It is this 'self' that we are aware
of when we go through the *cogito*, and it is the 'thinking thing', the *res cogitans*, that we discover in the *cogito*. Moreover, this 'self' is what exercises
acts of will, and it gives human beings a unified mental life lacking in
automata, which is why, cognitively sophisticated as these automata may
be, we do not treat them as being able to reflect epistemologically on
the nature of their cognitive states, why we do not hold them morally responsible, and why they are not capable of language.[15] A unified mental

---

[15] *Discours de la Méthode* Part V; AT VI. 56–7.

life is indispensable for these functions, and full modularity, of the kind Descartes effectively postulates in automata, is incompatible with everything from language to moral responsibility. *This* is what makes automata *machines*.

We saw in the last chapter that Descartes pursues a reductionist account of cognition much further than has been thought. It should also be noted in this connection that his sense of the limits of this project – the point beyond which the reductionist has to become an eliminativist, beginning to explain away, rather than explain, with all the implausibility that comes with this – is dictated less by some pre-given notion of the human 'soul' than by a well-founded judgement of the gap between the nature of human experience and the picture that a modularised psychophysiology is able to provide.

Concern with the question of the fragmentation of the soul arises primarily in the context of the passions, rather than that of cognitive states, however, and it is in the context of the passions that the importance of the sharp distinction between mind and body becomes particularly evident, for it is here that we begin to see a real rationale for Cartesian dualism, a rationale not always evident in the *Meditationes*, for example, where the defence of dualism can have the appearance of dogma.[16] In the seventeenth century, it was in fact in the context of accounts of the passions that discussions of the nature of the relation between mind and body generally occurred. The passions were associated with bodily conditions, bringing them under the purview of medicine and physiology, but they were also given ethical meanings, bringing them under the purview of moral psychology and theology. Treatises on the passions traditionally shared this combination of concerns, and Petrarch's *De remediis*, for example, a compendium of Stoic techniques for 'healing the passions', can be read as a treatise on morals, or as a treatise on psychotherapy: the distinction is simply not there to be made.[17] Much the same can be said of the whole tradition of writing about the passions, including Descartes' *Les Passions de l'Ame*, which takes its purview to include the physiology of the passions, psychosomatic states such as melancholia, and considerations bearing on the fact that 'all good and evil in this life depend on [the passions] alone'.[18] The practical aim of treatises on the passions is, generally

---

[16] Gordon Baker and Katherine J. Morris, *Descartes' Dualism* (London, 1996), establish in detail why this is only an appearance.

[17] See Letizia A. Panizza, 'Stoic Psychotherapy in the Middle Ages and the Renaissance: Petrarch's *De remediis*', in Margaret Osler, ed., *Atoms, Pneuma, and Tranquillity* (Cambridge, 1991), 39–66.

[18] *Passions*, art. 212; AT XI. 488.

speaking, the 'healing of the soul', something which involves moral and psycho-therapeutic considerations, and these require an understanding of the bodily conditions associated with various afflictions of the soul which may give rise to anything from immorality to madness. It is in this light that we must understand Descartes' remark in *La Discours* that 'even the mind depends so much on the temperament and disposition of the bodily organs that if it is possible to find some means of making men in general wiser and more skilful than they have been up to now, I believe I must look for it in medicine'.[19]

It is true that in the Preface to *Les Principes*, morals is listed along with mechanics and medicine as one of the three fundamental sciences, although we are to understand by the term 'the highest and most perfect moral system, which presupposes a complete knowledge of the other sciences [viz. medicine and mechanics] and is the ultimate level of wisdom'.[20] In other words, moral philosophy is not *sui generis*. It emerges naturally out of his natural philosophy, particularly his account of the psycho-physiology of affective states, which in turn rests upon his account of physiology and ultimately upon the general principles of his natural philosophy. In 1646, on hearing that his friend Chanut is undertaking a study of moral philosophy, Descartes writes:

I agree with you entirely that the safest way to find out how we should live is to discover first what we are, what kind of world we live in, and who is the creator of this world, or the master of the house we live in. But I cannot at all claim or promise that all I have written is true, and besides there is a very great distance between the general notion of heaven and earth, which I have tried to convey in my *Principia*, and a detailed knowledge of the nature of man, which I have not yet discussed. However, I do not want you to think I wish to divert you from your plan, and so I must say in confidence that what little knowledge of physics I have tried to acquire has been a great help to me in establishing sure foundations in moral philosophy. Indeed I have found it easier to reach satisfactory conclusions on this topic than on many others concerning medicine on which I have spent much more time. So instead of finding ways to preserve life, I have found another, much easier and surer way, which is not to fear death. But this does not depress me, as it commonly depresses those whose wisdom is drawn entirely from the teaching of others, and rests on foundations that depend only on human prudence and authority.[21]

A clue to the orientation of Descartes' whole approach is given in his statement at the beginning of *Les Passions* that he writes not as 'an orator,

---

[19] AT vi. 62.   [20] AT ixb. 14.   [21] Descartes to Chanut, 15 June 1646; AT iv. 441–2.

nor as a moral philosopher, but as a physicist [*physicien*]'.²² This means two things. First, his treatment of the passions is dependent upon the metaphysical foundations of natural philosophy set out in the *Principia*, and, in this respect, the passions have the same ultimate foundation as the two other basic sciences, mechanics and medicine. The first principles provide a framework within which the exposition of doctrine must proceed if any systematic certainty is to attach to one's conclusions. In writing as a '*physicien*' and not as a moral philosopher, Descartes is providing an account of the passions, and hence morality, which is not *sui generis* but rests upon a whole system of natural philosophy. Moreover, in virtue of this, he is also advocating something that aspires to a degree of certainty lacking in rival accounts. Descartes' image of philosophy as a tree, with metaphysics as the roots, physics (natural philosophy) the trunk, and the specific sciences of mechanics, medicine, and morals as the branches²³ is instructive. And just as it is from the ends of the branches of the tree that the fruits are gathered, so, too, the fruits of the perfect wisdom that he sought from his system are to be found in the practical benefits of his philosophy: power to control the environment through mechanics, the promotion of health and the prolongation of life through medicine, and the achievement of true happiness and a proper understanding of the relation between mind and body through ethics.²⁴

The traditional disputes over the nature of the passions had a number of features, but one basic polarity that pervades them is that between what can broadly be termed Stoic and Augustinian conceptions of the passions. The Stoics treated the passions as false judgements, and, following an already strong tradition of intellectualist ethics in Greek thought, they identified virtue and knowledge. Augustine was motivated by a number of theological problems that had concerned the Alexandrian Church Fathers generally about the relations between bodily passions and passions of the soul, but he was also very concerned with the question of how there could be evil in the world if God was good. His solution was to make human beings responsible for evil, and the philosophical tool that he uses to achieve this is the notion of free will. While earlier theories of moral behaviour had invoked the notion of responsibility for action, none of them introduced the notion of the will in this context. Augustine did, and he explained the existence of evil thereby. But the theory of the will had ramifications for his views on the intellect and sensation, freedom

---

²² *Les Passions*, Reply to Second Letter; AT XI. 326.   ²³ AT XIB. 14.
²⁴ See John Cottingham, *Philosophy and the Good Life* (Cambridge, 1998), 9.

and determination, and the moral evaluation of purpose and action.[25] In particular, the ethical consideration of the passions now comes to be formulated in terms of the action of the will. Affective states, which he treats as the soul's motions, cannot simply be referred to a criterion of rationality, as the Stoics had urged, but must be assessed in terms of the act of will from which they arise, and 'if the will is wrongly directed the emotions will be wrong; if the will is right, the emotions will be not only blameless but praiseworthy'.[26] The fundamental character of the will, which guides its inclinations, is love, and virtuous affections are to be distinguished from vicious ones in terms of the moral quality of the love that rules in the will.

Once the topic of the affections had been formulated in terms of the action of the will, a long exercise of classification and categorisation of them began, the most systematic account being that provided by Aquinas in Part II.i of the *Summa theologica*. Like Augustine, Aquinas is opposed to the Stoic doctrine, pointing out that the Stoics confuse sensitive and rational appetites, and hence the passions and the acts of will which alone are the seat of moral good and evil.[27] He begins by distinguishing 'passions of the body', such as physical suffering, which originate in the body and terminate in the soul, from 'passions of the soul', which originate in the soul and terminate in the body. The various passions of the soul generally recognised are then classified into concupiscible affections (desires and appetites) and irascible affections (the passions strictly speaking), the former regarding good or evil absolutely and directly, the latter regarding good and evil 'ratione ardui', that is, as something to be attained or avoided only with difficulty. The classification distinguishes between concupiscible affections directed towards a good object – love, desire, and pleasure or joy – concupiscible affections directed towards an evil object – hate, aversion, and pain or sorrow – irascible affections directed towards a good object – hope and despair – and irascible affections directed towards an evil object – fear, courage, and anger. But the point of the exercise goes beyond mere classification of affective states. Aquinas' aim is to provide a genealogy for the passions whereby they can all be derived from four: pleasure, pain, hope, and fear. Pleasure and pain are the termini of all the passions, in that all the passions result in one or other of these, and hope and fear are the termini of the movements of the

[25] On the difference between Augustine's account of moral responsibility and that of his predecessors, see Dihle, *The Theory of the Will.*
[26] Augustine, *De Civitate Dei*, XIV, cap. 6.   [27] Aquinas, *Summa theologica*, Qu. XXIV, art. 1–2.

appetite: to take Aquinas' example, love passes through desire to hope, hate through aversion to fear.[28] This classification and genealogy of the passions provided the model for subsequent discussion, and, despite the fact that the two most influential later writers on the passions, Vives and Descartes, rejected it, it continued well into the eighteenth century.[29]

Aquinas' account of the physiology of the passions reflects the traditional treatment, a treatment that was bequeathed to the seventeenth century. A passion arises when something good or evil is apprehended, exciting an appetite, which induces a bodily change. The passion is constituted by the dual movement of the appetite and the body: among the causes of the passion are the bodily 'complexion', which predisposes the body in various ways, and the particular bodily accompaniments of the passion which characterise that passion. This does not mean, however, that the state of mind that results is merely an effect of the bodily changes, a mere consciousness of them, for the bodily changes are merely an embodiment of the apprehension of good or evil seeking satisfaction. As Aquinas puts it, 'the affections of the soul are not caused by changes in the heart, but rather cause them ... A man does not seek vengeance because the blood about the heart is inflamed; this is what disposes him to anger, but the anger itself comes from the appetite of vengeance.'[30] Gardiner sums up the doctrine well, noting that, while Aquinas makes bodily changes essential to the constitution of a passion, the sensation of those changes is nowhere said to be essential to its psychical constitution. Aquinas' 'general representation is that of a process of apprehension and appetite on the one side resulting in expressive bodily movements on the other, the relation of the two being conceived in Aristotelian terms as one of "form" to "matter", so that the phenomenon may be described by either, but is best described, of course, by the determining factor, the form'.[31]

The most significant break with the Thomist account of the passions comes in the work of Vives.[32] Vives' conception of the passions differs significantly from that of Aquinas, for he considers only the more violent emotions to be passions, and the mind does not so much register the experience as share in it. In his *De anima et vita* (1538), Vives abandons the distinction between concupiscible and irascible passions and offers a

[28] Ibid., Qu. xxv, art. 4.
[29] See H. M. Gardiner, Ruth Clarke Metcalf, and John Beebe-Center, *Feeling and Emotion* (New York, 1937), 110.
[30] Quoted in ibid., 115.   [31] Ibid., 116.
[32] On Vives, see Carlos G. Noreña, *Juan Luis Vives and the Emotions* (Carbondale, Ill., 1989).

different classification. But the key feature of Vives' account for our purposes is the way he makes the intellect and the will into autonomous faculties whose acts are mutually independent. As Levi has noted, in Vives' theory of the passions there is discernible a breakdown in the traditional Scholastic psychology, and his work sets the stage for seventeenth-century debates.[33] Although the will should be guided by reason, which has as its object the rationally perceived good, the reason does not actually cause the will to choose in a particular way, for the will is essentially spontaneous in its liberty to choose. As Levi points out, what resulted was not only a blurring of the distinction between the passions and the virtues, but also a separation of the reason and the will such that it is difficult to see how an act can at the same time be both rational and free.[34] The ultimate upshot of this was that the will and the reason were gradually prized further apart, so that in the neo-Stoic revival of the sixteenth and seventeenth centuries (of which we may take Montaigne and Lipsius as early representatives) it began to be urged that the reason could be relied upon to the exclusion of the will.[35] One might expect disputes pursued along clear neo-Stoic versus Augustinian/Thomist lines to follow from this, focusing on the question of whether the will did or did not play a part, but this is not what happened. The issue was complicated by the fact that, although he regarded them as mutually dependent, Aquinas had defended a 'real' distinction between the intellect and the will as two faculties of the soul, one having the true as its object, the other having the good. There is a fundamental instability or unclarity on the question of the relation between the will and reason, and what one tends to find on the anti-Stoic side in the late sixteenth- and early seventeenth-century literature on the passions, whether Scholastic, devotional, or secular, is a basic adherence to a generally Augustinian/Thomist position tempered to a greater or lesser degree by elements drawn from Stoicism.

The deep problems in the literature can be glimpsed by considering the discussion of the passions in Part II of the second Book, on ethics, in Eustachius' *Summa philosophiae*.[36] Eustachius urges a sharp distinction between the higher and lower parts of the soul, holding that the will is related to the intellect in the higher part of the soul as the imagination

---

[33] Anthony Levi, *French Moralists* (Oxford, 1964), 26.   [34] Ibid., 27.

[35] So begins a complex history of the relative roles of the reason and the will, on which see Susan James, *Passion and Action: the Emotions in Seventeenth-century Philosophy* (Oxford, 1997).

[36] On Eustachius on the passions see Levi, *French Moralists*, ch. 6, and Leslie Armour, 'Descartes and Eustachius a Sancto Paulo: Unravelling the Mind–Body Problem,' *British Journal for the History of Philosophy* 1 (1993), 3–22.

is related to the sensitive appetite in the lower part. Aquinas had treated reason, sense, and imagination as part of a single cognitive process, but the Stoic tendency to use the term 'imagination' pejoratively, combined with a move to think of the imagination as being concerned with knowledge of material objects and the reason as being concerned with knowledge of immaterial objects (universals, etc.), had a significant impact on later Scholastic thinking and the imagination becomes insulated from reason and begins to be treated as the source of error. This opens up the possibility of an act of will being at variance with the sensitive appetite and exercising no control over it. More generally, what results is an extremely unstable amalgam of elements taken from the Scholastic tradition and Stoicism, and the price paid is a fragmentation of the soul which has no obvious benefits. This opened the door to an abandonment of the Scholastic account in favour of Stoicism, notwithstanding the well-known difficulties with the Stoic account, for above all it offers a unified conception of the soul.[37]

This, then, is the context within which Descartes was writing. Where the physiology of the passions was treated, there was an almost irresistible tendency to apply properly mental and corporeal attributes interchangeably, and even to conceive of animal spirits in a vitalistic fashion; and where the faculties were treated, there was an increasing fragmentation of the soul or mind with various 'lower' parts blending into the corporeal functions. And this occurred with no discernible improvement in our understanding of the nature of human affective states. Descartes' aim in producing a systematic account of the passions was, more than anything else, to restructure the whole question of the affective states around a clear understanding of the distinction between mind and body, and on the basis of such an understanding to formulate the appropriate notion of a substantial union needed to account for the source and nature of affective states.

In *Les Passions*, completed over the winter of 1645/6, Descartes sets out to provide a comprehensive account of the various ways in which mind and body interact. The three parts of the text are designated by Descartes himself as providing a general account of the mind/body relation and the general nature of passions (Part I), a classification of the passions (Part II), and an account of particular passions (Part III), although from near the end of Part II the discussion shifts to the moral/therapeutic questions surrounding the passions.

---

[37] See Levi, *French Moralists*, 155.

Descartes begins Part I by noting that whether something is called an action or a passion depends simply on whether it is considered with respect to the mind or the body, so the crucial thing is to start with the difference between the soul and the body (art. 2). As we have seen, contemporary accounts of the passions were very vague on the key question of what the relation between the mind and the body is, with many of them assuming that the action of the mind on the body is like the action of one body on another,[38] and Descartes insists that any serious discussion of the passions must begin with this question. Articles 7 to 16 set out in a very summary way the mechanistic physiology of *L'Homme* (and of the projected Part V, which we looked at in the previous chapter), and we are then provided with a division of the functions of the soul into two: actions and passions. Actions comprise volitions which either terminate in the soul, as 'when we will to love God', or in the body, as when we move our legs by willing to walk. They also include those perceptions which have their origin in the soul, as when we reflect upon our own existence. Perceptions which have their origin in the body, on the other hand, are passions. The treatment of the passions then proceeds, from article 21 onwards, in terms of functions of the soul which depend on its union with the body. Perceptions which do not derive from the soul itself can be caused either by external bodies acting upon us, or from natural appetites of the body such as hunger which we sense through bodily organs, or they can be felt 'as in the soul itself', in which case no immediate cause is evident (art. 25). These last are the 'passions of the soul', and Descartes is concerned with their phenomenology rather than their causes, for, while we may be deceived about their causes – they may be experienced whether we are awake or asleep, for example – we cannot be deceived about their existence or specific nature (art. 26). They are defined as being 'caused, maintained, and strengthened by a movement of the spirits', and take the form of 'excitations of the soul', as do volitions, but unlike volitions they do not have their source in the soul. Articles 30 to 47 then provide a psycho-physiology of the soul in terms of Descartes' doctrine that the pineal gland is the seat of the soul, much along the lines of *L'Homme*.

Two features of this account are worth noting. First, in article 36 he explains how different passions can arise in different people who are apparently stimulated in the same way. Clearly, any treatment of the passions is going to have to account for what we might call differences in

---

[38] See Descartes to Elizabeth, 21 May 1643; AT III. 666.

temperament. But the explanatory value of his account is minimal, to say the least, for he simply translates differences in response into differences in the disposition of the brain, so that the spirits are reflected differently in different people depending on the initial disposition of their brain, and hence pineal gland, something which results in different responses. Second, in article 47, he uses the doctrine of the pineal gland being the seat of the soul to undermine the prevalent account of the passions in terms of a conflict between higher and lower parts of the soul:

> All the struggles that people customarily imagine between the lower part of the soul, which is called sensitive, and the higher or 'rational' part, or between the natural appetites and the will, just consist in the opposition between the movements which the body, by its spirits, and the soul, by its will, tend to excite simultaneously in the gland. For there is only a single soul in us, and this soul has within itself no diversity of parts; one and the same soul is sensitive and rational, and all its appetites are volitions.

The conflicts that we experience are, then, conflicts between the soul and the body, for there is no sense in which they can be either conflicts between higher and lower parts of the soul, or conflicts between different powers of the soul. The spirits can move the pineal gland in a particular way, stimulating a desire for something, and, while the will cannot halt this directly, it can represent objects to itself so vividly that, by the principle of association, the course of the spirits will gradually be halted. In these circumstances, the soul will be impelled 'almost simultaneously' both to desire and not to desire the same thing, but the 'almost' is important, and this will not be a genuine conflict in the soul. A parallel case occurs in the body, when the passions cause the organs or limbs to act in a certain way, and the soul attempts to stop this, causing conflict in the body. What is required in both cases is mastery of one's passions, which derive from 'firm and determined judgements' (art. 48). There is no question of using one passion to offset another, and even less of trying to live without passions: the passions are crucial for fortifying and sustaining individual acts of will, and those who have no inclination for the passion of wonder, for example, are 'usually very ignorant' (art. 75). Mastery of the passions for the Stoics was a matter of overcoming or of purging them. For Descartes, by contrast, it was a matter of overcoming some and cultivating others. The passions are a necessary condition of a moral life: 'it is on the passions alone that all the good and evil of this life depends' (art. 212).

Part II of *Les Passions* deals with the classification of the passions. The basis for the classification is different from that of a writer like Aquinas, who attempts to provide a systematic genealogy in terms of an account of primitive passions from which others can be derived. Moreover, rejecting any distinction between parts of the soul, Descartes rejects the distinction between concupiscible and irascible appetites which depends on this, thereby removing the basis of the traditional classifications (art. 68). Although he lists six primitive passions – wonder, love, hate, desire, joy, and sadness – and although, except for the first, these are part of the standard Scholastic listing, Descartes takes a thoroughly functional approach, for the basis for identifying passions is in terms of the importance the perceivable objects have for us, how much difficulty we have in obtaining them, whether they are harmful or of benefit to us, and so on. Moreover, the full listing – as opposed to the six primitive passions – is explicitly open-ended for there are, Descartes tells us, an indefinite number of passions.

In the course of his discussion of joy and sadness in *Les Passions*, Descartes introduces an important distinction between joy and intellectual joy, and sadness and intellectual sadness. Intellectual joy and sadness are not passions properly speaking, for they 'come into the soul by the action of the soul itself' (art. 91) and not by the action of the body. In the *Principia*, Descartes had mentioned that, when we hear good news, 'it is first of all the mind that makes a judgement about it and rejoices with that intellectual joy which occurs without any bodily disturbance and which, for that reason, the Stoics allowed the wise man to experience' (Part IV, art. 190). Such 'inner excitations', as Descartes calls them, come to play an increasingly important role as *Les Passions* progresses, and at the end of Part II he introduces a fuller account of their nature:

Here I shall merely add one further consideration which, I believe, helps to prevent us from suffering any discomfort from the passions. This is that our well-being depends principally upon inner excitations which are excited in the soul only by the soul itself. In this respect they differ from the passions of the soul, which invariably depend on some movement of the spirits. Although these excitations of the soul are often joined with those passions which are similar to them, they may also frequently be found with others, and they may even originate in those to which they are opposed. For example, when a husband mourns his dead wife, it sometimes happens that he would be sorry to see her brought to life again. It may be that his heart is constricted by the sadness excited in him by the funeral display and by the absence of a person to whose company he was accustomed. And it may be that some remnants of love or pity occur in his imagination and draw genuine tears from his eyes, in spite of the fact that he feels at the same time a secret joy in his innermost soul, and the excitation of this joy has such a power that the concomitant sadness and tears can do nothing to diminish its force. Again, when we read of strange adventures in a book, or see them represented on stage, this sometimes arouses sadness in us, sometimes joy, or love, or hatred, and generally any of the passions, depending on which objects are presented to our imagination. But along with this we have pleasure of feeling them aroused in us, and this pleasure is an intellectual joy which can just as easily originate in sadness as in any of the other passions. (art. 147)

Here Descartes begins to show some influence of neo-Stoicism for he goes on to tell us that such inner excitations affect us more intimately than the passions, and hence, so long as our soul always has the means of happiness within itself, anything external is powerless to harm it (art. 148). At this point, considerations of the physiology of the passions recede into the background, as ethical questions are construed in terms of the true worth of things, which the passions exaggerate in one direction or the other. The traditional contrast between reason and passion now appears as a contrast between an inner excitation and a passion. He distinguishes, for example, between 'the love which is purely intellectual or rational and the love which is a passion'.[39] The former consists in the movement of the will that accompanies the knowledge that a good is possessed, the latter in the experience of possessing the good. Intellectual love is clear, love as a passion confused.[40] Our judgement of the worthiness of the object determines the degree of our intellectual emotion, whereas the extent of the passion depends on our degree of esteem for the object. Since the second must be proportional to the first, it is the intellectual or rational version of the emotion, the 'inner excitation', that provides the key to how we should behave.

The direction and regulation of the passions enables us to live a good life: 'good' both in the sense of being ethical and in the sense of being fulfilling, for the two are inseparable in Descartes' account. Consider, for example, his discussion of generosity, probably the most important concept in Descartes' ethics. Although the word *generosité* had much the same core meaning in ordinary seventeenth-century French as it has for us, the French moralists had added a connotation of nobility. In *Les Passions*, Descartes defines generosity as follows:

I believe that true generosity, which causes a man to esteem himself to the greatest degree which is legitimate, consists solely in this: partly in his under-standing that there is nothing which truly belongs to him except his free control of his volitions, and the only grounds for praise or blame are that he uses it well or badly; and partly in his feeling within himself a firm and constant

---

[39] Descartes to Chanut, 1 February 1647; AT IV. 601.   [40] Ibid., AT IV. 603–4.

resolution to use it well – that is, never to lack the will to undertake and carry out whatever he judges to be the best. To do this is to pursue virtue perfectly. (art. 153)

In article 158 he reaffirms that 'the volition we feel within ourselves always to make good use of our free will results . . . in generosity'. In article 160 he contrasts it with vanity as the vice corresponding to the virtue of generosity, where 'vanity and generosity consist simply in the good opinion we have of ourselves, the only difference being that this opinion is unjustified in the one case and justified in the other', and both are related to the same passion, which is produced 'by a movement made up of those of wonder, of joy, and of love (self-love as much as the love we have for the cause of our self-esteem)'. Generosity is both a necessary condition for self-esteem and something that turns on self-esteem: indeed, it is the paradigm expression of self-esteem. This is important because it is ultimately our degree of self-esteem that will determine the worth of what we do. Hence the importance of the therapeutic aspects of Descartes' moral programme, such as those set out in the letter to Elizabeth in the middle of 1645, which recommends exercises for ridding oneself of melancholia – the affliction of those drawn to intellectual reflection – by 'directing the imagination':

Consider a person who had every reason to be happy but who saw continually enacted before him tragedies full of disastrous events, and who spent all his time in consideration of sad and pitiful things. Let us suppose that he knew they are imaginary fables so that though they drew tears from his eyes and moved his imagination they did not touch his intellect at all. I think that this alone would be enough gradually to close up his heart and make him sigh in such a way that the circulation of his blood would be delayed and slowed down . . . On the other hand, there might be a person who had many genuine reasons for distress but who took such pains to direct his imagination that he never thought of them except under compulsion by some practical necessity, and spent the rest of his time in the consideration of things which could furnish contentment and joy. This would help him by enabling him to judge more soberly about the things that mattered because he would look on them without passion. Moreover, I do not doubt that this by itself would be capable of restoring him to health, even if his spleen and lungs were already in a poor condition because of the bad temperament of blood produced by sadness.[41]

The aim of these exercises is not to overcome passions but to reorder one's passions so that they are directed: so that we are in control of them,

---

[41] Descartes to Elizabeth, May or June 1645; AT IV. 219–20.

and not they in control of us:

> It seems that the difference between the greatest souls and those that are base and
> common consists principally in the fact that common souls abandon themselves
> to their passions and are happy or unhappy only according as the things that
> happen to them are agreeable or unpleasant; the greatest souls, on the other
> hand, reason in a way that is so strong and cogent that, although they also
> have passions, and indeed passions which are often more violent than those of
> ordinary people, their reason nevertheless always remains mistress, and even
> makes their afflictions serve them and contribute to the perfect happiness they
> enjoy in this life.[42]

THE PHILOSOPHER AS SAGE

'An examination of the principles of my philosophy, and the long chain of
truths that can de deduced from them', Descartes writes in the Prefatory
letter to *Les Principes*, 'will make people realise how important it is to
continue the search for these truths, and to what a high degree of wisdom,
and to what perfection and felicity of life, these truths can bring us'.[43] This
remark echoes that of Eustachius a Sancto Paulo, who, in the Preface
to Part II of his *Summa*, writes that 'the goal of a complete philosophy is
human happiness'.

Human happiness had been the business of philosophers in Greek and
Roman antiquity, and it was to them that one turned for guidance for how
life was to be lived. What philosophy offered was, as Cottingham puts it,
'a set of systematic reflections on the capacities and dispositions of human
beings, and how those capacities and dispositions can be utilized in the
construction of a rationally articulated plan for the conduct of life'.[44]
The systematic nature of these reflections derives in large part from their
incorporation within a system of natural philosophy, as Cicero makes
clear in *De finibus* III. 73:

> No one can make true judgements about good and evil without a grasp of the
> rational principles of nature and divine life, and an understanding of whether or
> not the nature of man accords with that of the cosmos. Without a knowledge of
> the principles of physics, no one can see the supreme significance of the ancient
> ethical maxims of the sages, such as 'yield to the times', 'follow God', 'know
> thyself' and 'nothing in excess'.[45]

---

[42] Descartes to Elizabeth, 18 May 1645; AT IV. 201.   [43] AT IXB. 20.
[44] See Cottingham, *Philosophy and the Good Life*, 15–16.   [45] Translated in ibid., 175 n. 11.

Moreover, when one has grasped these rational principles, morality comes naturally, as it were. At III. 7 of *De finibus*, Cicero tells us that, 'since the ultimate aim is to live in conformity and harmony with nature, it necessarily follows that those possessed of philosophical wisdom live their lives in a state of happiness, perfection, and good fortune, without any restriction, hindrance, or need'. The notion that Cicero is articulating here is the Stoic one of indifference to calamity and misfortune, a notion that is still readily familiar. Achieving this goal is not easy, however, and it requires philosophers to undergo training to prepare themselves for a life quite different from that of their fellows. What is required is set out by Philo of Alexandria, at the end of the Hellenistic era, when he examines how the *persona* of the philosopher or sage is to be formed:

Every person – whether Greek or Barbarian – who is in training for wisdom, leading a blameless, irreproachable life, chooses neither to commit injustice nor return it unto others, but to avoid the company of busybodies and hold in con-tempt the places where they spend their time – courts, councils, marketplaces, assemblies – in short, every kind of meeting or reunion of thoughtless people. As their goal is a life of peace and serenity, they contemplate nature and everything found within her . . . Thus, filled with every excellence, they are accustomed no longer to take account of physical discomforts or exterior evils, and they train themselves to be indifferent to indifferent things; they are armed against both pleasures and desires, and in short, they always strive to keep themselves above passions.[46]

There is a focus on moral questions here, but cognitive prescriptions were as often as not tied in to the general picture of the appropriate be-haviour for the philosopher, either implicitly, as in the case of Hellenistic writers generally, or occasionally explicitly, as in the case of Marcus Aurelius' advice:

Everywhere and at all times it is up to you to rejoice piously at what is occurring at the present moment, to conduct yourself with justice towards the people who are present here and now, and to apply rules of discernment to your present representations, so that nothing slips in that is not objective.[47]

We must not forget that these were questions that were paramount throughout antiquity, and at least from Socrates onwards the philoso-pher took on or fostered a distinct *persona* and attitude, depending on

[46] Quoted in Pierre Hadot, *Philosophy as a Way of Life* (Oxford, 1995), 264.
[47] Marcus Aurelius, *Meditations*, 7.54; quoted in Hadot, *Philosophy*, 132.

the philosophical doctrine or school. For Plato, for example, the *persona* of the philosopher fitted him for kingship. For Diogenes the Cynic, on the other hand, it fitted him to the life of a beggar or a slave, and this was by no means something one merely fell into. It required an *askesis*, a pattern of living, which involved indifference to hardship and suffering (*apatheia*), self-sufficiency and a refusal to engage in the responsibilities of civil society (*autarkia*), complete and blunt freedom of speech (*parrhesia*), and lack of shame in performing bodily functions (*anaideia*).[48]

This fostering of a philosophical *persona* is particularly marked in the Hellenistic era, where *ataraxia*, peace of mind, was explicitly the aim of all the major schools, and where regulation of the passions played a major role for Epicureans and Stoics alike in attaining the state of mind, and corresponding behaviour, worthy of or appropriate to a member of their philosophical school. Indeed, as Hadot has remarked, it is love of wisdom, 'which is foreign to the world, that makes the philosopher a stranger to it. So each school will elaborate its rational depiction of this state of perfection in the person of a sage, and each will make an effort to portray him.'[49] This philosophical self-fashioning was pursued in a different way in the Christian era. This is nowhere clearer than in the disputes of the 1260s and 1270s arising from the attempts to introduce an autonomous philosophical system, that of Aristotle, into Christian thought. The Averroist Boethius of Dacia, one of the strongest advocates of philosophical 'self-affirmation', argued that it was easier for the philosopher to be virtuous than for anyone else, and that whoever does not live the life of a philosopher does not live rightly or virtuously.[50] Tempier responded in the 1277 Condemnation by condemning the propositions 'that no station in life is to be preferred to the study of philosophy' and 'philosophers alone are the wise men of the world'.[51] No less striking is the idea of philosophical self-fashioning that pervaded the Renaissance thought, with Pico della Mirandola's eulogy on 'the dignity of man' being in fact an attempt to redefine the office of the philosopher as the paradigm sage, and to set out a programme for the attainment of this goal.[52] Works like Montaigne's

[48] See H. D. Rankin, *Sophists, Socratics and Cynics* (London, 1983), ch. 13.
[49] Hadot, *Philosophy*, 57.
[50] Boethius of Dacia, *On the Supreme Good*, ed. and trans. J. F. Wippel (Toronto, 1987), 32–5. See Georg Wieland, 'The Reception and Interpretation of Aristotle's *Ethics*', in Norman Kretzmann et al. eds., *The Cambridge History of Later Medieval Philosophy* (Cambridge, 1982), 657–72.
[51] Proposition 40: 'quod non est excellentior status quam vacare philosophiae'; proposition 154: 'quod sapientes mundi sunt philosophi tantum'; see P. Mandonnet, *Siger de Brabant et l'averroisme latin au XIIIme siècle, 2me partie, textes inédits*, 2nd edn (Louvain, 1908), 175.
[52] See William G. Craven, *Giovanni della Mirandola, Symbol of His Age* (Geneva, 1981), ch. 2.

Essais and Burton's *The Anatomy of Melancholy* show that the genre was alive and well in the early modern era, and although the way in which it was pursued differed, a theme that runs through all the literature is the mastery of the passions.

Philosophical self-fashioning had always turned on the understanding and regulation of the passions, and because of this they have a peculiar centrality, for they have not merely been one object of study among others for philosophers, but something which must be understood if one is to be 'philosophical' in the first place. Mastery of the passions was not only a theme in philosophy but a distinctive feature of the philosophical *persona* from Socrates onwards, and Renaissance and early modern philosophers pursue the theme of self-control with no less vigour than had the philosophers of antiquity.

In general terms, philosophers in antiquity, in the Middle Ages, and in the early modern era, were able, with varying degrees of success, to construct images of themselves as paradigmatic bearers of moral, aesthetic, and intellectual responsibility. Whatever deep philosophical quarrels they may have had among themselves, it was important to establish that the philosophical view was not simply one kind of opinion amongst others. What was required to establish this was the construction of a philosophical *persona* capable of bearing and displaying this authority: an authority which was very different from that borne and displayed by theologians and statesmen, for example, whose claims on moral, natural–philosophical and other questions may have overlapped with, and perhaps competed with, those of philosophers. The question raised here is one about the relation between philosophy and the behaviour appropriate for the philosopher, or at least the philosophically educated: what kind of *persona* philosophy does or should shape or encourage.[53]

THE MORALITY OF PHILOSOPHERS

We have seen that morality emerges from Descartes' theory of the passions, which in turn emerges from his psycho-physiology of affective states, the same psycho-physiology that underlies his account of cognitive states, and one in which what is distinctive about human beings is

---

[53] Note that there is no sense at all of 'philosopher kings' here. Descartes sees politics as the business of sovereigns, something quite distinct from considerations about the values and character of private individuals. See Nannerl O. Keohane, *Philosophy and the State in France* (Princeton, 1980), 203.

their ability to stand back from their mental states, reflect upon them, make judgements about them, and shape their behaviour accordingly. In some respects, the point is not a new one, and Charron, in his immensely popular *De la Sagesse* (1601), had identified two 'dispositions to wisdom', the first being 'knowledge of oneself and the human condition', and the second,

> which follows from the first (and frees us from internal and external captivity and confusion) is the full, complete, generous, and noble twofold freedom of the mind, namely freedom of judgement and freedom of the will.[54]

Descartes translates this twofold freeedom into an ability to focus the mind, and this stands out as a key theme in his work from his earliest discussion of cognitive states in the *Regulae* – where he tells us that his 'whole method consists in nothing but ordering and arranging the objects on which we must concentrate our mind's eye if we are to discover some truth'[55] and that we must survey everything 'in a continuous and wholly uninterrupted sweep of thought'[56] – to what, twenty-five years later, in the dedicatory letter to the *Principia*, is, in effect, the analogue for affective states:

> whoever possesses the firm and powerful resolve always to use his reasoning powers correctly, as far as he can, and to carry out whatever he knows to be best, is truly wise, so far as his nature permits.[57]

The power to concentrate in cognitive states, and the power to exercise one's will in affective states, which is above all the power to regard or disregard particular passions, are both the powers of an autonomous agent, powers absent in animals, and these powers are, in effect, constitutive of what it is that is distinctive about human agency.[58]

   The question that remains for us to ask is: Who are these autonomous agents? or, Where is this autonomy to be found in its fullest form? Here, I suggest we find a convergence in the thought of Descartes and Bacon, by contrast with the broad humanist tradition, in which we may include

---

[54] Pierre Charron, *De la Sagesse*, ed. Barbara de Nagroni (Paris, 1986), 385 (Book II, ch. 2).
[55] AT x. 379.   [56] AT x. 387.
[57] AT viiiA. 2. Cf. the second maxim of Descartes' provisional morality in *La Discours*: 'to be as firm and decisive in all my actions as I could, and to follow even the most doubtful opinions, once I had adopted them, with no less constancy than if they had been quite certain' (AT vi. 24). Note, however, Descartes' clarification of this maxim in his letter to Reneri for Pollot, April or May 1638; AT ii. 34–5.
[58] On the question of autonomy in the moral realm see J. B. Schneewind, *The Invention of Autonomy* (Cambridge, 1998).

figures otherwise as diverse as Montaigne, Lipsius, and Grotius. What is distinctive about the approach of Descartes and Bacon is that the *persona* of the philosophical sage is not in the first instance that of the moral philosopher, but rather that of the natural philosopher. Bacon's reasoning on this question is elaborate and pervades his natural–philosophical project, and his views were to have a great influence, both in Britain and in Continental Europe, from the mid-1620s onwards.[59] On the face of it, it might seem that Descartes' project could not be further from Bacon's. Descartes advocates starting from a radical form of scepticism, so that one effectively begins with a *tabula rasa* except for one clear and distinct idea, the certainty of one's own existence, throwing us back on the 'natural light of reason'. Bacon, by contrast, thinks our natural in- tuitive reasoning processes are fatally flawed, so that what is needed in the shaping of the natural philosopher is subjection to a purging of the mind, by identifying and countering, as far as is possible, the 'Idols of the Mind', and by replacing natural reasoning processes with other proce- dures, above all a method of eliminative induction.[60] In one sense, then, Descartes might be seen to be appealing to the autonomy and independ- ence of the philosopher, whereas Bacon might be seen to be denying it.

As I indicated in chapter 3, however, matters are not so straightfor- ward. Everyone has a capacity for clear and distinct ideas, which is why everyone can go through the foundational project of Descartes' episte- mologised metaphysics: sceptical doubt, the *cogito*, the recognition that our existence depends on God, the exploration of what God's essence consists in, the guarantee of clear and distinct ideas, and the elaboration of the nature of mental and material substance on the basis of clarity and distinctness. But the fact that everyone has a capacity for clear and distinct ideas does not mean that everyone is inclined to exercise this capacity to the same degree. In *La Recherche*, the *honnête homme* alone is identified as the kind of person who uses his natural faculty of clarity and distinctness to the highest degree: or, at least, it is he who, when called upon, uses it to the highest degree. This does not mean that the *honnête homme* alone is able to put himself through the rigours of hyperbolic doubt and discover the true foundations of knowledge: in theory, everyone is able to do that, Scholas- tics included. After all, hyperbolic doubt erases our beliefs – everyone's beliefs – to such an extent that everyone becomes a natural–philosophical *tabula rasa*.

---

[59] See my *Francis Bacon and the Transformation of Early-Modern Philosophy*.
[60] See ibid., chs. 4 and 5.

The route of hyperbolic doubt is one route that we can take to natural philosophy, and if we want a legitimation of this natural philosophy in terms of first principles, then this is the route we have to take, just as, if we want a rigorous proof of Pythagoras' theorem, we will take the Euclidean route from first principles, in which case the result can be demonstrated in a completely compelling way to someone of no mathematical skills or training, so long as this person can understand the proofs. However, if one thinks of oneself as a working mathematician then, as the *Regulae* and *La Géométrie* make clear, one will approach the theorem through problem-solving techniques which give one a feel for what is being shown and help one build up new techniques, enabling one to deal with cognate problems whose solutions have not yet been found. Analogously, if one simply wants to be taken through natural philosophy in such a way that the results are indisputable – and, incidentally, in such a way that the Roman Inquisition's 1633 ruling that natural philosophy alone cannot decide questions about the structure of the cosmos is observed – then the foundationalist metaphysical approach is that one must follow, for

an examination of the nature of many different minds has led me to observe that there are almost none at all so dull and slow as to be incapable of forming sound opinions or indeed of grasping all the most advanced sciences, provided they receive proper guidance. And this may be proved by reason. For since the principles in question [namely, those of the *Principia*] are clear, and nothing is permitted to be deduced from them except by very evident reasoning, everyone has enough intelligence to understand the things that depend upon them.[61]

But if the aim is to develop and refine natural–philosophical skills as one progresses, then we require something different:

As for the individual, it is not only beneficial to live with those who apply themselves to [the study of philosophy]; it is incomparably better to undertake it oneself. For by the same token it is undoubtedly much better to use one's eyes to get about, but also to enjoy the colours of beauty and light, than to close one's eyes and be led around by someone else. Yet even the latter is much better than keeping one's eyes closed and having no guide but oneself.[62]

'Using one's eyes to get about' is not something that everyone finds equally easy, however. What Descartes is seeking are those who can develop his system to completion:

the majority of truths remaining to be discovered depend on various particular observations/experiments which we can never happen upon by chance but

[61] AT IXB. 12.   [62] AT IXB. 3.

which must be sought out with care and expense by very intelligent people. It will not easily come about that the same people who have the capacity to make good use of these observations will have the means to make them. What is more, the majority of the best minds have formed such a bad opinion of the whole of philosophy that has been current up until now, that they certainly will not apply themselves to look for a better one.[63]

We must recognise that some are more fitted than others to follow the path of instruction/enlightenment in natural philosophy. And in *La Recherche*, as we have seen, Descartes realises, practically, that people come to natural philosophy not with a *tabula rasa* but with different sets of highly developed beliefs which are motivated in different ways and developed to different degrees.[64] These rest upon various things, and this is what leads him, in *La Recherche*, to construct an image of the *honnête homme* as a model in which the moral sage and the natural philosopher meet,[65] for, as he puts it in the prefatory letter to *Les Principes*, 'the study of philosophy is more necessary for the regulation of our morals and our conduct in this life than is the use of our eyes to guide our steps'.[66] Philosophy has a moral imperative, and in explaining his decision to publish his *La Discours* and *Les Essais*, for example, he tells us that not to publish would be 'to sin gravely against the law that obliges us to do all in our power to secure the general welfare of mankind'.[67] In *Les Principes*, philosophy is defined as

the study of wisdom, where by 'wisdom' I mean not only prudence in our everyday affairs but also perfect knowledge of all things that mankind is capable of knowing, both for the conduct of life and for the preservation of health and the discovery of all manner of skills.[68]

Such philosophy requires principles 'which are so clear and so evident that the human mind cannot doubt their truth when it attentively concentrates on them', principles that can be grasped by 'whoever possesses the firm and powerful resolve always to use his reasoning powers correctly',

---

[63] AT IXB. 20.

[64] Compare the remark in *La Discours*: 'I thought too how the same man with the same mind, had he been brought up from infancy among the French or Germans, develops otherwise than he would have had he always lived among the Chinese or cannibals ... Thus it is custom and example that persuade us, rather than any certain knowledge' AT VI. 16.

[65] Note in this respect the argument offered by John Marshall, in his *Descartes's Moral Theory* (Ithaca, 1998), 19–22, that the reasons Descartes gives for his vocation as a philosopher are moral reasons.

[66] AT IXB. 3–4.   [67] AT VI. 61.   [68] AT IXB. 2.

Descartes' system of natural philosophy

as he puts it in the dedicatory letter to the *Principia*. What prevents acceptance of this philosophy is the fact that

> the majority of those aspiring to be philosophers in the last few centuries have blindly followed Aristotle. Indeed they have corrupted the sense of his writings and attributed to him various opinions which he would not recognise to be his, were he now to return to this world. Those who have not followed Aristotle (and this group includes many of the best minds) have nevertheless been saturated with his opinions in their youth (since these are the only opinions taught in the Schools) and this has so dominated their outlook that they have been unable to arrive at knowledge of true principles.[69]

In the *Principia*, Descartes has set out to reform philosophy in its entirety, but he does not see the project as establishing the kind of stagnant system that Scholasticism had become, where what has caused the decline of the system was clearly in large part due, in his view (and, it should be said, in that of many of his contemporaries), to the slavish adherence of its proponents to Aristotle. In this respect, Descartes is not in the slightest interested in winning over Scholastic philosophers to his system: they are simply not the kind of people who can develop it, and would only lead it to the kind of stagnation to which they have led Aristotelianism. A fortiori, they cannot act as paradigm philosophers, as sages whose wisdom can guide the rest. This role falls instead to those who, reflecting upon the current state of philosophy, have formed a low opinion of it, and have avoided taking it up. This low opinion, wholly merited, is what makes them *honnêtes hommes*, and it is precisely these whom Descartes sees as being potentially the new paradigm philosophers, marked by an intellectual honesty which rescues philosophy from the intellectual disgrace into which it has fallen.[70] And what these *honnêtes hommes* have is the ability to foster their clear and distinct ideas, for this is the key to Descartes' philosophical system.

We have seen that Descartes' prime concern, from the hydrostatics manuscripts of 1619 to his last writing, *Les Passions*, was always in natural philosophy, but after 1633 he shifted from developing to legitimating his natural philosophy. This legitimation was effected through a completely new kind of metaphysics in which the driving force was not a

[69] AT IXB. 7.

[70] 'Intellectual honesty' will remain one of the keystones in the ideology of the scientist, reaching its apogee in Karl Popper, for whom the scientist is in effect the only truly intellectually honest person, for the scientist alone tries to falsify his theories, whereas everyone else tries to show theirs to be true.

reconciliation or balance between metaphysics, natural philosophy, and theology, as it had been within the Christianised Aristotelianism that set the agenda for philosophy from the thirteenth century onwards, but the epistemological doctrine of clear and distinct ideas. The doctrine of clear and distinct ideas was the means by which Descartes established a starting point in setting out a *scientia* of natural philosophy, a starting point that could not possibly lead in the direction of any of the late Scholastic versions of natural philosophy, but only in the direction of a quantitative, mechanistic model of the kind that Descartes was advocating. But I have also been at pains to stress that there is another dimension to the doctrine of clear and distinct ideas, which reflects one of the most pressing problems for those engaged in the reform of natural philosophy. This is the reform of natural philosophers – or, since the natural philosopher gradually becomes the philosopher *par excellence* in the seventeenth century, having taken over this role at the end of the Renaissance from the moral philosopher – the reform of philosophers per se.[71]

We have here one of the key developments in the emergence of a scientific culture in early modern Europe, the transformation of philosophers into what will later become known as scientists. As I have argued, the procedure of rendering the reader a *tabula rasa* by means of hyperbolic doubt is part of Descartes' legitimatory strategy, but it is not part of his strategy for developing the kinds of attitude, capacities, and skills required of a natural philosopher in the Cartesian mould. Yet the very criterion that the *tabula rasa* must have recourse to in finding a route to natural philosophy, that of clear and distinct ideas, is also that which marks out the potential true natural philosopher. Being a philosopher – in antiquity, in the Hellenistic era, and throughout the Middle Ages and Renaissance – had always been an activity for which preparation and training were required, and, because the philosopher was looked to as someone who could offer guidance on how to live one's life, being a philosopher had always carried with it a particular kind of moral standing. This was reflected above all in the idea that the philosopher was someone who had complete control over his affective or emotional life, and what Descartes offers in his theory of the passions is an account of how this control is possible. However, control over one's affective states had often been seen to be part of a more general control over one's mental life, and, as we have seen, control over affective states had occasionally been tied

---

[71] See my *Francis Bacon and the Transformation of Early-Modern Philosophy.*

in explicitly with control over cognitive states. This connection between cognitive and affective states is re-forged in Descartes. The *honnête homme*, someone who in the first instance has a certain quality, honesty, which is both intellectual and moral, is also identified as the material from which natural philosophers will be forged. For both morality, and the intellectual honesty required of the new natural philosopher, derive from a single quality of mind, the ability to stand back from our thoughts and feelings, and assess and control them according to a God-given criterion of clarity and distinctness, which no authority, religious or secular, can countermand.

Bibliography

PRIMARY SOURCES

Abra de Raconis, Charles François d', *Totius philosophiæ, hoc est logicae, moralis, physicae, et metaphysicæ*, 2 vols. (Paris, 1633).

Alembert, Jean le Rond d', *Traité de Dynamique* (Paris, 1743).

Aristotle, *De Anima*, ed. with introduction and commentary by David Ross (Oxford, 1961).

Arnauld, Antoine, *On True and False Ideas*, ed. and trans. Stephen Gaukroger (Manchester and New York, 1990).

Bacon, Francis, *The Works of Francis Bacon*, ed. James Spedding, Robert Leslie Ellis, and Douglas Denon Heath, 14 vols. (London, 1857–74).

Beeckman, Isaac, *Journal tenu par Isaac Beeckman de 1604 à 1634*, ed. Cornelius de Waard, 4 vols. (The Hague, 1939–53).

Boethius of Dacia, *On the Supreme Good*, ed. and trans. J. F. Wippel (Toronto, 1987).

Cano, Melchior, *Locorum Theologicorum Libri Duodecim* (Cologne, 1574).

Caus, Salomon de, *Les raisons des forces mouvantes avec diverses machines tant utiles que plaisantes ausquelles sont adjoints plusioeurs desseigns de grotes et fontaines* (Frankfurt, 1615).

Charron, Pierre, *De la Sagesse*, ed. Barbara de Nagroni (Paris, 1986).

Clavius, Christoph, *Opera mathematica, quinque tomis distributa*, 5 vols. (Mainz, 1611).

Copernicus, Nicholas, *De revolutionibus orbium cælestium, Libri VI* (Nuremberg, 1543).

Cureau de la Chambre, Marin, *Les Charactères des passions*, 4 vols. in 2 (Paris, 1658–1662).

Dasypodius, Conrad and Herlinus, Christian, *Analyseis geometricæ sex librorum Euclidis* (Strasbourg, 1566).

Descartes, René, *Oeuvres de Descartes*, ed. Charles Adam and Paul Tannery, 11 vols., 2nd edn (Paris, 1974–86).

Digby, Kenelme, *Two Treatises, In one of Which the nature of Bodies, in the Other the Nature of Man's Soule is Looked Into, in Way of Discovery of the Immortality of Reasonable Souls* (Paris, 1644).

Dupleix, Scipion, *Corps de philosophie, contenant la logique, l'ethique, la physique, et la metaphysique* (Geneva, 1623).

247

Euler, Leonhard, *Mechanica sive motus scientia analytice exposita*, 2 vols. (St Petersburg, 1738–40).

Eustachius a Sancto Paulo, *Summa philosophiæ quadripartita, de rebus Dialecticis, Ethicis, Physicis, & Metaphysicis* (Cologne, 1629).

Ficino, Marsilio, *Opera Omnia*, 2 vols. (Basle, 1576).

Fonseca, Pedro da, *Institutionum dialecticarum libri octo* (Lisbon, 1564).

Fontenelle, Bernard le Bouvier de, *Théorie des tourbillons cartésiens avec des réflections sur l'attraction* (Paris, 1752).

Galileo Galilei, *Dialogo . . . sopra i due Massimi Sistemi del Mondo* (Florence, 1632).

Two New Sciences, ed. and trans. Stillman Drake (Madison, 1974).

Gassendi, Petrus, *Opera Omnia*, 6 vols. (Lyon, 1658).

Gilbert, William, *De magnete, magnetisque corporibus, et de magno magnete tellure: Physiologia nova plurimis et argumentis et experimentis demonstrata* (London, 1600).

De mundo nostro sublunari nova (Amsterdam, 1651).

Havers, G., *A General Collection of the Discourses of the Virtuosi of France* (London, 1664).

Hobbes, Thomas, *The English Works of Thomas Hobbes*, ed. Sir William Molesworth, 11 vols. (London, 1839–45).

Huygens, Christiaan, *Oeuvres complètes de Christiaan Huygens*, ed. La Société Hollandaise des Sciences, 22 vols. (The Hague, 1888–1950).

Lagrange, Louis de, *Méchanique analytique* (Paris, 1788).

Leibniz, Gottfried Wilhelm, *Die philosophische Schriften von G. W. Leibniz*, ed. C. I. Gerhardt, 7 vols. (Berlin, 1875–90).

Malebranche, Nicholas, *De la recherche de la vérité, où l'on traite de la nature de l'esprit de l'homme, et de l'usage qu'il en droit faire pour éviter l'erreur dans les sciences*, ed. G. Rodis-Lewis, 3 vols. (Paris, 1945–56).

Mandonnet, P., *Siger de Brabant et l'averroisme latin au XIIIme siècle, 2me partie, textes inédits*, 2nd edn (Louvain, 1908).

Mersenne, Marin, *Quæstiones in Genesim* (Paris, 1623).

La Verité des Sciences, contre les septiques ou Pyrrhoniens (Paris, 1625).

More, Henry, *Enchiridium metaphysicum sive de rebus incorporeis succincta et luculenta dissertatio* (London, 1671).

A Collection of Several Philosophical Writings (London, 1712).

Newton, Isaac, *Unpublished Scientific Papers of Isaac Newton*, ed. and trans. A. Rupert Hall and Marie Boas Hall (Cambridge, 1962).

The Principia: Mathematical Principles of Natural Philosophy, ed. and trans. I. Bernard Cohen and Anne Whitman (Berkeley, 1999).

Patrizi, Francesco, *Nova de universis philosophia* (Ferrara, 1591).

Pomponazzi, Pietro, *De immortalitate animæ* (Padua, 1516).

Régis, Pierre-Sylvan, *Système de philosophie, contenant la logique, la métaphysique, la physique et la morale*, 3 vols. (Paris, 1690).

Regius, Henricus, *Fundamenta physices* (Amsterdam, 1646).

Rohault, Jacques, *Traité de Physique* (Paris, 1671).

Suárez, Francisco, *Metaphysicorum disputationum tomi dui* (Salamanca, 1597).

Vives, Juan Luis, *De anima et vita libri tres* (Basle, 1538).
Wright, Thomas, *Passions of the Minde* (London 1601).

SECONDARY SOURCES

Aiton, Eric J., *The Vortex Theory of Planetary Motions* (London, 1972).
Ariew, Roger, 'Les *Principia* et la *Summa Philosophica Quadripartita*', in Jean-Robert Armogathe and Giulia Belgioioso, eds., *Descartes: Principia Philosophiæ, 1644– 1994* (Naples, 1996), 473–89.
    Descartes and the Last Scholastics (Ithaca, 1999).
Ariew, Roger, Cottingham, John, and Sorell, Tom, *Descartes' Meditations: Background Source Materials* (Cambridge, 1998).
Armour, Leslie, 'Descartes and Eustachius a Sancto Paulo: Unravelling the Mind–Body Problem,' *British Journal for the History of Philosophy* 1 (1993), 3–22.
Baker, Gordon, and Morris, Katherine J., *Descartes' Dualism* (London, 1996).
Barbour, Julian B., *Absolute or Relative Motion? Volume 1: The Discovery of Dynamics* (Cambridge, 1989).
Beaune, Jean-Claude, *L'automate et ses mobiles* (Paris, 1980).
Berkel, Klaas van, 'Descartes' Debt to Beeckman: Inspiration, Cooperation, Conflict', in Stephen Gaukroger, John Schuster, and John Sutton, eds., *Descartes' Natural Philosophy* (London, 2000), 46–59.
Biagioli, Mario, *Galileo Courtier: the Practice of Science in the Culture of Absolutism* (Chicago, 1993).
Bitbol-Hespériès, Annie, *Le Principe de vie chez Descartes* (Paris, 1990).
Blackwell, Richard J., *Galileo, Bellarmine, and the Bible* (Notre Dame, 1991).
Blay, Michel, *La Naissance de la mécanique analytique* (Paris, 1992).
Bloch, Olivier, *La philosophie de Gassendi* (The Hague, 1971).
Blumenberg, Hans, *The Legitimacy of the Modern Age* (Cambridge, Mass., 1983).
    The Genesis of the Copernican World (Cambridge, Mass., 1987).
Brockliss, Laurence W. B., 'Rapports de structure et de contenu entre les *Principia* et les cours de philosophie des collèges', in Jean-Robert Armogathe and Giulia Belgioioso, eds., *Descartes: Principia Philosophiæ, 1644–1994* (Naples, 1996), 491–516.
Brown, Peter, *The Body and Society* (London, 1989).
Brundell, Barry, *Pierre Gassendi* (Dordrecht, 1987).
Capek, Milic, *The Philosophical Impact of Contemporary Physics* (New York, 1961).
Charlton, William, *Aristotle's Physics I, II* (Oxford, 1970).
Clarke, Desmond M., *Occult Powers and Hypotheses: Cartesian Natural Philosophy under Louis XIV* (Oxford, 1989).
Cottingham, John, 'A Brute to the Brutes?', *Philosophy* 53 (1978), 551–9.
    'Descartes' Trialism', *Mind* 44 (1985), 218–30.
    Philosophy and the Good Life (Cambridge, 1998).
Craven, William G., *Giovanni della Mirandola, Symbol of His Age* (Geneva, 1981).

Damerow, Peter, Freudenthal, Gideon, McLaughlin, Peter, and Renn, Jürgen, *Exploring the Limits of Preclassical Mechanics* (New York, 1992).

Daston, Lorraine and Park, Katherine, *Wonders and the Order of Nature, 1150–1750* (Cambridge, Mass., 1998).

Dear, Peter, *Discipline and Experience: the Mathematical Way in the Scientific Revolution* (Chicago, 1995).

Des Chene, Dennis, *Physiologia: Natural Philosophy in Late Aristotelian and Cartesian Thought* (Ithaca, 1996).

Life's Form: Late Aristotelian Conceptions of the Soul (Ithaca, 2000).

Spirits and Clocks: Machine and Organism in Descartes (Ithaca, 2001).

Dick, Steven J., *Plurality of Worlds: The Origins of the Extraterrestrial Life Debate from Democritus to Kant* (Cambridge, 1982).

Dihle, Albrecht, *The Theory of the Will in Classical Antiquity* (Berkeley, 1982).

Dijksterhuis, E. J., *The Mechanisation of the World Picture* (New York, 1961).

Dod, Bernard, 'Aristoteles Latinus', in N. Kretzman, Anthony Kenny, and Jan Pinborg, eds., *The Cambridge History of Later Medieval Philosophy* (Cambridge, 1982), 45–79.

Donahue, William H., 'The Solid Planetary Spheres in Post-Copernican Natural Philosophy', in Robert S. Westman, ed., *The Copernican Achievement* (Berkeley, 1975), 244–75.

Fraisse, Simone, *L'Influence de Lucrèce en France au Seizième Siècle* (Paris, 1962).

Gabbey, Alan, Review of Wilson L. Scott, *The Conflict between Atomism and Conservation Theory, 1644–1860*, *Studies in History and Philosophy of Science* 4 (1973), 373–85.

'Force and Inertia in the Seventeenth Century: Descartes and Newton', in Stephen Gaukroger, ed., *Descartes: Philosophy, Mathematics and Physics* (New York, 1980), 230–320.

'Huygens and Mechanics', in H. J. M. Bos, ed., *Studies on Christiaan Huygens* (Lisse, 1980), 166–99.

'Newton's "Mathematical Principles of Natural Philosophy": A Treatise on "Mechanics"?', in P. M. Harman and Alan Shapiro, eds., *The Investigation of Difficult Things* (Cambridge, 1992), 305–22.

'Descartes' Physics and Descartes' Mechanics: Chicken and Egg?' in Stephen Voss, ed., *Essays on the Philosophy and Science of René Descartes* (New York, 1993), 311–23.

'The *Principia Philosophiæ* as a Treatise in Natural Philosophy', in Jean-Robert Armogathe and Giulia Belgioiso, eds., *Descartes: Principia Philosophiæ, 1644–1994* (Naples, 1996), 517–29.

'New Doctrines of Motion', in Daniel Garber and Michael Ayers, eds., *The Cambridge History of Seventeenth-Century Philosophy* (Cambridge, 1998), 649–79.

Garber, Daniel, *Descartes' Metaphysical Physics* (Chicago, 1992).

'A Different Descartes: Descartes and the Programme for a Mathematical Physics in his Correspondence', in Stephen Gaukroger, John Schuster, and John Sutton, eds., *Descartes' Natural Philosophy* (London, 2000), 113–30.

Gardiner, H. M., Metcalf, Ruth Clarke, and Beebe-Center, John, *Feeling and Emotion* (New York, 1937).

Gaukroger, Stephen, 'Aristotle on the Function of Sense Perception', *Studies in History and Philosophy of Science* 12 (1981), 75–89.

'The Metaphysics of Impenetrability: Euler's Conception of Force', *British Journal for the History of Science* 15 (1982), 132–54.

'The Sources of Descartes' Procedure of Deductive Demonstration in Metaphysics and Natural Philosophy', in John Cottingham, ed., *Reason, Will, and Sensation* (Oxford, 1994), 47–60.

Descartes, An Intellectual Biography (Oxford, 1995).

'The Ten Modes of Aenesidemus and the Myth of Ancient Scepticism', *British Journal for the History of Philosophy* 3 (1995), 371–87.

'The Foundational Role of Statics and Hydrostatics in Descartes' Natural Philosophy', in Stephen Gaukroger, John Schuster, and John Sutton, eds., *Descartes' Natural Philosophy* (London, 2000), 60–80.

'The Role of Matter Theory in Baconian and Cartesian Cosmologies', *Perspectives on Science*, 8 (2000), 201–22.

Francis Bacon and the Transformation of Early Modern Philosophy (Cambridge, 2001).

Gaukroger, Stephen and Schuster, John, 'The Hydrostatic Paradox and the Origins of Cartesian Dynamics', *Studies in History and Philosophy of Science*, forthcoming.

Gilbert, Neal W., *Renaissance Concepts of Method* (New York, 1960).

Gilson, Etienne, *La philosophie de St. Bonaventure* (Paris, 1945).

History of Christian Philosophy in the Middle Ages (London, 1955).

'Autour de Pomponazzi: problématique de l'immortalité de l'âme en Italie au début du XVIe siècle', *Archives d'histoire doctrinale et littéraire du moyen âge* 18 (1961), 163–279.

Glacken, Clarence J., *Traces on the Rhodian Shore* (Berkeley, 1967).

Gomez, Joaquim F., 'Pedro da Fonseca: Sixteenth Century Portuguese Philosopher', *International Philosophical Quarterly* 6 (1966), 632–44.

Gouhier, Henri, *Cartésianisme et Augustinisme au XVIIe Siècle* (Paris, 1978).

Gracia, Jorge, *Individuation in Scholasticism: the Later Middle Ages and the Counter-Reformation, 1150–1650* (Albany, N.Y., 1994).

Greenberg, Sidney Thomas, *The Infinite in Giordano Bruno* (New York, 1978).

Gueroult, Martial, 'The Metaphysics and Physics of Force in Descartes', in Stephen Gaukroger, ed., *Descartes: Philosophy, Mathematics and Physics* (New York, 1980), 196–229.

Hadot, Pierre, *Philosophy as a Way of Life* (Oxford, 1995).

Harrison, Peter, *The Bible, Protestantism, and the Rise of Natural Science* (Cambridge, 1998).

'Reading Les Passions: the Fall, Les Passions, and Dominion over Nature', in Stephen Gaukroger, ed., *The Soft Underbelly of Reason* (London, 1998), 49–78.

'The Influence of Cartesian Cosmology in England', in Stephen Gaukroger, John Schuster, and John Sutton, eds., *Descartes' Natural Philosophy* (London, 2000), 168–92.

Heilbron, J. L., *Electricity in the Seventeenth and Eighteenth Centuries* (New York, 1999).

Jacquart, Danielle, 'Aristotelian Thought in Salerno', in Peter Dronke, ed., *A History of Twelfth-Century Western Philosophy* (Cambridge, 1988), 407–28.

James, Susan, *Passion and Action: the Emotions in Seventeenth-Century Philosophy* (Oxford, 1997).

Keohane, Nannerl O., *Philosophy and the State in France* (Princeton, 1980).

Knowlson, James, *Universal Language Schemes in England and France, 1600–1800* (Toronto, 1975).

Koyré, Alexandre, *From the Closed World to the Infinite Universe* (Baltimore, 1957).

Kripke, Saul, *Wittgenstein on Rules and Private Language* (Oxford, 1982).

Kristeller, Paul Oskar, *Renaissance Thought and its Sources* (New York, 1979).

Kuhn, Thomas S., *The Copernican Revolution* (Cambridge, Mass., 1957).

Kusukawa, Sachiko, *The Transformation of Natural Philosophy: The Case of Philip Melanchthon* (Cambridge, 1995).

Lenoble, Robert, *Mersenne ou la naissance du mécanisme*, 2nd edn (Paris, 1971).

Levi, Anthony, *French Moralists* (Oxford, 1964).

Lohr, Charles, 'Renaissance Latin Aristotle Commentaries: Authors D–F', *Renaissance Quarterly*, 30 (1976), 714–45.

'Metaphysics', in Charles B. Schmitt, Quentin Skinner, and Eckhard Kessler, eds., *The Cambridge History of Renaissance Philosophy* (Cambridge, 1988), 537–638.

'The Sixteenth-Century Transformation of the Aristotelian Division of the Speculative Sciences', in D. R. Kelley and R. H. Popkin, eds., *The Shapes of Knowledge from the Renaissance to the Enlightenment* (Dordrecht, 1991), 49–58.

'Metaphysics and Natural Philosophy as Sciences: the Catholic and Protestant Views in the Sixteenth and Seventeenth Centuries', in Constance Blackwell and Sachiko Kusukawa, eds., *Philosophy in the Sixteenth and Seventeenth Centuries* (Aldershot, 1999), 280–95.

Marshall, John, *Descartes's Moral Theory* (Ithaca, 1998).

McLaughlin, Peter, 'Force, Determination and Impact', in Stephen Gaukroger, John Schuster, and John Sutton, eds., *Descartes' Natural Philosophy* (London, 2000), 81–112.

Meschini, Franco Aurelio, *Indice dei Principia Philosophiæ di René Descartes* (Florence, 1996).

Michel, Paul Henri, *The Cosmology of Giordano Bruno* (Paris, 1973).

Mouy, Paul, *Le Développement de la physique cartésienne, 1646–1712* (Paris, 1934).

Noreña, Carlos G., *Juan Luis Vives and the Emotions* (Carbondale, Ill., 1989).

Panizza, Letizia A., 'Stoic Psychotherapy in the Middle Ages and the Renaissance: Petrarch's *De remediis*', in Margaret Osler, ed., *Atoms, Pneuma, and Tranquillity* (Cambridge, 1991), 39–66.

Peghaire, J., *Intellectus et ratio selon S. Thomas d'Aquin* (Paris and Ottawa, 1936).

Pelikan, Jaroslav, *Christianity and Classical Culture* (New Haven, 1993).

Pumfrey, Stephen, 'Magnetical Philosophy and Astronomy, 1600–1650', in René Taton and Curtis Wilson, eds., *Planetary Astronomy from the Renaissance to the Rise of Astrophysics, Part A: Tycho Brahe to Newton* (Cambridge, 1989), 45–53.

Ranea, Alberto Guillermo, 'A "Science for *honnêtes hommes*": *La Recherche de la Vérité* and the Deconstruction of Experimental Knowledge,' in Stephen Gaukroger, John Schuster, and John Sutton, eds., *Descartes' Natural Philosophy* (London, 2000), 313–29.

Rankin, H. D., *Sophists, Socratics and Cynics* (London, 1983).

Reventlow, Henning Graf, *The Authority of the Bible and the Rise of the Modern World* (Philadelphia, 1985).

Roger, Jacques, 'The Cartesian Model and its Role in Eighteenth-Century "Theory of the Earth"', in T. Lennon, J. Nicholas, and J. Davis, eds., *Problems of Cartesianism* (Kingston, 1982), 95–112.

Buffon: A Life in Natural History (Ithaca, 1997).

Rorty, Amélie, 'Descartes on Thinking with the Body', in John Cottingham, ed., *The Cambridge Companion to Descartes* (Cambridge, 1992), 371–92.

Rosenfield, Leonora Cohen, *From Beast–Machine to Man–Machine*, rev. edn (New York, 1968).

Rossi, Paolo, *The Dark Abyss of Time: The History of the Earth and the History of Nations from Hooke to Vico* (Chicago, 1984).

Ryle, Gilbert, *The Concept of Mind* (London, 1949).

Sabra, A. I., *Theories of Light from Descartes to Newton* (Cambridge, 1981).

Schlanger, Judith, *Les métaphores de l'organisme* (Paris, 1971).

Schmitt, Charles B., 'The Rise of the Philosophical Textbook', in Charles B. Schmitt, Quentin Skinner, and Eckhard Kessler, eds., *The Cambridge History of Renaissance Philosophy* (Cambridge, 1988), 792–804.

Schneewind, J. B., *The Invention of Autonomy* (Cambridge, 1998).

Schuster, John, *Descartes and the Scientific Revolution, 1618–1634*, 2 vols. (Ann Arbor, Mich., 1977).

'Descartes' *Mathesis Universalis*, 1619–28', in Stephen Gaukroger, ed., *Descartes, Philosophy, Mathematics and Physics* (New York, 1980), 41–96.

'Descartes *Opticien*: The Construction of the Law of Refraction and the Manufacture of its Physical Rationales, 1618–29', in Stephen Gaukroger, John Schuster, and John Sutton, eds., *Descartes' Natural Philosophy* (London, 2000), 258–312.

Scott, Wilson L., *The Conflict between Atomism and Conservation Theory, 1644–1860* (London, 1970).

Secada, Jorge, *Descartes' Metaphysics* (Cambridge, 2000).

Shea, William, *Galileo's Intellectual Revolution* (New York, 1972).

The Magic of Numbers and Motion (Canton, Mass., 1991).

Slaughter, M. M., *Universal Language and Scientific Taxonomy in the Seventeenth Century* (Cambridge, 1982).

Slowik, Edward, 'Perfect Solidity: Natural Laws and the Problem of Matter in Descartes' Universe', *History of Philosophy Quarterly* 13 (1996), 187–204.

Bibliography

Sorabji, Richard, *Necessity, Cause and Blame: Perspectives on Aristotle's Theory* (London, 1980).

Matter, Space, and Motion: Theories in Antiquity and Their Sequel (London, 1988).

Sorabji, Richard, ed., *Philoponus and the Rejection of Aristotelian Science* (London, 1987).

Steinmetz, D. C., *Luther and Staupitz* (Durham, NC, 1980).

Sutton, John, *Philosophy and Memory Traces* (Cambridge, 1998).

Swerdlow, Noel M., 'The Derivation and First Draft of Copernicus' Planetary Theory: A Translation of the *Commentariolus* with Commentary', *Proceedings of the American Philosophical Society* 117 (1973), 423–512.

'*Pseudodoxia Copernicana*: Or, Enquiries into Very Many Received Tenets and Commonly Presumed Truths, Mostly Concerning Spheres', *Archives internationales d'histoire des sciences* 26 (1976), 108–58.

Thomas, Keith, *Man and the Natural World: Changing Attitudes in England 1500–1800* (London, 1983).

Trompf, G. W., *The Idea of Historical Recurrence in Western Thought: From Antiquity to the Reformation* (Berkeley, 1979).

Truesdell, Clifford, 'Rational Fluid Mechanics, 1687–1765', *Leonhardi Euleri opera omnia*: series 2, vol. 12 (Zurich, 1954), ix–cxxv.

'The Rational Mechanics of Flexible or Elastic Bodies, 1638–1788', *Leonhardi Euleri opera omnia*: series 2, vol. 11, section 2 (Zurich, 1960), 11–435.

Tweedale, Martin, 'Logic (i): From the late Eleventh Century to the Time of Abelard', in Peter Dronke, ed., *A History of Twelfth-Century Western Philosophy* (Cambridge, 1988), 196–226.

Vartanian, Aram, *La Mettrie's L'Homme Machine: A Study in the Origins of An Idea* (Princeton, 1960).

Verbeek, Theo, 'Le contexte historique des *Notæ in Programma Quoddam*', in Theo Verbeek, ed., *Descartes et Regius* (Amsterdam, 1993), 1–34.

'The Invention of Nature: Descartes and Regius', in Stephen Gaukroger, John Schuster, and John Sutton, eds., *Descartes' Natural Philosophy* (London, 2000), 149–67.

Weber, Jean-Paul, *La Consitution du texte des Regulæ* (Paris, 1964).

Westfall, Richard S., *Force in Newton's Physics: The Science of Dynamics in the Seventeenth Century* (London, 1971).

Westman, Robert, 'The Melanchthon Circle, Rheticus, and the Wittenberg Interpretation of the Copernican Theory,' *Isis* 66 (1975), 165–93.

'The Astronomer's Role in the Sixteenth Century: A Preliminary Study', *History of Science* 18 (1980), 105–47.

Wieland, Georg, 'The Reception and Interpretation of Aristotle's *Ethics*', in Norman Kretzmann, Anthony Kenny, and Jan Pinborg, eds., *The Cambridge History of Later Medieval Philosophy* (Cambridge, 1982), 657–72.

Yolton, John, *Perceptual Acquaintance* (Oxford, 1984).

Index